REVELATIONS
of DIVINE LOVE
Recorded by JULIAN,
Anchoress at NORWICH
ANNO DOMINI 1373

In lumine tuo videbimus lumen.

A version from the MS.
in the BRITISH MUSEUM
edited by
GRACE WARRACK

Methuen & Company
36 Essex Street Strand
London
1901

DOMINE, REFUGIUM FACTUS ES NOBIS, A GENERATIONE IN GENERATIONEM.
RESPICE IN SERVOS TUOS, ET IN OPERA TUA: ET DIRIGE FILIOS EORUM.
ET SIT SPLENDOR DOMINI DEI NOSTRI SUPER NOS, ET OPERA MANUUM
NOSTRARUM DIRIGE SUPER NOS: ET OPUS MANUUM NOSTRARUM DIRIGE.

"Truth seeth God, and Wisdom beholdeth God, and of these two cometh the third: that is a holy, marvelling delight in God; which is Love."

CONTENTS

viii CONTENTS

CONTENTS

The Title-page is from a design by Phoebe Anna Traquair.

NOTES ON MANUSCRIPTS AND EDITIONS

THIS English book exists in two Manuscripts : No. 30 of the Bibliothèque Nationale, Paris (*Bibliotheca Bigotiana*, 388), and No. 2499 *Sloane*, in the British Museum.

The Paris Manuscript is of the Sixteenth Century, the Sloane is in a Seventeenth Century handwriting ; the English of the Fourteenth Century seems to be on the whole well preserved in both, especially perhaps in the later Manuscript, which must have been copied from one of mixed East Anglian and northern dialects. This manuscript has no title-page, and nothing is known as to its history. Delisle's catalogue of the *Biblioth. Bigot.* (1877) gives no particulars as to the acquisition of No. 388. The two versions may be compared in these sentences :—

Chap. II., *Paris* MS. : "This revelation was made to a Symple creature unlettyrde leving in deadly flesh the yer of our Lord a thousande and thre hundered and lxxiii the xiii Daie of May."

Sloane : "These Revelations were shewed to a simple creature that cowde no letter the yeere of our Lord 1373 the xiij day of may."

Chap. LI., *Paris* MS. : "The colour of his face was feyer brown whygt with full semely countenaunce. his eyen were blakke most feyer and semely shewyng full of lovely pytte and within hym an heyward long and brode all full of endlesse hevynlynes. And the lovely lokyng that he lokyd on his servant contynually. And namely in his fallyng ÷ me thought it myght melt oure hartys for love. and brek them on twoo for Joy."

Sloane: "The color of his face was faire browne, with ful semely features, his eyen were blak most faire and semely shewand ful of lovely pety and within him an heyward long and brode all full of endles hevyns, and the lovely lokeing that he loked upon his servant continuly and namely in his fallyng me thowte it myte molten our herts for love & bresten hem on to for joy."

The Sloane MS. does not mention the writer of the book, but the copyist of the Paris version has, after the *Deo Gratias* with which it ends, added or transcribed these words : *Explicit liber Revelationem Julyane anatorite* [sic] *Norwyche cujus anime propicietur Deus.*

Blomefield, in his *History of Norfolk* (iv. p. 81), speaks of "an old vellum Manuscript, 36 pages of which contained an account of the visions, etc.," of the Lady Julian, anchoress at St. Julian's, Norwich, and quotes the title written by a contemporary : " Here es a Vision shewed by the godenes of God to a devoute Woman : and her name is Julian, that is recluse at Noryche, and yett is on life, Anno Domini mccccxlii. In the whilke Vision er fulle many comfortabyll words, and greatly styrrande to alle they that desyres to be Crystes Looverse "— greatly stirring to all that desire to be lovers of Christ. This Manuscript, possibly containing the writing of Julian herself, was in the possession of the Rev. Francis Peck (1692-1743). The original MSS. of that antiquarian writer went to Sir Thomas Cave, and ultimately to the British Museum, but his general library was sold in 1758 to Mr T. Payne (of Payne & Foss), bookseller, Strand, and this old Manuscript of the " Revelations," which has been sought for in vain in the catalogues of public collections, may perhaps have been bought and sold by him.[1] It may be extant in some private library.

Tersteegen, who, in his *Auserlesene Beschreibungen Heiliger Seelen*, gives a long extract from Julian's book (vol. iii. p. 252,

[1] v. Nichol's *Literary Anecdotes*, vol. iii. p. 653.

3rd ed. 1784), mentions in his preface that he had seen "in the Library of the late Poiret" an old Manuscript of these Revelations. Pierre Poiret, author of several works on mystical theology, died in 1719 near Leyden, but the Manuscript has not found its way to the University there.

Poiret himself refers thus to Julian and her book in his *Catalogus Auctorum Mysticorum*, giving to her name the asterisk denoting greatness : "*Julianae Matris Anachoretae, Revelationes de Amore Dei. Anglice. Theodidactae, profundae, ecstaticae.*" (*Theologiae Pacificae itemque Mysticae*, p. 336. Amsterdam, 1702.)

The earliest printed edition of Julian's book was prepared by the Benedictine Serenus de Cressy, and published in 1670 by permission of his ecclesiastical Superior, the Abbot of Lambspring, under the title of *Sixteen Revelations of Divine Love*. It agrees with the Manuscript now in Paris, but the readings that differ from the Sloane Manuscript are very few and are quite unimportant. This version of de Cressy's is in Seventeenth Century English with some archaic words, which are explained on the side margins ; it was re-printed in 1843. A modernised version taken from the Sloane MS. was published, with a preface, by Henry Collins in 1877 (T. Richardson & Sons).

These three, the only printed editions, are now all of great rarity.

For the following version, the editor having transcribed the Sloane MS., divided its continuous lines into paragraphs, supplied to many words capital letters, and while following as far as possible the significance of the commas and occasional full stops of the original, endeavoured to make the meaning clearer by a more varied punctuation. As the book is designed for general use, modern spelling has been adopted, and most words entirely obsolete in speech have been rendered in modern English, though a few that seemed of special significance or charm have been retained. Archaic forms of construction have been almost invariably left as they are, without regard to modern grammatical usage. Occasionally a word has been underlined for the sake of clearness or as a help in preserving the measure of the original language, which in a modern version must lose a little in rhythm, by altered pronunciation and by the dropping of the termination " en " from verbs in the infinitive. Here and there a clause has been put within parentheses. The very few changes made in words that might have any bearing on theological or philosophical questions, any historical or personal significance in the presentment of Julian's view, are noted on the margin and in the Glossary. Where prepositions are used in a sense now obscure they have generally been left as they are (*e.g.*, *of* for *by* or *with*), or have been added to rather than altered (*e.g.*, *for* is rendered by the archaic but intelligible *for that*, rather than by *because*, and *of* is amplified by words in square brackets, as [*by virtue*] *of*, [*out*] *of* rather than changed into *through* or *from*). The editor has desired to follow the rule of never omitting a word from the Manuscript, and of enclosing within square brackets the very few words added. It may be seen that these words do not alter the sense of the passage, but are interpolated with a view to bringing it out more clearly, in insignificant references (*e.g.* " in this [Shewing] "), and once or twice in a passage of special obscurity (see chap. xlv.).

NOTE AS TO THE LADY JULIAN, ANCHORESS AT ST JULIAN'S, AND THE LADY JULIAN LAMPET, ANCHORESS AT CARROW

IN *Carrow Abbey*, by Walter Rye (privately printed, 1889), is given a list of Wills, in which the name of the Lady Julian Lampet frequently occurs as a legatee between the years 1427 (Will of Sir John Erpingham) and 1478 (Will of William Hallys). Comparing the Will of Hallys with that of Margaret Purdance, which was made in 1471 but not proved till 1483, and from which the name of Lady Julian Lampet as a legatee is stroked out, no doubt because of her death, we find evidence that this anchoress died between 1478 and 1483. As even the earlier of these dates was a hundred and thirty-six years after the birth of the writer of the "Revelations," who in May 1373 was over thirty years of age, the identity of the "Lady Julian, recluse at Norwich," with the Lady Julian Lampet, though it has naturally been suggested, is surely an impossibility. There were anchorages in the churchyards both of St Julian's, Conisford (which belonged to the nuns of Carrow in the sense of its revenues having been made over to them by King Stephen for the support of that Priory or "Abbey"), and of St Mary's, the Convent Church of the nuns. See the Will of Robert Pert —proved 1445—which left "to the anchoress of Carhowe 1s., to ditto at St Julian's 1s.," and that of the Lady Isobel Morley, who in 1466 left bequests to "Dame Julian, anchoress at Carrow, and Dame Agnes, anchoress at St Julian's in Cunisford"— no doubt the same Dame Agnes that is mentioned by Blomefield as being at St Julian's in 1472. This Agnes may have been the immediate successor of Julian the writer of the "Revelations," who is spoken of as "yet in life"—as if in great age—in 1442, when she would be a hundred years old.

Perhaps the almost invariable use of the surname of the Carrow Dame Julian (who was, no doubt, of the family of Sir Ralph Lampet—frequently mentioned by Blomefield and in the *Paston Letters*) may go to establish proof that there had been before her and in her earlier years of recluse life another anchoress Julian, who most likely had been educated at Carrow, but who lived as an anchoress at St Julian's, and was known simply as Dame or "the Lady" Julian.

———————

From Blomefield's *History of Norfolk*, vol. iv. p. 524: "Carhoe or Carrow stands on a hill by the side of the river, about a furlong from Conisford or Southgates, and was always in the liberty of the City [of Norwich]. . . . Here was an ancient Hospital or Nunnery, dedicated to Saint Mary and Saint John, to which King Stephen having given lands and meadows without the South-gate, Seyna and Lescelina, two of the sisters, in 1146 began the foundations of a new monastery called Kairo, Carrow, Car-hou, and sometimes Car-Dieu, which was dedicated to the Virgin Mary and Saint John, and consisted of a prioress and nine (afterwards twelve) Benedictine black nuns. . . . Their church was founded by King Stephen and was dedicated to the Blessed Virgin, and had a chapel of St John Baptist joined to its south side, and another of St Catherine to its north ; there was also an anchorage by it, and in 1428 Lady Julian Lampet was anchoress there." . . . "This nunnery for many years had been a school or place of education for the young ladies of the chief families of the diocese, who boarded with and were educated by the nuns."

From Dr Jessopp's *Visitations of the Diocese of Norwich*, 1492-1532, Introduction, p. xliv.: "The priory of Carrow had always enjoyed a good reputation, and the house had for long been a favourite retreat for the daughters of the Norwich citizens who desired to give themselves to a life of religious retirement."

INTRODUCTION

PART I

THE LADY JULIAN

Beati pauperes spiritu : quoniam ipsorum est regnum cælorum
S. Matth. v. 3

VERY little is known of the outer life of the woman
that nearly five hundred years ago left us this
book.

It is in connection with the old Church of St Julian
in the parish of Conisford, outlying Norwich, that
Julian is mentioned in Blomefield's *History of Norfolk*
(vol. iv. p. 81): "In the east part of the churchyard stood an anchorage in which an ankeress or recluse
dwelt till the Dissolution, when the house was de-
molished, though the foundations may still be seen
(1768). In 1393 Lady Julian, the ankeress here was
a strict recluse, and had two servants to attend her in
her old age. This woman was in these days esteemed
one of the greatest holiness. In 1472 Dame Agnes
was recluse here; in 1481, Dame Elizabeth Scott;
in 1510, Lady Elizabeth; in 1524, Dame Agnes
Edrygge."

The little Church of St Julian (in use at this day) still keeps from Norman times its dark round tower of flint rubble, and still there are traces about its foundation of the anchorage built against its south-eastern wall. "This Church was founded," says the History of the County, "before the Conquest, and was given to the nuns of Carhoe (Carrow) by King Stephen, their founder; it hath a round tower and but one bell; the north porch and nave are tiled, and the chancel is thatched. There was an image of St Julian in a niche of the wall of the Church, in the Churchyard." Citing the record of a burial in "the churchyard of St Julian, the King and Confessor," Blomefield observes: "which shews that it was not dedicated to St Julian, the Bishop, nor St Julian, the Virgin."

The only knowledge that we have directly fom Julian as to any part of her history is given in her account of the time and manner in which the Revelation came, and of her condition before and during and after this special experience. She tells how on the 13th day of May, 1373,[1] the Revelation of Love was shewed to her, "a simple creature, unlettered," who had before this time made certain special prayers from out of her longing

---

[1] This must have been a Friday—sacred Day of the Passion of Christ—for Easter Sunday of 1373 was on the 17th of April (O.S.). So when the Revelation finally closed and Julian was left to "keep it in the Faith"—the Common Christian Faith—it was Sunday morning, and the words and voices she would hear through her window opening into the Church would be from the early worship of "the Blessed Common" assembled there.

after more love to God and her trouble over the sight
of man's sin and sorrow. She had come now, she
mentions, to the age of thirty, for which she had in
one of these prayers, desired to receive a greater consecration,—thinking, perhaps, of the year when the
Carpenter's workshop was left by the Lord for wider
ministry,—she was "thirty years old and an half."
This would make her birth-date about the end of 1342,
and the old Manuscript says that she "was yet in life"
in 1442. Julian relates that the Fifteen consecutive
"Shewings" lasted from about four o'clock till after
nine of that same morning, that they were followed by
only one other Shewing (given on the night of the next
day), but that through later years the teaching of these
Sixteen Shewings had been renewed and explained and
enlarged by the more ordinary enlightenment and in-
fluences of "the same Spirit that shewed them." In
this connection she speaks, in different chapters, of
"fifteen years after and more," and of twenty years
after, "save three months"; thus her book cannot have
been finished before 1393.

Of the circumstances in which the Revelations came,
and of all matters connected with them, Julian gives a
careful account, suggestive of great calmness and power
of observation and reflection at the time, as well as
of discriminating judgment and certitude afterwards.
She describes the preliminary seven days' sickness, the
cessation of all its pain during the earlier visions, in

which she had spiritual sight of the Passion of Christ, and indeed during all the five hours' "special Shewing"; the return of her physical pain and mental distress and "dryness" of feeling when the vision closed; her falling into doubt as to whether she had not simply been delirious, her terrifying dream on the Friday night, —noting carefully that "this horrible Shewing" came in her sleep, "and so did none other"—none of the Sixteen Revelations of Love came thus. Then she tells how she was helped to overcome the dream-temptation to despair, and how on the following night another Revelation, conclusion and confirmation of all, was granted to strengthen her faith. Again her faith was assayed by a similar dream-appearance of fiends that seemed as it were to be mocking at all religion, and again she was delivered, overcoming by setting her eyes on the Cross and fastening her heart on God, and comforting her soul with speech of Christ's Passion (as she would have comforted another in like distress) and rehearsing the Faith of all the Church. It may be noted here that Julian when telling how she was given grace to awaken from the former of these troubled dreams, says, "anon all vanished away and I was brought to great rest and peace, without sickness of body or dread of conscience," and that nothing in the book gives any ground for supposing that she had less than ordinary health during the long and peaceful life wherein God "lengthened her patience." Rather it would seem that one so wholesome in mind, so happy in spirit, so wisely moderate, no doubt, in self-guidance, must have kept that general health that *she* could not despise who speaks of God having "no disdain" to serve the body, for love of the soul, of how we are "soul and body clad in the Goodness of God," of how "God hath made waters plenteous in earth to our service and to our bodily ease,"[1] and of how Christ waiteth to minister to us His gifts of grace "unto the time that we be waxen and grown, our soul with our body and our body with our soul, either of them taking help of other, till we be brought unto stature, as nature worketh."[2]

Julian mentions neither her name not her state in life; she is "the soul," the "poor" or "simple" soul that the Revelation was shewed to—"a simple creature," in herself, a mere "wretch," frail and of no account.

Of her parentage and early home we know nothing: but perhaps her own exquisite picture of Motherhood —of its natural (its "kind") love and wisdom and know-ledge—is taken partly from memory, with that of the kindly nurse, and the child, which by nature loveth the

---

[1] See the *Ancren Riwle*, Part viii. *Of Domestic Matters*, for counsels to anchoresses as to judicious care of the body: diet, washing, needful rest, avoidance of idleness and gloom, reading, sewing for Church and Poor, making and mending and washing of clothes by the anchoress or her servant. "Ye may be well content with your clothes, be they white, be they black; only see that they be plain, and warm, and well made—skins well tanned; and have as many as you need. . . . Let your shoes be thick and warm."

[2] *cf.* Robert Browning, *Rabbi Ben Ezra*, xii.

Mother and each of the other children, and of the training by Mother and Teacher until the child is brought up to "the Father's bliss" (lxi.-lxiii.).

The title "Lady," "Dame" or "Madame" was commonly accorded to anchoresses, nuns, and others that had had education in a Convent.[1]

Julian, no doubt, was of gentle birth, and she would probably be sent to the Convent of Carrow for her education. There she would receive from the Benedictine nuns the usual instruction in reading, writing, Latin, French, and fine needlework, and especially in that Common Christian Belief to which she was always in her faithful heart and steadfast will so loyal,—"the Common Teaching of Holy Church in which I was afore informed and grounded, and with all my will having in use and understanding" (xlvi.).

It is most likely that Julian received at Carrow the consecration of a Benedictine nun; for it was usual, though not necessary, for anchoresses to belong to one or other of the Religious Orders.

The more or less solitary life of the anchorite or hermit, the anchoress or recluse, had at this time, as earlier, many followers in the country parts and large towns of England. Few of the "reclusoria" or women's

[1] S. de Cressy was probably the originator of the designation "Mother Juliana." The old name was *Julian*. The Virgin-Martyr of the Legend entitled "The Life of St Juliana" (Early English Text Society) is called in the Manuscripts, Iulane, Iuliene, and Iuliane and Julian. So also *Lady Julian Berners* is a name in the history of Fifteenth Century books.

anchorholds were in the open country or forest-lands like those that we come upon in Medieval romances, but many churches of the villages and towns had attached to them a timber or stone " cell "—a little house of two or three rooms inhabited by a recluse who never left it, and one servant, or two, for errands and protection. Occasionally a little group of recluses lived together like those three young sisters of the Thirteenth Century for whom the *Ancren Riwle*, a Rule or Counsel for " Ancres," was at their own request composed. The recluse's chamber seems to have generally had three windows : one looking into the adjoining Church, so that she could take part in the Services there ; another communicating with one of those rooms under the keeping of her " maidens," in which occasionally a guest might be entertained ; and a third—the " parlour " window—opening to the outside, to which all might come that desired to speak with her. According to the *Ancren Riwle* the covering-screen for this audience-window was a curtain of double cloth, black with a cross of white through which the sunshine would penetrate—sign of the Dayspring from on high. This screen could of course be drawn back when the recluse ' held a parliament ' with any that came to her.[1]

---

[1] " So he kneeled at her window and anon the recluse opened it, and asked Sir Percival what he would. ' Madam,' said he, ' I am a knight of King Arthur's Court and my name is Sir Percival de Galis.' So when the recluse heard his name, she had passing great joy of him, for greatly she loved him before all other knights of the world ; and so of right she ought to do, for she was his aunt."—Malory's *Morte d'Arthur*, xiv. i.

Before Julian passed from the sunny lawns and meadows of Carrow, along the road by the river and up the lane to the left by the gardens and orchards of the Coniston of that day, to the little Churchyard house that would hide so much from her eyes of outward beauty, and yet leave so much in its changeful perpetual quietude around her (great skies overhead like the ample heavenly garments of her vision "blue as azure most deep and fair"; little Speedwell's blue by the crannied wall of the Churchyard—*Veronika*, true Image, like the Saint's "Holy Vernacle at Rome") her vow[1] might be: "I offering yield myself to the divine Goodness[2] for service, in the order of anchorites: and I promise to continue in the service of God after the rule of that order, by divine grace and the counsel of the Church: and to shew canonical obedience to my ghostly fathers."

The only reference that Julian makes to the life dedicated more especially to Contemplation is where she is speaking, as if from experience, of the temptation to despair because of falling oftentimes into the same sins, "especially into sloth and losing of time. For that is the beginning of sin, as to my sight,—and especially to the creatures that have given themselves to serve our Lord with inward beholding of His blessed Goodness."[3]

[1] *Manuale ad usum insignis ecclesie Sarisburiensis* (ed. of 1555), fo. lxix. *Servitium includendorum.*   [2] "*pietatis.*"

[3] The sins that Julian mentions, "despair or doubtful dread," "sloth and losing of time," "unskilful [unpractical, unreasoning] heaviness and vain sorrow," seem to be all akin to that dreaded sin, besetting particularly the Contemplative life, *Accidia*. See *Ancren Riwle* p. 287.

*" One thing have I desired of the Lord, that will I
seek after: that I may dwell in the house of the Lord all the
days of my life, to behold the beauty of the Lord, and to enquire
in His temple "*—His Sanctuary of the Church or of the
soul. *That* was her calling. She had heard the Voice
that comes to the soul in Spring-time and calls to the
Garden of lilies, and calls to the Garden of Olive-trees
(where all the spices offered are in one Cup of Heavenly
Wine): *" Surge, propera amica mea: jam enim Hyems
transiit, imber ambiit et recessit. Surge, propera amica mea,
speciosa mea, et veni." " Arise: let us go hence."* [1] *" For
this is the natural yearnings of the soul by the touching
of the Holy Ghost: God of Thy Goodness, give me Thyself,
for Thou art enough to me; . . . and if I ask anything
that is less, ever me wanteth; but only in Thee I have
all "* (v.).

" A soul that only fasteneth itself on to God with
very trust, either by seeking or in beholding, it is the
most worship that it may do to Him, as to my sight "
(x.). "To enquire" and "to behold"—no doubt it

" *Accidies salue is gostlich gledshipe.* The remedy for indolence is
spiritual joy, and the consolation of joyful hope from reading and
from holy meditation, or when spoken by the mouth of man. Often,
dear sisters, ye ought to pray less, that ye may read more. Reading is good prayer. Reading teacheth how, and for what ye ought
to pray. In reading, when the heart feels delight, devotion ariseth,
and that is worth many prayers. Everything, however, may be
overdone. Moderation is always best."—(Pub. by the Camden
Society).

[1] Canticles ii. 10. St John xiv. 31.

was for these that Julian sought time and quiet. For she had urgent questionings and "stirrings" in her mind over "the great hurt that is come by sin to the creature"—"afore this time often I wondered why by the great foreseeing wisdom of God the beginning of sin was not letted" ("mourning and sorrow I made over it without reason and discretion"); and also she was filled with desire for God: "the longing that I had to Him afore" (xxvii.).

Moreover, this life to which Julian gave herself was to be a life of "meek continuant prayers" "for enabling" of herself in her weakness, and for help to others in all their needs. For thought and worship could only be held together by active prayer: the pitiful beholding of evil and pain and the joyful beholding of Goodness and Love would be at war, as it were, with each other, unless they were set at peace for the time by the prayer of intercession. And *that* is the call of the loving soul, strong in its infant feebleness to wake the answering Revelation of Love to faith that "all shall be well," and that "all is well" and that when all are come up above and the whole is known, all shall be seen to be well, and to have been well through the time of tribulation and travail.

"At some time in the day or night," says the *Ancren Riwle*, which Julian perhaps may have read, though as to such prayers her compassionate heart was its own

director—" At some time in the day or night think upon
and call to mind all who are sick and sorrowful,
who suffer affliction and poverty, the pain which
prisoners endure who lie heavily fettered with iron;
think especially of the Christians who are amongst the
heathen, some in prison, some in so great thralldom
as is an ox or an ass; compassionate those who are
under strong temptations; take thought of all men's
sorrows, and sigh to our Lord that He may take
care of them and have compassion and look upon them
with a gracious eye; and if you have leisure, repeat
this Psalm, *I have lifted up mine eyes. Paternoster. Return,
O Lord, how long, and be intreated in favour of Thy servants:
Let us pray.* 'Stretch forth, O Lord, to thy servants and
to thy handmaids the right hand of thy heavenly aid,
that they may seek thee with all their heart, and obtain
what they worthily ask through Jesus Christ our Lord.'"
Julian tells how in her thinking of sin and its hurt there
passed before her sight all that Christ bore for us, "and
His dying; and all the pains and passions of all His
creatures, ghostly and bodily; *and the beholding of this*—
with all pains that ever were or ever shall be" (xxvii).
From sin, except as a general conception, Julian's natural
instinct was to turn her eyes; but with this Christly
compassion in her heart in looking on the sorrows of the
world she could not but take account of its sin. As she
came to be convinced that "though we be highly lifted
up into contemplation, it is needful for us to see our own

sin,"—albeit we should not accuse ourselves "overdone much" or "be heavy or sorrowful indiscreetly"—so when sins of others were brought before her she would seek with compassion to take the sinner's part of contrition and prayer. "The beholding of other man's sins, it maketh as it were a thick mist afore the eyes of the soul, and we cannot, for the time, see the fairness of God, but if we can behold them with contrition with him, with compassion on him, and with holy desire to God for him" (lxxvi.).

And notwithstanding all the stir and eager revival of the Fourteenth Century in religion, politics, literature and general life, there was much both of sin and of sorrow then to exercise the pitiful soul — troubles enough in Norwich itself, of oppression and riot and desolating pestilence—troubles enough in Europe, West and East,—wars and enslaving and many cruelties in distant lands, and harried Armenian Christians coming to the Court of Edward to plead for succour in their long-enduring patience. There was trouble wherever one looked; but to prayer, and to that compassion which is in itself a prayer, the answer came. Indeed the compassion was its own first immediate answer: for "then I saw that each kind compassion that man hath on his *even-Cristen* (his fellow-Christians) with charity, *it is Christ in him*." This is the comfort that both comforts in waiting and calls to deeds of help. And such "charity" of social service was not beyond the scope

of the life "enclosed,"—whether it might be by deed
or, as more often, by speech.[1]

It is in her seeking for truth and her beholding of
Love that we best know Julian.   Of the opening of the
Revelation she says : "In all this I was greatly stirred
in charity to mine even-Christians, that they might see
and know the same that I saw : for I would it were
comfort to them," and again and again throughout the
book she declares that the "special Shewing" is given not
for her in special, but for all—for all are meant to be
one in comfort as all are one in need.   "Because of the

[1] See the chapter "How an Anchoress shall behave herself to them
that come to her," in "The Scale of Perfection," by Walter Hilton
(died 1396), edition of 1659, p. 106.   "Since it is so that thou
oughtest not to goe out of thy house to seek occasion how thou
mightest profit thy Neighbour by deeds of Charity, because thou
art enclosed ; . . . therefore who so will speake with thee . . . be
thou soon ready with a good will to aske what his will is . . .
for thou knowest not what he is, nor why he cometh, nor what
need he hath of thee, or thou of him, till thou hast tryed.   And
though thou be at prayer, or at thy devotions, that thou thinkest
loth to break off, for that thou thinkest that thou oughtest not
leave God for to speake with any one, I think not so in this case,
for if thou be wise, thou shalt not leave God, but thou shalt find
him, and have him, and see him in thy Neighbour as well as in
prayer, onely in another manner.   If thou canst love thy Neighbour
well, to speake with thy Neighbour with discretion shall be no
hindrance to thee. . . . If he come to tell thee his disease [distress]
or trouble, and to be comforted by thy speech, heare him gladly,
and suffer him to say what he will for ease of his own heart ; And
when he hath done, comfort him if thou canst, gladly, gently, and
charitably, and soon break off.   And then, after that, if he will fall
into idle tales, or vanities of the World, or of other men's actions,
answer him but little, and feed not his speech, and he will soon be
weary, and quickly take his leave," etc.

Shewing I am not good, but if I love God the better: and in as much as ye love God the better it is more to you than to me. . . . For we are all one in comfort. For truly it was not shewed me that God loved me better than the least soul that is in grace; for I am certain that there be many that never had any Shewing nor sight but of the common teaching of Holy Church that love God better than I. For if I look singularly to myself I am right nought; but in general [manner of regarding] I am, I hope, in oneness of charity with all mine even-Christians. For in this oneness standeth the life of all mankind that shall be saved, and that which I say of me, I say in the person of all mine even-Christians: for I am taught in the Spiritual Shewing of our Lord God that He meaneth it so. And there-fore I pray you for God's sake, and counsel you for your own profit that ye leave the beholding of a worth-less creature [a "wretch"] it was shewed to and mightily, wisely and meekly behold God that of His special good-ness would shew it generally, in comfort of us all" (ix.).

Thus Julian turns our eyes from looking *on* her to looking *with* her on the Revelation of Divine Love.

Yet surely in her we have also "a shewing"—a shewing of the same. She tells us little of her own story, and little is told us of her by any one else, but all through her recording of the Revelation the simple creature to whom it was made unconsciously shews herself, so that soon we come to know her with a pleasure that surely she would not think too "special" in its regard. (For she herself in speaking of Love makes note that the general does not exclude the special). Perhaps we are helped in this friendly acquaintanceship by those endearingly characteristic little formulas of speech disavowing any claim to dogmatic authority in the statements of her views of truth : those modest parentheses "as to my sight," "as to mine understanding." "Wisdom and truth and love," the dower that she saw in the Gracious soul, were surely in the soul of this meek woman ; but enclosing these gifts of nature and grace are qualities special to Julian : depth of passion, with quietness, order, and moderation ; loyalty in faith, with clearest candour—"I believe . . . but this was not shewed me"—(xxxiii., lxxvii., lxxx.) pitifulness and sympathy, with hope and a blithe serenity ; sound good sense with a little sparkle upon it—as of delicate humour (that crowning virtue of saints) ; and beneath all, above all, an exquisite tenderness that turns her speech to music. "*I will lay thy Stones with fair Colours.*"

"Thou hast the dews of thy youth." Hundreds of years have gone since that early morning in May when Julian thought she was dying and was "partly troubled" for she felt she was yet in youth and would gladly have served God more on earth with the gift of her days— hundreds of years since the time that her heart would fain have been told by special Shewing that "a certain creature I loved should continue in good living"—but still we have "mind" of her as "a gentle neighbour and of our knowing." For those that love in simplicity are always young; and those that have had with the larger Vision of Love the gift of love's passionate speech, to God or man, in word or form or deed, as treasure held —live yet on the earth, untouched by time, though their light is shining elsewhere for other sight.

"From that time that the Revelation was shewed I desired oftentimes to learn what was our Lord's meaning. And fifteen years afterwards and more, I was answered in ghostly understanding, saying thus : *Wouldst thou learn thy Lord's meaning in this thing? Learn it well: Love was His meaning. Who shewed it thee? Love. What shewed He thee? Love. Wherefore shewed it He? For Love. Hold thee therein and thou shalt learn and know more in the same. But thou shalt never know nor learn other thing without end.*"

And if we, with no special shewing, might ask and, in trust of "spiritual understanding," might answer more—asking *to whom*, and *for whom* was the Revelation shewed, we might answer : *To one that loved*; for all that would learn in love.

"*Ecco chi crescerà li nostri amori*"![1]

"Here is one who shall increase our love."

Blessed are they that mourn : for they shall be comforted.
Blessed are the meek : for they shall inherit the earth.
Blessed are the pure in heart : for they shall see God.

[1] Dante, *Paradiso*, v. 105.

PART II

THE MANNER OF THE BOOK

As an hert desirith to the wellis of watris :
  so thou God, my soule desirith to thee. . . .
The Lord sent his merci in the day :
  and his song in the nyght.

Ps. '*Quemadmodum*' ; from the *Prymer*.

WITHOUT any special study of the literature of Mysticism for purposes of comparison, in reading Julian's book one is struck by a few characteristics wherein it differs from many other Mystical writings as well as by qualities that belong to most or all of that general designation.

The silence of this book both as to preliminary ascetic exercises and as to ultimate visions of the Absolute, might be attributed to Julian's being wholly concerned with giving, for comfort to all, that special sight of truth that came to her as the answer to her own need. She sets out not to teach methods of any kind for the gradual drawing near of man to God, but to record and shew forth a Revelation, granted once, of God's actual nearness to the soul, and for this Revelation she herself had been prepared by the " stirring " of her conscience, her love and her understanding, in a word of her *faith*, even as she was in short time to be left " neither sign nor token," but only the Revelation to hold " in faith." Moreover, the means that in general she looks to for realising God's nearness, in whatever measure or manner the revelation of it may come to any soul, is the immediate one of faith as a gift of nature and a grace from the Holy Ghost: faith leading by prayer, and effort of obedience, and teachableness of spirit, into actual experience of oneness with God. The natural and common heritage of love and faith is a theme that is dear to Julian: in her view, longing toward God is grounded in the love to Him that is native to the human heart, and this longing (painful through sin) as it is stirred by the Holy Spirit, who comes with Christ, is, in each naturally developed Christian, spontaneous and increasing;—" for the nearer we be to our bliss, the more we long after it " (xlvi., lxxii., lxxxi.). " This is the kinde [the natural] yernings of the soule by the touching of the Holy Ghost: *God of Thy goodness give me Thyself: for Thou art enow to me, and I may nothing ask that is less that may be full worshippe to Thee.*" God is the first as well as the last: the soul begins as well as ends with God: begins by Nature, begins again by Mercy, and ends—yet " without end "—by Grace. Certainly on the way—the way of these three, by falling, by succour, by upraising—to the more perfect knowing of God that is the soul's Fulfilment in Heaven, there is a less immediate knowledge to be gained through experience: " *And if I aske anything that is lesse, ever me wantith,*" for " It needyth us to have knoweing of the littlehede of creatures and to nowtyn all thing that is

made, for to love and have God that is onmade." But
this knowing of the littleness of creatures comes to
Julian first of all in a sight of *the Goodness of God*; "For
[to] a soule that seith the Maker of all, all that is made
semith full litil." By the further beholding, indeed, of
God as Maker and Preserver, that which has been rightly
" noughted " as of no account, is seen to be also truly
of much account. For that which was seen by the soul
as so little that it seemed to be about to fall to nothing
for littleness, is seen by the understanding to have " three
properties " :—God made it, God loveth it, God keepeth
it. Thus it is known as " great and large, fair and
good "; " it lasteth, and ever shall, for God loveth it."
—Yet again the soul breaks away to its own, with the
natural flight of a bird from its Autumn nest at the call
of an unseen Spring to the far-off land that is nearer still
than its nest, because it is in its heart. " But what is to
me sothly [in verity] the Maker, the Keper and the Lover,
—I cannot tell, for till I am Substantially oned [deeply
united] to Him, I may never have full rest ne very blisse ;
that is to sey, that I be so festined to Him, that there is
right nowte that is made betwix my God and me " (v.,
viii.). This " fastening " is all that in Julian's book represents that needful process wherein the truth of asceticism
has a part. It is not essentially a process of detaching
the thought from created things of time—still less one
of detaching the heart from created beings of eternity—
but a process of more and more allowing and presenting

the man to be fastened closely to God by means of the original longing of the soul, the influence of the Holy Ghost, and the discipline of life with its natural tribulations, which by their purifying serve to strengthen the affections that remaining pass through them. "*But only in Thee I have all.*" On the way this discovery of the soul at peace must needs be sometimes a word for exclusion, in parting and pressing onward from things that are made : in the end it is the welcome, all-inclusive. And Julian, notwithstanding her enclosure as a recluse, is one of those that, happy in nature and not too much hindered by conditions of life, possess for large use *by the way* the mystical peace of fulfilled possession through virtue of freedom from bondage to self. For it is by means of the tyranny of the "self," regarding chiefly itself in its claims and enjoyments, that creature things can be intruded between the soul and God ; and always, in some way, the meek inherit the earth. "All things are yours ; and ye are Christ's."

The life of a recluse demanded, no doubt, as other lives do, a daily self-denial as well as an initiatory self-devotion, and from Julian's silence as to "bodily exercises" it cannot of course be assumed that she did not give them, even beyond the incumbent rule of the Church, though not in excess of her usual moderation, some part in her Christian striving for mastery over self. Nor could this silence in itself be taken as a proof that ascetic practices had not in her view a preparatory

function such as has by many of the Mystics been
assigned to them during a process of self-training in
the earlier stages of the soul's ascent to aptitude for
mystical vision.   It is, however, to be noted that neither
in regard to herself nor others do we hear from Julian
anything about an undertaking of this kind.   To her
the "special Shewing" came as a gift, unearned, and
unexpected : it came in an abundant answer to a prayer
for other things needed by every soul.[1]   Julian's desires
for herself were for three "wounds" to be made more
deep in her life : contrition (in sight of sin), compassion
(in sight of sorrow) and longing after God : she prayed
and sought diligently for these graces, comprehensive as
she felt they were of the Christian life and meant for all ;
and with them she sought to have for herself, in par-

[1] The soon-forgotten petition of Julian's youth for a "bodily sickness"
does not seem to have had any connection in her mind with special
Revelation : it was desired neither as in any way a sign of invisible things
nor as a direct means of beholding them.   And probably, as a matter of
fact, the sickness that was granted helped her in the way that she had
desired, helped her to the sight of the Revelation, not directly, but by
drawing her spirit to that utter dependence on and trust in God that is
death's first lesson for all, that uttermost self-devotion to God that is
life's last exercise.   This spiritual state, with all that through years had
gone before of feeling and thought and life's experience, made her ready
to be shewn with special largeness and clearness God's love : how it filled
the empty place of sin and pain and sorrow with its divine fulness.   As
to the "bodily sight" introducing the Revelation, a sight of "parts of the
Passion," which may be compared with "The XV. Oos "—'Orationes'—
Passion-prayers each beginning with ' O ' (v. Horæ of Sarum), it was
recognised by Julian herself, even at the time of her seeing it, as being a
sight of things "not in substance or nature."   In this recognition it was
proved to be neither *mental delusion* nor mere "raving" delirium.   But it

ticular regard to her own difficulties, a sight of such truth as it might " behove " her to know for the glory of God and the comfort of men. According to Julian the " special Shewing " is a gift of comfort for all, sent by God in a time to some soul that is chosen in order that it may have, and so may minister, the comfort needed by itself and by others (ix.). In her experience this Revelation, soon closed, is renewed by influence and enlightenment in the more ordinary grace of its giver, the Holy Ghost. But a still fuller sight of God shall be given, she rejoices to think, in Heaven, to *all* that shall reach that Fulfilment of blessed life—the only mount of the soul set forth in this book. Thither, by the high-road of Christ, all souls may go, making the steep ascent

---

would, it seems, be natural that in her weakness of body and her exaltation of spirit (so tense that the strength of her self-surrender to death seemed to cast her back upon bodily life in the painless world between the two) some sort of *physical illusion* should be brought about by her prolonged gaze upon the Face of the Crucifix, and that in her desire to enter into the sufferings of the Passion as fully as those friends of her Lord's that beheld it, Julian thus gazing in the midst of night's shadows and the dim light of dawn should seem to herself to behold the sacred drops, depicted beneath the painted or sculptured Crown of Thorns, flow down " right plenteously." Julian gave thanks for this and all the " bodily sight " as a gift from God. By Him sickness and illusion, as well as things evil, are " suffered " to come, and by Him Revelation is given according to sundry times in diverse manners. Gain of the spirit through failure of the body—and no less by illusions of fever than by trance-state visions their seers speak of, when Death passes the Spirit half through the gates —would indeed be accordant with the truth of the Shewing that came to Julian, how man is raised through shame and death into glory and life, since in the weakness of failing men the strength of Christ is made perfect.

through "longing and desire,"—longing that embodies itself in desire towards God, that is, in Prayer.

Nothing is said by Julian as to successive stages of Prayer, though she speaks of different *kinds* of prayer as the natural action of the soul under different experiences or in different states of feeling or "dryness." Prayer is *asking* ("beseeching"), with submission and acquiescence; or *beholding*, with the *self* forgotten, yet offered-up; it is a thanking and a praising in the heart that sometimes breaks forth into voice; or a silent joy in the sight of God as all-sufficient. And in all these ways "Prayer oneth the soul to God."

To Julian's understanding the only Shewing of God that could ever be, the highest and lowest, the first and the last, was the Vision of Him as Love. "Hold thee therein and thou shalt witten and knowen more in the same. But thou shalt never knowen ne witten other thing without end. Thus was I lerid that Love was our Lord's menyng" (lxxxvi.). Alien to the "simple creature" was that desert region where some of the lovers of God have endeavoured to find Him,—desiring an extreme penetration of thought (human thought, after all, since for men there is none beyond it) or an utmost reach of worship (worship from fire and ice) in proclaiming the Absolute One not only as All that *is*, but as All that is *not*. Julian's desire was truly for God in Himself, through Christ by the Holy Spirit of Love : for God in "His homeliest home," the soul, for God in

His City. Therefore she follows only the upward way of the light attempered by grace, not turning back to the *Via Negativa*, that downward road that starting from a conception of the Infinite "as the antithesis of the finite,"[1] rather than as including and transcending the finite, leads man to deny to his words of God all qualities known or had by human, finite beings. Julian keeps on the way that is natural to her spirit and to all her habits of thought as these may have been directed by reading and conversation: it does not take her towards that Divine Darkness of which some seers have brought report. Hers was not one of those souls that would, and must, go silent and alone and strenuous through strange places: "homely and courteous" she ever found Almighty God in Jesus Christ our Lord.

Julian's mystical sight was not a negation of human modes of thought: neither was it a torture to human powers of speech nor a death-sentence to human activities of feeling. "He hath no despite of that which He hath made" (vi.). This seer of the littleness of all that is made saw the Divine as containing, not as engulfing, all things that truly are, so that in some way "all things that are made" because of His love last ever. Certainly she passes sometimes beyond the language of earth, seeing a love and a Goodness "more than tongue can tell," but she is never inarticulate in any painful,

[1] See the Bampton Lectures on *Christian Mysticism*. W. R. Inge. (P. 111.)

struggling way—when words are not to be found that can tell all the truth revealed, she leaves her Lord's "meaning" to be taken directly from Him by the understanding of each desirous soul. So is it with the Shewing of God as the Goodness of everything that is good: "It is I—it is I" (xxvi.). Certainly Julian looks both downward and upward, sees Love in the lowest depth, far below sin, below even Mercy; sees Love as the highest that can be, rising higher and higher far above sight, in skies that as yet she is not called to enter: "abysses" there are, below and above, like Angela di Foligno's "double abyss"; but here is no desert region like that where Angela seems as "an eagle descending"[1] from heights of unbreathable air, baffled and blinded in its assault on the Sun, proclaiming the Light Unspeakable in anguished, hoarse, inarticulate cries; here is a mountain-path between the abysses and the sound as of a chorus from pilgrims singing:

"Praise to the Holiest in the height
And in the depth be praise";—
'ALL IS WELL: ALL IS WELL: ALL SHALL BE WELL.'

Moreover, Julian while guided by Reason is *led* by the "Mind" of her soul—pioneer of the path through the wood of darkness though Reason is ready to disentangle the lower hindrances of the way; and where her instructed soul "finds rest," those things that are hid from

[1] See the Introduction to *Le Livre des Visions et Instructions de la Bienheureuse Angèle de Foligno*, traduit par Ernest Hello. Paris, 1895.

the wisdom and prudence of Reason only are to its simplicity of obedience revealed. Even as her Way is Christ-Jesus, and her walk by "longing and desire" is of faith and effort, so the End and the Rest that she seeks is the *fulness* of God, in measure as the soul can enter upon His fulness here and in that heavenly "oneing" with Him which shall be by grace the "fulfilling" and "overpassing" of "Mankind." "The Mid-Person willed to be Ground and Head of this fair Kind," "out of Whom we ben al cum, in Whom we be all inclosid, into Whom we shall all wyndyn, in Him fynding our full Hevyn in everlestand joye" (liii.).[1] The soul that participates in God cannot be lost in God, the soul that wends into oneness with God finds there at last its Self. Words of the Spirit-nature fail to describe to man, as he is, this fulness of personal life, and Julian falls back in one effort, daring in its infantine concreteness of language, on acts of all the five senses to symbolise the perfection of spiritual life that is in oneness with God (xliii.).

It may be noted that in these "Revelations" there is absolutely no regarding of Christ as the "Bridegroom" of the individual soul: once or twice Julian in passing uses the symbol of "the Spouse," "the Fair Maiden," "His loved Wife," but this she applies only to the Church. In her usual speech Christ when unnamed is our "Good" or our "Courteous" Lord, or sometimes simply

---

[1] "When that which drew from out the boundless deep
Turns again home."

" God," and when she seeks to express pictorially His union with men and His work for men, then the soul is the Child and Christ is the Mother. In this symbolic language the love of the Christian soul is the love of the Child to its Mother and to each of the other children.

Julian's Mystical views seem in parts to be cognate with those of earlier and later systems based on Plato's philosophy, and especially perhaps on his doctrine of Love as reaching through the beauties of created things higher and higher to union with the Absolute Beauty above, Which is God—schemes of thought developed before her and in her time by Plotinus, Clement, Augustine, Dionysius " the Areopagite," John the Scot, Eckhart, the Victorines,[1] Ruysbroeck, and others. One does not know what her reading may have been, or with what people she may have conversed. Possibly the learned Austin Friars that were settled close to St Julian's in Conisford may have lent her books by some of these writers, or she may have been influenced through talks with a Confessor, or with some of the Flemish weavers of Norwich, with whom Mystical views were not uncommon. Yet the Mysticism of the " Revelations " is peculiarly of the English type. Less exuberant in language than Richard Rolle, the Hermit of Hampole, Julian resembles him a little in her blending of practical sense with devotional fervour ; but the writer to whom

[1] *v.* pp. 27, 57, 126, 156, 168 ; *cf.* Dionysius : " *On Divine Names.*" Cap. iv. (tr. by Parker). S. Aug. *Conf.* : b. i. ch. 2 ; iii. 7 ; iv. 10-16 ; vii. 12-18.

she seems, at any rate in some of her phrases, most akin is Walter Hilton, her contemporary.[1] Hilton, however, is very rich in quotations from the Bible, while Julian's only direct quotations from any book—beyond her reference to the legend of St Dionysius—are one that belongs to Christ: "I thirst" (xvii.), and two that belong to the soul: "Lord, save me: I perish!" "Nothing shal depart me from the charite of Criste" (xv.). (And indeed these three are a fit embodiment of the Christian Faith as seen in her "Revelations.") But Julian, while perhaps more speculative than either of these typical English Mystics, is thoroughly a woman. Lacking their literary method of procedure, she has a high and tender beauty of thought and a delicate bloom of expression that are her own rare gifts—the beauty of the hills against skies in summer evenings, of an orchard in mornings of April. Again and again she stirs in the reader a kind of surprised gladness of the simple perfection wherewith she utters, by few and adequate words, a thought that in its quietness convinces of truth, or an emotion deep in life. Of a little child it has been said: "He thought great thoughts simply," and Julian's deepness of insight and simplicity of speech are like the Child's.[2] "For ere that He made

---

[1] See the extract from Hilton given as a note to chapter lvii.

[2] *Little Flowers of a Childhood* (in Mem. J. D. W., Oct. 1894—March 1899). Some of the thoughts of children,—some of the rising thoughts of a very little child who, like Julian, faced the darkness of time (steadfast as Dürer's pilgrim Knight, gentle as Chaucer's,) and

us He loved us, and when we were made we loved
Him" (liii.). " I love thee, and thou lovest me, and our
love shall not be disparted in two" (lxxxii.). *"Thou
art my Heaven."* " I had liefer have been in that pain
till Doomsday than have come to Heaven otherwise
than by Him." " Human is the vehemence," says a
writer on Julian's " Revelations," of that reiterated exclusion of all other paths to joy. ' Me liked,' she
says, ' none other heaven.' Once again she touches
the same octave, condensing in a single phrase which
has seldom been transcended in its brief expression of
the possession that leaves the infinity of love's desire

---

beheld on his journey the shining of the Eternal City,—might be set
beside words of the Mystics as shewing, perhaps, through their very
simplicity, the oneness of truth that there is to see, and the oneness of
souls that see it. Here are convictions that the Cause of love, felt within,
" must be Jesus' Good Spirit"; comfort in discovering of death's
unreality (for if only the body, not the spirit, dies, " Oh, then it is only
pretending-dying !"); a flash of discernment, perhaps, as to the passing
away of lifeless evil since although, to the child, indeed " it is a pity that
some one did not come and kill the devil; and then he would be dead," yet
he has his own eschatology: " Well, when *we* are all dead, the devil
will be dead too." More significant is a sudden overawed realisation of
the great universe (setting pause to his own run round in play),
one door to a quick perception in the child's devout spirit of analogy
binding truths unseen by sense: " Is this world always going round,
now ? " (' Yes.') " It stays still ! still !—Jesus is looking down now :
we don't see Him."—Here, too, are habitual references to the things that
are *meant to be*,—musings over the goodness and knowledge, the braveness
and courtesy " meant to be " in a *man*; and here is a grateful, trusting
sense of the real ' kindness ' of ' wild ' creatures and of hurting
remedies. Many of those simple utterances, careless yet arresting like a
blackbird's song, and personal with the ardent love and clear reason of
a child faithfully living and bravely dying, seem to attest a kinship with

still unsatiated : ' *I saw Him and sought Him, I had Him, and I wanted Him.*' Fletcher's tenderness, Ford's passion lose colour placed side by side with the utterances of this worn recluse whose hands are empty of every treasure." [1] Sometimes with her subject her language assumes a majestic solemnity : " The pillars of Heaven shall tremble and quake " (lxxv.) ; sometimes it seems to march to its goal in an ascent of triumphal measure as with beating of drums : " The body was in the grave till Easter-morrow and from that time He lay nevermore. For then was rightfully ended " . . . (close of Chap. li.). Generally, perhaps, the style in its move-

---

seers of truth to whom longer trial has offered a sterner strength of complex thinking, for wider service here, but who, although they may have learnt thus '*more*' in the knowledge of love, " shall never know nor learn *other* thing without end."—" I understood none higher stature in this life than childhood."

> " It is not growing like a tree
> In bulk, doth make man better be.
>
> .   .   .   .   .
>
> A lily of a day
> Is fairer far in May,
> Although it fall and die that night,
> It was the plant and flower of Light."

For all of the Company of saints have the sight of One Vision, and be it in the steadfast fulfilment of labour, or from out of the merriment of play,—through the strong, bright peace of endurance, or the silent acquiescence of the will, led along valleys of darkness,—or again in some swift rush of prayer into the morning light,—*all* of the saints, the babe and the ancient, beholding " the Blissful Countenance " say " with one voice ": " IT IS WELL." " *Amen. Amen.*"

[1] " Catholic Mystics of the Middle Ages." *Edinburgh Review*, October 1896.

ment recalls the rippling yet even flow of a brook, cheerfully, sweetly monotonous : " If any such lover be in earth which is continually kept from falling, I know it not : for it was not shewed me. But this was shewed : that in falling and in rising we are ever preciously kept in one love " (lxxxii.). But now and again the listener seems to be caught up to Heaven with song, as in that time when her " marvelling " joy in beholding love " breaks out with voice ":—" Behold and see ! the precious plenty of His dearworthy blood descended down into Hell, and braste her bands, and delivered all that were there that belonged to the Court of Heaven. The precious plenty of His dearworthy blood overfloweth all Earth and is ready to wash all creatures of sin which be of goodwill, *have* been and *shall* be. The precious plenty of His dearworthy blood ascended up into Heaven to the blessed body of our Lord Jesus Christ, and there is in Him, bleeding and praying for us to the Father, and is and shall be as long as it needeth ; and ever shall be as long as it needeth ; and evermore it floweth in all Heavens, en-joying the salvation of all mankind that *are* there, and *shall* be—fulfilling the Number that faileth " (xii.).

The Early English Mystics make good reading,— even as to the mere manner of their writings we might say, if it were possible to separate the style from the freshness of feeling and the pointedness of thought that inform it ; and though we do not, of course, have from

Julian,—a woman writing of the *Revelations of Love*,—
the delightfully trenchant, easy address of Hilton in his
counsels as to how to scale the *Ladder of Perfection*—
counsels both wise and witty—yet Julian, too, with all
her sweetness, is full of this every day vigour and common sense. And sometimes she puts things in a naïve,
engaging way of her own, grave and yet light—as if
with a little understanding smile to those to whom she
is speaking :—" Then ween we, who *be* not all wise " ;
"That the outward part should draw the inward to assent
was not shewed to me, but that the inward draweth the
outward by grace and both shall be oned in bliss without
end by the virtue of Christ, *this* was shewed " (lxi., xix.).

Rolle, Hilton, and more especially the *Ancren Riwle*,
give examples of that custom of allegorical interpretation
of Sacred Scriptures that has fascinated many mystical
authors, but one can scarcely suppose that this method
would ever have been a favourite one with Julian even if
she had been in the way of dealing with literary parallels
and references. For though she uses " examples," or
illustrations (sometimes calling them " shewings," or
" bodily examples ") and also metaphorically figurative
speech, she does not shew any interest in elaborate,
arbitrary symbolism. At any rate she is too directly
simple, it seems, and too much in the centre of realities,
to be a writer that (without constraint of following the
lines of others) would take as foundation for an argu-
ment or an exposition outward resemblances or verbal

connections, fit perhaps to illustrate or enforce the truth in question, but lacking in relation to it that inward vital oneness whereby certain things that to man seem below him may become symbolic to him of others that he beholds as within or above him.

Exposition by analysis has been reckoned to be characteristic of the Schoolmen rather than of the Mystics,[1] though surely a mystical sight may be served by an analytical process, and to see God in a part before or while He is seen in the whole is effected not without analysis of the subtlest kind. So we find analysis in Julian's sight (Rev. iii.): "*I saw God in a point*"; and in her conclusions from this: "*By which sight I saw that He is in all things*"; and in her immediate raising, from this conclusion, of the question: "*What is sin?*" and throughout her treatment of the problem in the scheme of her book. Even for the merely formal task of distinguishing by number, Julian, we see, will set briskly forward (though we may not feel much inclined to follow) and often she begins her careful dissections with: "In this I see"—four, five, or six things, as the case may be. Her speech of spiritual Revelations is, however, helped out less by numbers than by living and homely things of sight: the mother and the children and the nurse; lords and servants, kings and their subjects (with echoes of the language of Court and

---

[1] In reference to introspection M. Maeterlinck speaks of Ruysbroeck as "the one analytical mystic." *Ruysbroeck and the Mystics*, p. 19.

d

chivalry) ; the deep sea-ground, waters for our service ; clothing, in its warmth, grace and colour ; the light that stands in the night, the hazel-nut, the scales of herrings.[1]

As one grows familiar with the "Revelations" one finds oneself in the midst of a great scheme : a network of ideas that cross and re-cross each other in a way not very clear at first, perhaps, but not really in confusion. All through this treatise from its beginning, the Revelation as a whole is in the mind of Julian; interpolation by another writer is out of the question : the book is all of a piece, both as the expression of one person, in mind and character, and as the setting forth of a theological system. From the first we find Julian holding her diverse threads of nature and mercy and grace for the fabric of love she is weaving, and all through she guides them in and out, with no hesitation, till at last the whole design lies fair before her, shewing the *Goodness of God*.

With regard to this scheme it may be noted that apart from her merely intellectual pleasure in arithmetical methods of statement, Julian shews throughout a mystical sense of numerical correspondences. Life, both as being and action, is, to her sight, in its perfection full of *trinities*,—while there are *doubles*,—incident to its imperfection, as we may put it, perhaps, though the book itself does not mark this distinction in so many words—there are doubles wherein two things are partially opposed and require for their reconciling a

[1] In ch. vii. de Cressy's " the Seal of her Ring " gives a misreading.

doubles

third that will complete them into trinity. First, as the Centre of all, there is the BLESSED TRINITY: All-Might, All-Wisdom, All-Love : one Goodness: FATHER and SON and HOLY GHOST: one Truth. To the First, Second, and Third Persons correspond the verbs MAY, for all-powerful freedom to do ; CAN, for all-skilful ability to do; WILL, for all-loving will to do. So also "the Father *willeth*, the Son *worketh*, the Holy Ghost *confirmeth*." Another nomenclature of the Holy Trinity is, Might, Wisdom, Goodness : one Love ; but that of Might, Wisdom, Love (employed by Abelard, Aquinas, and the Schoolmen generally) is the usual one, while *Truth, Wisdom, Love*, is employed in reference to that Image of God wherein Man is made : for man has not *created might* : his might is all in the uncreated might of God. Man in his essential Nature is " made-trinity," " like to the unmade Blessed Trinity " —a human trinity of truth, wisdom, love ; and these respectively *see, behold, and delight in* the Divine Trinity of Truth, Wisdom, Love.

Man possesses *Reason*, which *knows*, *Mind*, or a feeling wisdom, which *wits*, and *Love*, which *loves*. The making of Man by the Son of God as Eternal Christ, is the work of *Nature* ; the falling of Man is " suffered " (allowed), and afterwards healed, by *Mercy* ; the raising of Man to a higher than his first state is the work of *Grace*. " In Nature we have our Being ; in Mercy we have our Increasing ; in Grace we have our Fulfilling."

The work of grace by means of our natural Reason en-
lightened by the Holy Ghost to see our sins, is *Contrition*; by means of our naturally-feeling Mind, touched
by the Holy Ghost to behold the pain of the world, is
Compassion; by means of our nature- and grace-in-
inspired Love, which loves our Maker and Saviour (still
by the separation of sin partially, painfully, hid from our
sight) is greater *Longing toward God*. This longing must
become an active " desire " : for the chief work that we
can do as fellow-workers with God in achieving full
oneness with Him is *Prayer*; of which there are three
things to understand : its *Ground* is God by whose
Goodness it springeth in us; its *use* is " to turn our
will to the will of our Lord " ; its *end* is " that we
should be made one with and like to our Lord in all
things." And lastly we have for this life, both by
nature and grace, the comprehensive virtue of *Faith*,
" in which all our virtues come to us " and which has in
its own nature three elements : *understanding*, *belief*, and
trust. With Faith, which belongs perhaps chiefly to
Reason,—" Faith is " nought else but a right understanding, with true belief and sure trust, of our Being :
that we are in God, and God in us, Whom we see not,"
" A light by nature coming from our endless Day, that
is our Father, God " (liv., lxxxiii.)—is also *Hope*,
which belongs to our feeling Mind (our Remembrance)
and to the work of Mercy in this our fallen state :
" Hope that we shall come to our Substance (our

high and heavenly nature) again." Moreover, " Charity
keepeth us in Hope and Hope leadeth us in Charity ;
and in the end all shall be *Charity* " (lxxxv.).

With these trinities and groups of threes are others,
belonging to God and man, mentioned successively in
the closing chapters of the book : three manners of God's
Beholding (or Regard of Countenance) : that of the
Passion, that of Compassion, and that of Bliss ; three
kinds of longing God has : to teach us, to have us, to
fulfil us ; three things that man needs in this life from
God : Love, Longing, and Pity—" pity in love," to keep
him now, and " longing in the same love" to draw him
to heaven ; three things by which man standeth in this
life and by which God is worshipped : " use of man's
reason natural ; common teaching of Holy Church ; inward gracious working of the Holy Ghost " ;—and last
of all, " three properties of God, in which the strength
and effect of all the Revelation standeth," " *Life, Love
and Light*."

Again, Julian speaks of things that are *double*, and this
double state seems to be one of imperfection, though she
does not explicitly say so. Man's nature, she says, was
created " double" : " *Substance*," or Spirit essential from
out of the Spirit Divine, and " *Sensuality* " or spirit related to human senses and making human faculties, intellectual and physical. These two, the Substance and
Sense-soul, in their imperfection of union through the
frailty of created love (which needs the divine in its

might to support it), became partially sundered by the failing of love. "For failing of love on our part, therefore, is all our travail"—from that comes the falling, the dying, and the painful travail between death from sin and life from God—both in the race and the individual. But Christ makes the double into trinity : for Christ is "the Mean [the medium] that keepeth the Substance and Sense-soul together" in his Eternal, Divine-Human Nature, because of His perfect love ; and Christ-Incarnate in His Mercy, by this same perfect love brings these two parts anew and more closely together ; and Christ up-risen, indwelling in the soul thus united, will keep them forever together, in oneness growing with oneness to Him. Moreover, Man being double also as "soul and body," needs to be "saved from double death," and this salvation, given, is Jesus-Christ, who joined Himself to us in the Incarnation and "yielded us up from the Cross with His Soul and Body into His Father's hands."

In a mere reading of the Book these repeated correspondences may be felt as wearisome, formal, fantastic, —or rather they may seem so when, as here, they are brought together and noted, for Julian herself simply speaks of these different groups as they come in her theme. But when one tries to follow the *thought* of this book amongst the heights and depths of the things that are seen and temporal and the things unseen and eternal, these likenesses, found in all, seem to afford one guidance and surety of footing, like steps cut out in a steep

and difficult path.   And as one goes on, and the whole
of the meaning takes form, these significations of something all-prevailing give one a partial understanding
such as Julian perhaps may have had : the feeling, the
" Mind," of a certain half-caught measure in "all things
that are," a proportion, a oneness.   We are amongst
free nature's mountains, but they do not rise haphazard :
they shew a strange, a balanced beauty of line and light
and shade, as convincing, if not as clear in its intention
as the sunrise-lines and colouring of the euphrasy
flower at our feet.   We hear as we walk the wandering
sound of " the vagrant, casual wind," but there is something in its rise and fall, and rising again, that has kinship with the flow and ebb and onrush of the lingering,
punctual waves on the shore.   *Sursum Corda.*

PART III

The Theme of the Book

" THE phase of thought or feeling which we call
Mysticism has its origin in . . . that dim consciousness
of the *beyond* which is part of our nature as human beings.
. . . Mysticism arises when we try to bring this higher
consciousness into relation with the other contents of
our minds.   Religious Mysticism may be defined as the
attempt to realise the presence of the living God in the
soul and in nature, or, more generally, as the attempt to

realise in thought and feeling, the immanence of the temporal in the eternal, and of the eternal in the temporal."—W. R. Inge, *Christian Mysticism*. The Bampton Lectures for 1900, p. 4.

"What is Paradise? All things that are; for all are goodly and pleasant and therefore may fitly be called a Paradise. It is said also that Paradise is an outer Court of Heaven. Even so this world is an outer court of the eternal, or of Eternity, and especially whatever in time, or any temporal creature manifesteth or remindeth us of God or Eternity; for the creature is a guide and a path to God and Eternity."[1] "God is althing that is gode, as to my sight," says Julian, "and the godenes that althing hath, it is He" (viii.).

"*Truth seeth God*," and every man exercising the human gift of Reason may in the sight and in the seeing of truths, attain to some sight of God as Truth. But "*Wisdom beholdeth God*," and although the enlightenment of the Spirit of Wisdom for the discernment of vital truth is a grace that is granted in needful measure to him that seeks to be guided by it, it is perhaps those receivers of grace that are mystics by nature and habit that are the most ready in reaching forward while still on earth to Wisdom's fullest and most immediate beholding of God as All in all. For theirs in the largest (and it may be the highest) efficiency, and in the fullest

[1] *Theologia Germanica*, Chap. 1.

accordance with man's first gift of "Reason Natural," is the further gift that Julian calls "*Mind*": the gift of a certain spiritual sensitiveness whereby they are quick to take impression of eternal things unseen (seeing them either within or beyond the things of time that are seen) with surrender of self to partake of their life.   For in this Beholding of Wisdom, response of the heart in purity and insight of the imagination in faith enhance each other, while the vision of the soul through both takes clearness.

The mystic, who sees the wide-ruling oneness of God with all that is good—and thus, as the Mystics say, with all that *is*,—may begin at any point the beholding of Goodness and therein the beholding of God.   "He is in the mydde poynt of all thyng, and all He doeth" (xi.).   It is in the way of those thus fully endowed for the reaching to truth in its highest wisdom here, while they walk amongst the many manifestations of earth, to take them as delicate partial signs instinct with a single meaning.   Here is mystical perception :—

> "To see a world in a grain of sand,
>   And a heaven in a wild flower;
> Hold infinity in the palm of your hand,
>   And eternity in an hour " ; [1]

by a blackbird's sudden song overhear, "in woodlands within," a joy out of the heart of the Life of life.[2] Speak-

---

[1] Blake's Poems.   [2] *Memorabilia of Jesus*, by W. Peyton, p. 33.

ing of the spiritual sight Julian relates: "I saw God in a point,—by which sight I saw that He is in all things." To the mystical soul, quiet to listen to " the music of the spheres," all sweet accordant sounds are singing *Holy, Holy, Holy*; to the mystical soul, " full of eyes within "—like those *Creatures of Life* seen on the plain by the prophet of the Law of Life as renewed for Hope, and seen in the heights by the herald of the Evangel of life as fulfilled in Love—all symmetrical sights are as doors that are opened in Heaven. But it is most of all in the music and the symmetry made of adverse life and death by the power of love, as this is seen from highest to lowest, from lowest to highest, that the Revelation of God as Love that is All in all is received. And looking thereon in the highest manifestation, the manifestation of Christ, which is made for all men, the mystics meet other beholders, who are not called " mystics," yet who have not merely in greater or less degree, with them, the common gift of Reason, but, after their different manner and in their own share, the gift of the feeling " Mind." For both from the seeing of Truth and from the beholding of Wisdom comes the " holy wondering delight in God " that is simply delight of love in Love. So they of the East and they of the West sit down together to partake of the Bread and the Wine of the Table of God in His Kingdom.

There is no other than one Food of the Divine Life consecrated and made ready and offered to man for his human spirit to feed on; but the Christian mystic finds an offering of that Food, which is the sanctified Life of the Christ of God, not only in its constant presentment to the spirit alone, by the Spirit of God through Christ. To him, as to other Christians, the sight and the offering of the Life in God is given in that memorial, mediate, expectant Sacrament consecrated for the spirit's nurture through those elected Symbols of sense that are the most perfect and sacred symbols because in their earlier, natural use they most immediately minister to the whole human life on earth of the Giver and of the receivers. But along with this chosen Sacrament, and as one with it, there is shewn to the mystic the Life Divine in diverse manners of working: he sees God's Christ from afar, *fore-sees* the Eucharistic Sacrament of His most sacred Death and Life, *now* raised in the Bread and the Wine on high,—seeing its promise low in the ground in the earliest, ageless life of the wheat and the vine: seed cast away, bruised corn of wheat, and dying Body, and broken Bread, and daily obedience; a hidden root, crushed fruit of the vine, and Blood poured forth, and uplifted Wine, and joy of Love over Death: one Life.

Sometimes there is for the mystics a partaking of these lesser " wayside sacraments," sometimes a turning aside from their symbols; sometimes the old song of life in the lower creation awakens singing, sometimes it scarcely is heard. But always the *spirit* of nature's signs as interpreted in Man, above all in Christ, lays its claim on the soul; always as sung by the chorus of human spirits that live on the " Righteousness, Peace, and Joy " of the Will of God, the New Song of Life through Death has in it a summons and receives from one and another here, passing through much tribulation, its fuller concord of human achievement, or at least the desirous *Amen*. So whether the mystic dwell much or little with the sights and sounds of sense, those things that are seen and heard by the *soul* bear to him the command of his home, and the merest doorway glimpses, the echoes most distant, making their proffer of more and more within and beyond, say *Come*.

> " I give you the end of a golden string :
>   Only wind it into a ball,
> It will lead you in at Heaven's Gate,
>   Built in Jerusalem wall." [1]

(Although this " following on to know," this winding of the truth caught hold of into a " perfect round " of thought and will and life, is probably not more easy for the mystics than for other people.

> " Amore, amor, tu sei cerchio rotondo ! " [2])

God is in all; but " our soul may never have rest in things that are beneath itself " (lxvii.). " Well I wot," says Julian, " that heaven and earth and all that is made is great and large, fair and good," yet " all that is made "

---

[1] Gilchrist's *Life and Works of William Blake*, vol. ii.

[2] *Amor de Caritade*, by Jacopone da Todi (formerly ascribed to S. Francis of Assisi).

is seen as a little thing, the size of a hazel nut, held in the palm of her hand, when along with it her spiritual sight beholds the Maker.   And though we may find the Maker in all things, we find Him, both as Maker and Restorer, first and best, First and Last, in the soul. There He is *Alpha*, there *Omega*.   " It is readier to us to come to the knowing of God than to know our own Soul" (in its fullest powers).   " For our soul is so deep-grounded in God and so endlessly treasured, that we may not come to the knowing thereof till we have first knowing of God, which is the Maker, to whom it is oned."   And yet, " we may never come to full knowing of God till we know first clearly our own soul" (lvi.).   The knowledge begins with God, but it begins with Him in the lowest place of the soul rescued from sin by mercy and entered by grace.   " For Himself is nearest and meekest, highest and lowest, and doeth all" (lxxx.).   To the soul that looks on Christ a remembrance rises of its own " fair nature" made in His image; yet "our Lord of His mercy sheweth us our sin and our feebleness by the sweet gracious light of Himself" (lxxviii.).   Thus in the working of grace the soul comes to the knowledge both of its higher and lower parts. For in finding in itself both a natural response to the working of grace by its love and its longing after God, and a contrariness to the goodness of grace by its often failing and falling, it experiences both the action of the " Godly Will" (which is within it as a part of, and a gift from, its higher nature, "the Substance") and the action of a "beastly will" (from the simple animal nature) which can will no moral good and which, "failing of love," falls into sin: whereby comes pain, with all the "travail" of good and evil in conflict during the course of restoration. But it is only when the Sense-soul (wherein the higher will must overcome the lower) is at last brought up to heaven, enriched by all the profits of tribulation, and is united to the Substance waiting there, "hid with Christ in God," that we come to the perfect knowledge of God. For that knowledge, perfect in kind though always growing, can only begin when, being in our "full powers" and "all fully holy," we come to know clearly our own united perfected Soul. This seems to be Julian's view (lvi., etc.).

Julian says elsewhere that we have in us here such a "medley" of good and evil that sometimes we hardly know of others or of ourselves wherein we stand, but that each "holy assent" that we make (by the Godly Will) to the grace and will of God, is a witness that we are of God. A witness to our sonship, it might be said; and perhaps, taking Julian's view for the time, we might think that as the Lost Son "came to himself," so the soul comes to the consciousness of the Godly Will; that as he arose and came to his Father and found Him, or rather was found by his Father, so the soul receives the healing of Christ in Mercy and the leading of the Holy Ghost in Grace; and that as at last, the

son not only found his father but found his lost sonship
—yet a better sonship than ever he had known before
—so the soul comes at last to find, more and more
fully, that new sonship which is of its nature, yet is
more than its nature. For it finds the nature oneness
which by creation it had with the Son of God, enhanced
and for ever sustained by grace.

Sometimes, truly, the Mystical doctrine leads by tracks
that are not easily followed, but it is perhaps only when
her views are regarded in single parts, that any harm
could be found in Julian's statements—all qualified as
they are by her " as to my sight." At first indeed it
may startle one to read of her saints that are known in
the Church and in Heaven " by their sins," to hear that
the wounds left by sin are made " medicines " on earth
and turned to " worships " in Heaven ; but then we
remember the joy that shall be in Heaven over " one
sinner that repenteth," the love that loves much because
much is forgiven. And yet we remember the little
children in *their* high faith and love and innocent days ;
and of such is the Kingdom of God. But the Child,
with many " fair virtues," albeit imperfect, was likewise
Julian's type of the Christian soul : " I understood no
higher stature in this life than Childhood."

" To know our own soul "—it behoveth us to know
our own soul—our high-nature soul, which is enclosed
in God, and also our soul on the earth which Christ-
Jesus inhabits, which has in it the " medley " : " we

have in us our Lord Jesus uprisen, we have in us the wretchedness and the mischief of Adam's falling, dying" (lii.). But elsewhere Julian gives this name "our own soul" to the Church, seeing the Church likewise as the dwelling and working-place of Christ (lxii.). She has been speaking of the Divine Wisdom being as it were the Mother of the soul, and now she seems to lead us to the Church as to the Nursery where He tends His children. "For one single person may oftentimes be broken, but the whole Body of Holy Church was never broken, nor ever shall be, without end. And therefore a sure thing it is, a good and a gracious, to will meekly and mightily to be fastened to our Mother, Holy Church, that is Christ Jesus. For the Food of Mercy that is His dearworthy blood and precious water is plenteous to make us fair and clean; the sweet gracious hands of our Mother be ready and diligently about us. For He in all this working useth the office of a kind nurse that hath not else to do but to entend about the salvation of her child" (lxi.). Each soul is indeed the soul of a person and most intimately knows itself in its personal experience, through which indeed alone it can come to knowledge of others. Yet the single soul knows itself *best* in the souls of all the saints, in the fellowship of the "Blessed Common," where every virtue is found, not in each, at this time, but in *all*—not now in the perfect height nor the fairest flowering, but at growth in that ground where each plant holds some likeness to Christ.

With Julian the Christian Faith is not a thing added to the Mystical sight : these are, as again and again she says, seen both as one.   It is the *inherent* Christianity of her system that makes her teaching always, in a large way, practical.   For the system came at first to be seen by prayerful searching made out of her practical need of an answer to the problem of sin and sorrow ; the Mystical Vision came with " contrition, compassion, and longing after God," those wounds that her contrite, pitiful, longing heart had desired should be made more deep in her life.   It is through the work of grace that Julian reaches back to the gift of nature, its ground ; and from the depths of this root-ground she rises soon again to the " springing and spreading " grace.   So in the First of her Shewings the " higher " truth is seen : " we are all in Him beclosed," but in the Last—the conclusion and confirmation of all—the lower, yet nearer, truth, which *all* may know : " and He is beclosed in us."   And speaking of this dwelling within the soul she speaks of His working us all into Him : " in which working He willeth that we be His helpers, giving to Him all our entending, learning His lores, keeping His laws, desiring that all be done that He doeth ; truly trusting in Him " (lvii.).

Julian had prayed to feel Christ's dying pains, if it should be God's will, in order that she might feel compassion, and the visionary sight of His pain in the Face of the Crucifix filled her with pain as it grew upon her.

e

" How might any pain be more to me than to see Him
that is all my life, all my bliss, and all my joy suffer ? "
Yet the Shewing of Pain was but the introduction to,
and for a time the accompaniment of, the Revelation ;
the Revelation, itself, as a whole, was of Love—the
Goodness or Active Love of God.   So the First Shewing, as the Ground of all the rest, was a large view of
this Goodness as the Ground of all Being.   Although
through these earlier Shewings the Saviour's bodily pain is
felt by Julian so fully in " mind " that she feels it indeed
as if it were bodily anguish she bore, it is in this very
experience that the shewing of Joy is made to her spirit.
So when in the opening of the Revelation she tells
of beholding the Passion of Christ, her first unexpected
word is of sudden joy from the inner sight of the Love
that God is : the sight of the Trinity :—" And in the
same Shewing suddenly the Trinity fulfilled my heart
most of joy.   (For where JESUS appeareth, the blessed
Trinity is understood, as to my sight.) "   And even
as Julian finds afterwards that the Last Word of the
Revelation is the same as the First : " *Thou shalt not be
overcome*," so the opening Sight already shews her that
which shall be revealed all through, for learning of
" more in the same," and uplifts her heart to the fulness
of joy that is shewn at the close.   For she feels that
this shock, as it were, of Revelation—this sudden joy of
seeing Love in the midst of earth's evil, beyond and
beneath and in the pain that is passing, is the entrance

into the joy of the Lord. "Suddenly the Trinity fulfilled my heart with utmost joy.—And so I understood it shall be in heaven without end to all that shall come there" (iv.). So at the close, when the vision was not of the Love Divine in that bending Face beneath the Crown of Thorns, but of the human love that shall spring up to meet the Divine out of the lowness of earth,—the vision of how from this body of death, as from an unsightly, shapeless, and stagnant mass of quagmire, there "sprang a full fair creature, a little Child, fully shapen and formed, agile and lively, whiter than lily; which swiftly glided up into heaven" —the spiritual shewing to the soul is this : "*Suddenly thou shalt be taken from all thy pain. . . . and thou shalt come up above and thou shalt have me . . . and thou shalt be fulfilled of love and of bliss*" (lxiv.). And so in that early experience of Julian's when in her love, abandoned to pity and worship, she wonld not look up to Heaven from the Cross, it was also the inward sight by the higher part of her soul of the higher part of Christ's life, that Heavenly Love that could only rejoice, that overcame her frailty of flesh unwilling to suffer, and made her choose "only Jesus in weal and in woe." "Thou art my Heaven" (xix.-lv.). "All the Trinity wrought in the Passion of Jesus Christ," though only the Son of the Virgin suffered, and in seeing this, Julian saw "the Bliss of Christ's works," "the joy that is in the blissful Trinity [by reason] of the Passion of Christ" ;

the Father willing all, the Son working all, the Holy Ghost confirming all."

This complexity of the Divine-Human life in the Son of God, this union in Christ Jesus of serene untouched blessedness in the heavenly regions of His spirit with His bearing, in the active joy of a "glad giver," all the sin and sorrow of the world, is revealed as the comfort and confidence of man, whose own deepest experience is love that suffers, whose highest worship therefore must be of Love that is strong to suffer.

It was a double joy that was shewn in Christ besides the bliss of the impassible Godhead, which is the bliss of Love without all time and beyond all deeds. For there was joy in the Passion itself: "*If I might suffer more, I would suffer more,*" and joy in its fruits: "*If thou art pleased, I am pleased.*" Thus, too, we are told of three ways in which our Lord would have us behold His Passion: first, "the hard pains He suffered on earth"; second, "the love that made Him to suffer passeth as far all His pains as Heaven is above earth"; third, "the joy and the bliss that made Him to be well-satisfied in it."—"With a glad countenance He looked unto His wounded Side, rejoicing" (xxii., xxiii., xxiv.).

From the sight of Love that is higher than pain comes the sight of Love that is deeper than sin. Julian had had the mystical shewing that God is all that is good,[1]

---

[1] "*Quid me interrogas de bono? Unus est bonus, Deus.*"—S. Matt. xix. 17.

and is only good, is the life of all that is, and doeth all that is done, and she had reasoned, as others before her had reasoned, that therefore "sin hath no substance" and "sin is no deed." But perhaps it is those that are most concerned with God in creature things, that suffer most shaking from the sight of evil. Those that seek God's Kingdom in this present world, finding "the dark places of the earth" full of the habitations of cruelty, have continually the enemy as with a sword in their bones saying within them: "Where is now thy God?" "I saw," says Julian, "that He is in all things. I beheld and considered, with a soft dread, and thought: *What is sin?*" (xi.). So also it is immediately after the coming of the mystical Shewing made "yet more highly": "*It is I, it is I, it is I that am all,*" that the memory of her own experience is brought to her and she sees how in her longings after God, who is all the time so close about us, around us and within,— she had always been hindered from seeing and reaching Him fully by the darkening, disturbing power of sin. "And so I looked generally upon us all, and methought: *If sin had not been, we should have all been clean, and like to our Lord as He made us*" (xxvii.). Thus came again the stirring of that old question over which "afore this time often I wondered," with "mourning and sorrow," "why the beginning of sin was not letted —for then, methought, all should have been well."

To this darkness, crying to God, the light came first

as by a soft general dawning of comfort for faith. "*Sin is behoveable* (it behoved that sin should be suffered to rise) *but all shall be well, and all shall be well, and all manner of things shall be well.*" Yet Julian, unable to take comfort to her heart over that which was still so dark to her intellect, stands "beholding things general, troublously and mourning," saying thus in her thoughts: "*Ah good Lord, how might all be* well, for the great hurt that is come by sin to the creature?" (xxix.).

The answer to this double question as to sin and pain is the central theme of the Revelation, though much is still hidden and much is but dimly revealed as yet to faith. In brief account, the sight, enough for us now, is this: "Mercy, by love, suffereth us to fail [of love] in measure, and in as much as we fail, in so much we die: for it needs must be that we die in so much as we fail of the sight and feeling of God that is our life. . . . And grace worketh our dreadful failing into plenteous, endless solace, and grace worketh our shameful falling into high, worshipful rising; and grace worketh our sorrowful dying into holy, blissful life" (xlviii.). "By the assay of this falling we shall have an high marvellous knowing of love in God, without end. For strong and marvellous is that love that may not and will not be broken for trespass. And this is one understanding of our profit. Another is the lowness and meekness that we shall get by the sight of our falling" (lxi.). "And by this meek knowing after this manner, through contrition and grace, we shall be broken from all that is not our Lord. And then shall our blessed Saviour perfectly heal us and one us to Him" (lxxviii.).

Theodidacta, Profunda, Ecstatica—so Julian has been designated; perhaps she might in fuller truth be called *Theodidacta, Profunda, Evangelica*. She is indeed a mystic, evangelical, practical. With all her fellow-Christians and in the most deeply personal concern she looks with a tender mind on the redeeming work of God by Christ in the "glorious satisfaction" ("*Asseth*"), and in fervent response of love and thankfulness trusts in the blessed Passion of Christ, and in His sure keeping, and in all the restoring, fulfilling work by the Holy Ghost. But after the Mystical manner she seeks "the beyond": that is, while in no way leaving the works of mercy and grace she seeks to go back to the ground or source of them, the Goodness of God,—yes, to God Himself. "I could not have perceived of the part of Mercy but as it were alone in Love." "The Passion was a noble worshipful deed done in a time, but Love was without beginning, is, and shall be without ending."

The Mystical Vision is that which in outward nature sees the unseen within the seen, but it is also that which in spiritual things sees behind and beyond the temporal means, the eternal causes and ends (vi.). And it is surely here in the spiritual things, in the heart and centre of human existence, in the stress of

sin and suffering, rather than amongst the gentle growing things, and flaming lights, and songs, and blameless
creatures of Nature that the Beatific Vision on earth is
at its highest. For here are found united the *Evangel*
and the *Vision* and the *Life* of love. "There the soul
is highest, noblest, and worthiest, where it is lowest,
meekest, and mildest": it is not in nature's goodness
alone that we have our life, "all our life is in three," in
nature, in mercy, in grace; "whereof we have meekness, mildness, patience and pity" (lviii., lix.). Man's
"spirit," the higher nature that Julian talks of, may
indeed be there in the Heavenly places, as an infant's
angel lying in the Father's arms, always beholding His
Face in love's silence of waiting ; but here in earthly
places is the Prodigal Son returning, here too is the
Father's embrace, and here is His earliest greeting of
the son that was lost and is found. And already here
in the Kingdom of Heaven on Earth (where *all* grow
pure in the sonship obedience of Jesus Christ), are
those that are kept from the first as little children, taken
up in His arms and suffered to sing their Hosannahs,
which perfect His praise.

The Revelation of Love is all centred in the Passion,
and looking on the Passion in time the soul sees, in
vision, the Lamb that was slain from the foundation
of the world, the mind conceives how before all time
the Divine Love took to itself in the Wisdom of God
the mode of Manhood, and in time created Man in the

same, and how thus God could be and do all that man could be and do, could exercise Love Divine in human Faith and Courage: could "take our flesh" and live on the earth as "the Man, Christ-Jesus," "in all points tempted like as we are," finding His daily Bread in the will of the Father, drinking with joy of the Wine of Life in the evening cup of Death. "Pain is passing," says Julian, but in passing it leads forth love in man to its deepest living, its fairest height of pureness and strength and fulfilment. Thus it behoved the Captain of man's salvation to have His perfection here through suffering. It is the *Lamb* in the midst of the Throne, the Almighty Love that was slain, that is Shepherd to the Martyrs, leading them unto living fountains of waters. He that bore the yoke gives rest to the heavy-laden; blessed is He that mourned: for He comforteth with His comfort.

So in the Mediæval story,[1] the highest Mystical Vision, the sight of the Holy Grail, comes only to him that is pure from self, and looks on the bleeding wound that sin has left in man, and is compassionate, and gives himself to service and healing.—*Can ye* drink *of the Cup I drank of?*—Love's Cup that is Death and Life.—

> Wine of Love's joy I see thy cup
> Red to the trembling brim
> With Life outpoured, once lifted up,
> I drink, remembering Him.—

[1] *A Key to Wagner's Parsifal*, by H. von Wolzogen, tr. by Ashton Ellis.

It is the mourners who are comforted : those that bear griefs of their own, or bear griefs of others fully, do not despair, though the mere onlooker may well despair. Thus the compassionate Julian's vision is of *Comfort*—comfort not for herself "in special," but for "the general Man" — for all her fellow-Christians. She who had long time mourned for the hurt that is come by sin to the creature, came to the sight of comfort not by turning her eyes away but by deeper compassion that found through the very wounds the healing of Love on earth, the glory of Love in Heaven. She was "filled with compassion for the Passion of Christ," and thus she saw *His joy*; so afterwards, she tells, "I was fulfilled in part with compassion of all mine even-Christians, for that well, well-beloved people that shall be saved. For God's servants, Holy Church, shall be shaken in sorrow and anguish and tribulation in this world, as men shake a cloth in the wind. And as to this our Lord answered in this manner : A great thing shall I make hereof in Heaven of endless worship and everlasting joys. Yea so far forth as this I saw : that our Lord joyeth of the tribulations of His servants, with ruth and compassion." "For He saith : *I shall wholly break you of your vain affections and of your vicious pride : and after that I shall together gather you, and make you mild and meek, clean and holy, by oneing to me*" (xxviii.). Sin is indeed " the sharpest scourge," " viler and more painful than hell, without comparison," " an horrible thing to see for the loved soul that would be all fair and shining in the sight of God, as Nature and Grace teacheth." And darkness, which overhangs the soul while here it is " meddling with any part of sin," " so that we see not clearly the Blissful Countenance of our Lord," is a lasting, life-long " natural penance " from God, the feeling of which indeed does not depart with actual sinning : "for ever the more clearly that the soul seeth this Blissful Countenance by grace of loving, the more it longeth to see it in fulness " (lxxii.). All this is in man's experience, with many other pains—pains which in individual lives have no proportionate relation to sin, though, in general, " sin is cause of pain " and " pain purgeth."— (" *For I tell thee, howsoever thou do thou shalt have woe* "), (lxxvii., xxvii.). But the Comfort Revealed shews how sin, which " hath no part of being " and " could not be known but by the pain it is cause of," (sin which in this view may be compared to the nails of the Passion— mere dead matter, though with power to wound unto death for a time the blessed Life), sin, which is failure of human love,—leaves, notwithstanding all its horror, an opening for a fuller influx of Divine love and strength.[1] And as to *darkness*, " seeking is as good as beholding, for

---

[1] Goodness is Active Love—love that moves. Drawing back from the finite creature, as a wave from the shore, it " suffers " sin's void to appear. But this lack of itself is allowed for the time, that so return- ing again in its force, to which evil is nothing, it may cover the desolate nature with deepness and highness and fulness unknown before. (See lvii.).

the time that God will suffer the soul to be in travail"
(x.). And as to tribulation of every kind, " the Passion
of our Lord is comfort to us against all this, and so is
His blessed will" (xxvii.).

The parts may seem to come by chance and to be
" amiss," but the whole, and in the whole each part, is
ordered. " And when we be all brought up above, then
shall we see clearly in God the secret things which be
now hid to us. Then shall none of us be stirred to say :
Lord, if it had been thus, then it had been full well : but we
shall all say with *one* voice : *Lord, blessed mayst Thou be,
for it is thus : it is well ; and now we see verily that all
things are done as it was then ordained before that anything
was made* " (xi., lxxxv.). " Moreover He that shall be
our bliss when we are there, is our Keeper while we are
here " ; and the Last Word of the Revelation is the same
as the First ; " *Thou shalt not be overcome.*" " He said not :
*Thou shalt not be tempested, thou shalt not be travailed, thou shalt
not be distressed* ; but He said : *Thou shalt not be overcome.*"

This is God's comfort. And that here, meanwhile,
we should take His comfort is Julian's chief desire and
instruction. For Julian, who speaking so much of sin
as a strange and troubling sight, yet gives as examples
of sin only a slothful mistrusting despondency,—speaks
indeed of faith and hope and charity, compassion and meekness, but scarcely *exhorts* except to the
cheerful enduring of tribulation. So she gives counsel
as to " rejoicing more in His whole love than sorrowing

in our often fallings"; as to "living gladly and merrily for love's sake" in our penance of darkness (lxxii.-lxxxi.). And in general, for all experiences of life, "It is God's will that we take His promises and His comfortings as largely and as mightily as we may take them, and also He willeth that we take our abiding and our troubles as lightly as we may take them, and set them at nought" (lxiv., lxv., xv.).

"We are all one in comfort," says Julian, "all the gracious comfort was for all mine even-Christians." Sin separates, pain isolates, but salvation and comfort unite.

And lastly, in this mystical vision of the oneness of man with God in Christ, man is seen not only as united in himself in the diverse parts of his nature, and as one with his fellow man, but as joined to that which is below him. How often of one good and another, as of that fair and sacred "service of the Mother"—"nearest, readiest, and surest"—"in the creatures by whom it is done," do we hear Julian's confident word of Sacramental declaration: "*It is Christ.*" "For God is all that is good, as to my sight, and God hath made all that is made: and he that loveth generally all his even-Christians for God, he loveth all that is. For in Mankind that shall be saved is comprehended all: that is to say, all that is made and the Maker of all. For in Man is God, and God is in all. And I hope," adds Julian, in words that are fitting to take for her courteous, her tender, "*Good Speed*" ere we pass to her book—altogether like her as they are, even to the careful, conditional "if" (for *nothing*, not even comfort, behoves to be "overdone much"), "I hope by the grace of God he that beholdeth it thus shall be truly taught and mightily comforted, if he needeth comfort" (ix.).

Deus ubique est, et totus ubique est. All things are gathered up in Man, and Man is gathered up in Christ; and Christ is gathered up in the Bosom of the Father. So the world of the lower creation makes promise: *All things are yours*; and the Church says over its offering, lifted up: *Ye are Christ's*; and from the stillness the voice of peace is heard: *And Christ is God's.* "All the promises of God in HIM are *Yea* and in HIM *Amen*, unto the glory of God by us." All the promises of God: the blossom that floated to the ground; "the lily of a day" that "fell and died that night"; the "little Child, whiter than lily, that swiftly glided up into Heaven" —all the utterances silenced here—in Him are *Yea* and in Him *Amen*: *Yea* on earth and *Amen* for ever. "*He turneth the shadow of death into the morning.*"

May 1901.

REVELATIONS OF DIVINE LOVE

REVELATIONS OF DIVINE LOVE

CHAPTER I

" A Revelation of Love—in Sixteen Shewings "

THIS is a Revelation of Love that Jesus Christ, our endless bliss, made in Sixteen Shewings, or Revelations particular.

Of the which the First is of His precious crowning with thorns; and therewith was comprehended and specified the Trinity, with the Incarnation, and unity betwixt God and man's soul; with many fair shewings of endless wisdom and teachings of love: in which all the Shewings that follow be grounded and oned.[1]

The Second is the changing of colour of His fair face in token of His dearworthy [2] Passion.

The Third is that our Lord God, Allmighty Wisdom, All-Love, right as verily as He hath made everything that is, all-so verily He doeth and worketh all-thing that is done.

The Fourth is the scourging of His tender body, with plenteous shedding of His blood.

The Fifth is that the Fiend is overcome by the precious Passion of Christ.

The Sixth is the worshipful [3] thanking by our Lord

---

[1] made one, united.   [2] precious, honoured.   [3] honour-bestowing.

A

God in which He rewardeth His blessed servants in Heaven.

The Seventh is [our] often feeling of weal and woe; (the feeling of weal is gracious touching and lightening, with true assuredness of endless joy; the feeling of woe is temptation by heaviness and irksomeness of our fleshly living;) with ghostly understanding that we are kept all as securely in Love in woe as in weal, by the Goodness of God.

The Eighth is of the last pains of Christ, and His cruel dying.

The Ninth is of the pleasing which is in the Blissful Trinity by the hard Passion of Christ and His rueful dying: in which joy and pleasing He willeth that we be solaced and mirthed [1] with Him, till when we come to the fulness in Heaven.

The Tenth is, our Lord Jesus sheweth in love His blissful heart even cloven in two, rejoicing.

The Eleventh is an high ghostly Shewing of His dearworthy Mother.

The Twelfth is that our Lord is most worthy Being.

The Thirteenth is that our Lord God willeth we have great regard to all the deeds that He hath done: in the great nobleness of the making of all things; and the excellency of man's making, which is above all his works; and the precious Amends [2] that He hath made for man's sin, turning all our blame into endless worship.[3] In which Shewing also our Lord saith: *Behold and see! For by the same Might, Wisdom, and Goodness that I have done all this, by the same Might, Wisdom, and Goodness I shall*

---

[1] made glad.   [2] MS. "Asseth" = Satisfaction, making-enough.
[3] honour, glory.

make well all that is not well ; and thou shalt see it. And in this He willeth that we keep us in the Faith and truth of Holy Church, not desiring to see into His secret things now, save as it belongeth to us in this life.

The Fourteenth is that our Lord is the Ground of our Prayer. Herein were seen two properties : the one is rightful prayer, the other is steadfast trust ; which He willeth should both be alike large ; and thus our prayer pleaseth Him and He of His Goodness fulfilleth it.

The Fifteenth is that we shall suddenly be taken from all our pain and from all our woe, and of His Goodness we shall come up above, where we shall have our Lord Jesus for our meed and be fulfilled with joy and bliss in Heaven.

The Sixteenth is that the Blissful Trinity, our Maker, in Christ Jesus our Saviour endlessly dwelleth in our soul, worshipfully ruling and protecting all things, us mightily and wisely saving and keeping, for love ; and we shall not be overcome of our Enemy.

CHAPTER II

"A simple creature unlettered.—Which creature afore desired three gifts of God"

THESE Revelations were shewed to a simple creature unlettered,[1] the year of our Lord 1373, the Thirteenth day of May. Which creature [had] afore desired three gifts of God. The First was mind of His Passion ; the Second was bodily sickness in youth, at thirty years

---

[1] " that cowde no letter "=unskilled in letters.

of age ; the Third was to have of God's gift three wounds.

As to the First, methought I had some feeling in the Passion of Christ, but yet I desired more by the grace of God. Methought I would have been that time with Mary Magdalene, and with other that were Christ's lovers, and therefore I desired a bodily sight wherein I might have more knowledge of the bodily pains of our Saviour and of the compassion of our Lady and of all His true lovers that saw, that time, His pains. For I would be one of them and suffer with Him. Other sight nor shewing of God desired I never none, till the soul were disparted from the body. The cause of this petition was that after the shewing I should have the more true mind in the Passion of Christ.

The Second came to my mind with contrition; [I] freely desiring that sickness [to be] so hard as to death, that I might in that sickness receive all my rites of Holy Church, myself thinking that I should die, and that all creatures might suppose the same that saw me : for I would have no manner of comfort of earthly life. In this sickness I desired to have all manner of pains bodily and ghostly that I should have if I should die, (with all the dreads and tempests of the fiends) except the out-passing of the soul. And this I meant [1] for [that] I would be purged, by the mercy of God, and afterward live more to the worship of God because of that sickness. And that for the more furthering [2] in my death : for I desired to be soon with my God.

These two desires of the Passion and the sickness I desired with a condition, saying thus : *Lord, Thou knowest*

---

[1] thought of, designed.   [2] MS. " speed."

what I would,—if it be Thy will that I have it—; and if it be not Thy will, good Lord, be not displeased: for I will nought but as Thou wilt.

For the Third [petition], by the grace of God and teaching of Holy Church I conceived a mighty desire to receive three wounds in my life: that is to say, the wound of very contrition, the wound of kind [1] compassion, and the wound of steadfast [2] longing toward God.[3] And all this last petition I asked without any condition.

These two desires aforesaid passed from my mind, but the third dwelled with me continually.

CHAPTER III

"I desired to suffer with Him"

AND when I was thirty years old and a half, God sent me a bodily sickness, in which I lay three days and three nights; and on the fourth night I took all my rites of Holy Church, and weened not to have lived till day. And after this I languored forth [4] two days and two nights, and on the third night I weened oftentimes to have passed; [5] and so weened they that were with me.

And being in youth as yet, I thought it great sorrow to die;—but for nothing that was in earth that meliked to live for, nor for no pain that I had fear of: for I

[1] *i.e.* natural.   [2] MS. "wilful"=earnest, with set will.
[3] For these wounds see xvii. p. 40, xxvii. p. 56, xxviii., lxxii. and xxxix.
[4] "I langorid forth"=languished on.
[5] I thought often that I was about to die.

trusted in God of His mercy. But it was to have lived that I might have loved God better, and longer time, that I might have the more knowing and loving of God in bliss of Heaven. For methought all the time that I had lived here so little and so short in regard of that endless bliss,—I thought [it was as] nothing. Wherefore I thought: *Good Lord, may my living no longer be to Thy worship!*[1] And I understood by my reason and by my feeling of my pains that I should die; and I assented fully with all the will of my heart to be at God's will.

Thus I dured till day, and by then my body was dead from the middle downwards, as to my feeling. Then was I minded to be set upright, backward leaning, with help,—for to have more freedom of my heart to be at God's will, and thinking on God while my life would last.

My Curate was sent for to be at my ending, and by that time when he came I had set my eyes, and might[2] not speak. He set the Cross before my face and said: *I have brought thee the Image of thy Maker and Saviour : look thereupon and comfort thee therewith.*

Methought I was well [as it was], for my eyes were set uprightward unto Heaven, where I trusted to come by the mercy of God; but nevertheless I assented to set my eyes on the face of the Crucifix, if I might ;[2] and so I did. For methought I might longer dure to look even-forth[3] than right up.

After this my sight began to fail, and it was all dark about me in the chamber, as if it had been night, save in

---

[1] Or it may be, as in de Cressy's version : *May my living be no longer to Thy worship?*

[2] *i.e.* could.   [3] straight forward.

the Image of the Cross whereon I beheld a common light; and I wist not how. All that was away from [1] the Cross was of horror to me, as if it had been greatly occupied by the fiends.

After this the upper [2] part of my body began to die, so far forth that scarcely I had any feeling;—with shortness of breath. And then I weened in sooth to have passed.

And in this [moment] suddenly all my pain was taken from me, and I was as whole (and specially in the upper part of my body) as ever I was afore.

I marvelled at this sudden change; for methought it was a privy working of God, and not of nature. And yet by the feeling of this ease I trusted never the more to live; nor was the feeling of this ease any full ease unto me: for methought I had liefer have been delivered from this world.

Then came suddenly to my mind that I should desire the second wound of our Lord's gracious gift: that my body might be fulfilled with mind and feeling of His blessed Passion. For I would that His pains were my pains, with compassion and afterward longing to God. But in this I desired never bodily sight nor shewing of God, but compassion such as a kind [3] soul might have with our Lord Jesus, that for love would be a mortal man: and therefore I desired to suffer with Him.

---

[1] MS. "beside."   [2] MS. "over."

[3] "kinde," true to its nature that was made after the likeness of the Creating Son of God, the type and the Head of Mankind,—therefore loving, and sympathetic with Him, and compassionate of His earthly sufferings: Who, Himself, for Love's sake, suffered as man.

THE FIRST REVELATION

CHAPTER IV

" I saw . . . as it were in the time of His Passion . . . And
in the same Shewing suddenly the Trinity filled my heart
with utmost joy "

IN this [moment] suddenly I saw the red blood trickle
down from under the Garland hot and freshly and
right plenteously, as it were in the time of His Passion
when the Garland of thorns was pressed on His blessed
head who was both God and Man, the same that suffered
thus for me. I conceived truly and mightily that it was
Himself shewed it me, without any mean.[1]

And in the same Shewing suddenly the Trinity fulfilled my heart most of joy. And so I understood it
shall be in heaven without end to all that shall come
there. For the Trinity is God: God is the Trinity;
the Trinity is our Maker and Keeper, the Trinity is our
everlasting love and everlasting joy and bliss, by our
Lord Jesus Christ. And this was shewed in the First
[Shewing] and in all: for where Jesus appeareth, the
blessed Trinity is understood, as to my sight.

And I said: *Benedicite Domine!* This I said for
reverence in my meaning, with mighty voice; and full
greatly was astonied for wonder and marvel that I
had, that He that is so reverend and dreadful will be
so homely with a sinful creature living in wretched
flesh.

This [Shewing] I took for the time of my temptation,

---

[1] intermediary—thing or person. See vi., xix., xxxv., lv.

—for methought by the sufferance of God I should be tempted of fiends ere I died. Through this sight of the blessed Passion, with the Godhead that I saw in mine understanding, I knew well that *It* was strength enough for me, yea, and for all creatures living, against all the fiends of hell and ghostly temptation.

In this [Shewing] He brought our blessed Lady to my understanding. I saw her ghostly, in bodily likeness : a simple maid and a meek, young of age and little waxen above a child, in the stature that she was when she conceived. Also God shewed in part the wisdom and the truth of her soul : wherein I understood the reverent beholding in which she beheld her God and Maker, marvelling with great reverence that He would be born of her that was a simple creature of His making. And this wisdom and truth : knowing the greatness of her Maker and the littleness of herself that was made,— caused her to say full meekly to Gabriel : *Lo me, God's handmaid!* In this sight [1] I understood soothly that she is more than all that God made beneath her in worthiness and grace ; for above her is nothing that is made but the blessed [Manhood [2]] of Christ, as to my sight.

[1] Either : *In this sight*—Shewing—*of her ;* or *In this her sight,*—insight —beholding (vii., xliv., lxv.). See Rev. xi. ch. xxv., "For our Lord shewed me nothing in special but our Lady Saint Mary ; and her He shewed three times." The first shewing is here (a *sight* referred to in ch. vii. and elsewhere); the second, in ch. xviii. ; the third, in ch. xxv.

[2] This word is in S. de Cressy's edition.

CHAPTER V

*" God, of Thy Goodness, give me Thyself ;—only in Thee
I have all "*

IN this same time our Lord shewed me a spiritual[1]
sight of His homely loving.

I saw that He is to us everything that is good and
comfortable for us : He is our clothing that for love
wrappeth us, claspeth us, and all encloseth[2] us for
tender love, that He may never leave us ; being to us
all-thing that is good, as to mine understanding.

Also in this He shewed me a little thing, the quantity
of an hazel-nut, in the palm of my hand ; and it was as
round as a ball. I looked thereupon with eye of my
understanding, and thought : *What may this be ?* And it
was answered generally thus : *It is all that is made.* I
marvelled how it might last, for methought it might
suddenly have fallen to naught for little[ness]. And I
was answered in my understanding : *It lasteth, and ever
shall [last] for that God loveth it.* And so All-thing hath
the Being by the love of God.

In this Little Thing I saw three properties. The first
is that God made it, the second is that God loveth it,
the third, that God keepeth it. But what is to me verily
the Maker, the Keeper, and the Lover,—I cannot tell ;
for till I am Substantially oned[3] to Him, I may never have
full rest nor very bliss : that is to say, till I be so
fastened to Him, that there is right nought that is made
betwixt my God and me.

---

[1] MS. "ghostly," and so, generally, throughout the MS.
[2] " Becloseth," and so generally.   [3] *i.e.* in essence united.

It needeth us to have knowing of the littleness of creatures and to hold as nought [1] all-thing that is made, for to love and have God that is unmade. For this is the cause why we be not all in ease of heart and soul: that we seek here rest in those things that are so little, wherein is no rest, and know not our God that is All-mighty, All-wise, All-good. For He is the Very Rest. God willeth to be known, and it pleaseth Him that we rest in Him; for all that is beneath Him sufficeth not us. And this is the cause why that no soul is rested till it is made nought as to all [2] things that are made. When it is willingly made nought, for love, to have Him that is all, then is it able to receive spiritual rest.

Also our Lord God shewed that it is full great pleasance to Him that a helpless soul come to Him simply and plainly and homely. For this is the natural yearnings of the soul, by the touching of the Holy Ghost (as by the understanding that I have in this Shewing): *God, of Thy Goodness, give me Thyself: for Thou art enough to me, and I may nothing ask that is less that may be full worship to Thee; and if I ask anything that is less, ever me wanteth,—but only in Thee I have all.*

And these words are full lovely to the soul, and full near touch they the will of God and His Goodness. For His Goodness comprehendeth all His creatures and all His blessed works, and overpasseth [3] without end. For He is the endlessness, and He hath made us only to Himself, and restored us by His blessed Passion, and keepeth us in His blessed love; and all this of His Goodness.

---

[1] " to nowtyn."
[2] " nowtid of." de Cressy: " *naughted* (emptied)."   [3] surpasseth.

CHAPTER VI

"The Goodness of God is the highest prayer, and it cometh down to the lowest part of our need"

THIS Shewing was made to learn our soul wisely to cleave to the Goodness of God.

And in that time the custom of our praying was brought to mind: how we use for lack of understanding and knowing of Love, to take many means [whereby to beseech Him].[1]

Then saw I truly that it is more worship to God, and more very delight, that we faithfully [2] pray to Himself of His Goodness and cleave thereunto by His Grace, with true understanding, and steadfast by love, than if we took all the means that heart can think. For if we took all these means, it is too little, and not full worship to God: but in His Goodness is all the whole, and *there* faileth right nought.

For this, as I shall tell, came to my mind in the same time: We pray to God for [the sake of] His holy flesh and His precious blood, His holy Passion, His dear-

---

[1] MS. "To make many menys." So in *Letter* 385 of *The Paston Letters*, 1422-1509 A.D.—"Our Soverayn Lord hath wonne the feld, & upon the Munday next after Palmesunday, he was resseved in York with gret solempnyte & processyons. And the Mair & Comons of the said cite mad ther menys to have grace be [by] Lord Montagu & Lord Barenars, which be for the Kyngs coming in to the said cite, which graunted hem [them] grace." *Letter* 472 (from Margaret Paston).— "Your ryth wele willers have kounselyd me that I xuld kownsell you to maken other menys than ye have made, to other folks, that wold spede your matyrs better than they have done thatt ye have spoken to therof" (ed. by James Gairdner, vol i.). See ch. iv. p. 8.

[2] *i.e.* trustingly.

worthy death and wounds : and all the blessed kindness,[1] the endless life that we have of all this, is His Goodness. And we pray Him for [the sake of] His sweet Mother's love that Him bare ; and all the help we have of her is of His Goodness. And we pray by His holy Cross that he died on, and all the virtue and the help that we have of the Cross, it is of His Goodness. And on the same wise, all the help that we have of special saints and all the blessed Company of Heaven, the dearworthy love and endless friendship that we have of them, it is of His Goodness. For God of His Goodness hath ordained means to help us, full fair and many : of which the chief and principal mean is the blessed nature that He took of the Maid, with all the means that go afore and come after which belong to our redemption and to endless salvation. Wherefore it pleaseth Him that we seek Him and worship through means, understanding that He is the Goodness of all.

For the Goodness of God is the highest prayer, and it cometh down to the lowest part of our need. It quickeneth our soul and bringeth it on life, and maketh it for to waxen in grace and virtue. It is nearest in nature ; and readiest in grace : for *it* is the same grace that the soul seeketh, and ever shall seek till we know verily that He hath us all in Himself enclosed.

For He hath no despite of that He hath made, nor hath He any disdain to serve us at the simplest office that to our body belongeth in nature, for love of the soul that He hath made to His own likeness.

For as the body is clad in the cloth, and the flesh in the skin, and the bones in the flesh, and the heart in the

---

[1] bond as of relationship.

whole,[1] so are we, soul and body, clad in the Goodness of God, and enclosed. Yea, and more homely: for all these may waste and wear away, but the Goodness of God is ever whole; and more near to us, without any likeness; for truly our Lover desireth that our soul cleave to Him with all its might, and that we be evermore cleaving to His Goodness. For of all things that heart may think, this pleaseth most God, and soonest speedeth [the soul].

For our soul is so specially loved of Him that is highest, that it overpasseth the knowing of all creatures: that is to say, there is no creature that is made that may [fully] know[2] how much and how sweetly and how tenderly our Maker loveth us. And therefore we may with grace and His help stand in spiritual beholding, with everlasting marvel of this high, overpassing, inestimable[3] Love that Almighty God hath to us of His Goodness. And therefore we may ask of our Lover with reverence all that we will.

For our natural[4] Will is to have God, and the Good Will of God is to have us; and we may never cease from willing nor from longing till we have Him in fullness of joy: and then may we no more desire.

For He willeth that we be occupied in knowing and loving till the time that we shall be fulfilled in Heaven; and therefore was this lesson of Love shewed, with all that followeth, as ye shall see. For the strength and the Ground of all was shewed in the First Sight. For

---

[1] "the bouke"=the bulk, the thorax.   [2] "witten."

[3] or, as in S. de Cressy, "unmeasurable." The word, however, looks like "oninestimable" with the "on" blotted or erased.

[4] "kindly."

of all things the beholding and the loving of the Maker maketh the soul to seem less in his own sight, and most filleth him with reverent dread and true meekness; with plenty of charity to his even-Christians.[1]

CHAPTER VII

" The Shewing is not other than of faith, nor less nor more "

AND [it was] to learn us this, as to mine understanding, [that] our Lord God shewed our Lady Saint Mary in the same time: that is to say, the high Wisdom and Truth *she* had in beholding of her Maker so great, so holy, so mighty, and so good. This greatness and this nobleness of the beholding of God fulfilled her with reverent dread, and withal she saw herself so little and so low, so simple and so poor, in regard of[2] her Lord God, that this reverent dread fulfilled her with meekness. And thus, by this ground [of meekness] she was fulfilled with grace and with all manner of virtues, and overpasseth all creatures.

In all the time that He shewed this that I have told now in spiritual sight, I saw the bodily sight lasting of the plenteous bleeding of the Head. The great drops of blood fell down from under the Garland like pellots, seeming as it had come out of the veins; and in the coming out they were brown-red, for the blood was full

---

[1] " to his even cristen "—fellow-Christians (" even "=equal). *Hamlet*, Act v. Sc. i. " great folk . . . more than their even Christian."

[2] *i.e.* seen at the same time as, or in comparison with. See the note to ch. iv. p. 9.

thick; and in the spreading-abroad they were bright-red; and when they came to the brows, then they vanished; notwithstanding, the bleeding continued till many things were seen and understood. The fairness and the lifelikeness is like nothing but the same; the plenteousness is like to the drops of water that fall off the eaves after a great shower of rain, that fall so thick that no man may number them with bodily wit; and for the roundness, they were like to the scale of herring, in the spreading on the forehead. These three came to my mind in the time: pellots, for roundness, in the coming out of the blood; the scale of herring, in the spreading in the forehead, for roundness; the drops off eaves, for the plenteousness innumerable.

This Shewing was quick and life-like, and horrifying and dreadful, sweet and lovely. And of all the sight it was most comfort to me that our God and Lord that is so reverend and dreadful, is so homely and courteous: and this most fulfilled me with comfort and assuredness of soul.

And to the understanding of this He shewed this open example :—

It is the most worship that a solemn King or a great Lord may do a poor servant if he will be homely with him, and specially if he sheweth it *himself*, of a full true meaning, and with a glad cheer, both privately and in company. Then thinketh this poor creature thus: *And what might this noble Lord do of more worship and joy to me than to shew me that am so simple this marvellous homeliness? Soothly it is more joy and pleasance to me than [if] he gave me great gifts and were himself strange in manner.*

This bodily example was shewed so highly that man's

heart might be ravished and almost forgetting itself for joy of the great homeliness. Thus it fareth with our Lord Jesus and with us. For verily it is the most joy that may be, as to my sight, that He that is highest and mightiest, noblest and worthiest, is lowest and meekest, homeliest and most courteous : and truly and verily this marvellous joy shall be shewn us all when we see Him.

And this willeth our Lord that we seek for and trust to, joy and delight in, comforting us and solacing us, as we may with His grace and with His help, unto the time that we see it verily. For the most fulness of joy that we shall have, as to my sight, is the marvellous courtesy and homeliness of our Father, that is our Maker, in our Lord Jesus Christ that is our Brother and our Saviour.

But this marvellous homeliness may no man fully see in this time of life, save he have it of special shewing of our Lord, or of great plenty of grace inwardly given of the Holy Ghost. But faith and belief with charity deserveth the meed : and so it is had, by grace ; for in faith, with hope and charity, our life is grounded. The Shewing, made to whom that God will, plainly teacheth the same, opened and declared, with many privy points belonging to our Faith which be worshipful to know. And when the Shewing which is given in a time is passed and hid, then the faith keepeth [it] by grace of the Holy Ghost unto our life's end. And thus through the Shewing it is not other than of faith, nor less nor more ; as it may be seen in our Lord's teaching in the same matter, by that time that it shall come to the end.

B

CHAPTER VIII

" In all this I was greatly stirred in charity to my fellow-Christians that they might see and know the same that I saw "

AND as long as I saw this sight of the plenteous bleeding of the Head I might never cease from these words : *Benedicite Domine !*

In which Shewing I understood six things :—The first is, the tokens of the blessed Passion and the plenteous shedding of His precious blood. The second is, the Maiden that is His dearworthy Mother. The third is, the blissful Godhead that ever was, is, and ever shall be: Almighty, All-Wisdom, All-Love. The fourth is, all-thing that He hath made.—For well I wot that heaven and earth and all that is made is great and large, fair and good ; but the cause why it shewed so little to my sight was for that I saw it in the presence of Him that is the Maker of all things : for to a soul that seeth the Maker of all, all that is made seemeth full little.— The fifth is : He that made all things for love, by the same love keepeth them, and shall keep them[1] without end. The sixth is, that God is all that is good, as to my sight, and the goodness that each thing hath, it is He.[2]

And all these our Lord shewed me in the first Sight, with time and space to behold it. And the bodily sight stinted,[3] but the spiritual sight dwelled in mine under-

[1] " it is kept, and shall be."

[2] " God is althing that is gode, as to my sight, and the godenes that al thing hath, it is he."

[3] *i.e.* ceased.

standing, and I abode with reverent dread, joying in
that I saw. And I desired, as I durst, to see more, if
it were His will, or else [to see for] longer time the
same.

In all this I was greatly stirred in charity to mine
even-Christians, that they might see and know the same
that I saw : for I would it were comfort to them. For
all this Sight was shewed [with] general [regard]. Then
said I to them that were about me : *It is to-day Doomsday
with me.* And this I said for that I thought to have died.
(For that day that a man dieth, he is judged [1] as shall be
without end, as to mine understanding.) This I said for
that I would they might love God the better, for to
make them to have in mind that this life is short, as they
might see in example. For in all this time I weened to
have died; and that was marvel to me, and troublous
partly : for methought this Vision was shewed for them
that should live. And that which I say of me, I say in
the person of all mine even-Christians : for I am taught
in the Spiritual Shewing of our Lord God that He
meaneth so. And therefore I pray you all for God's
sake, and counsel you for your own profit, that ye leave
the beholding of a poor creature [2] that it was shewed to,
and mightily, wisely, and meekly behold God that of
His courteous love and endless goodness would shew it
generally, in comfort of us all. For it is God's will
that ye take it with great joy and pleasance, as if Jesus
had shewed it to you all.

[1] " deemed."　　　　　　　　[2] " a wretch."

CHAPTER IX

"If I look singularly to myself, I am right nought"

BECAUSE of the Shewing I am not good but if I love
God the better: and in as much as ye love God
the better, it is more to you than to me. I say[1] not
this to them that be wise, for they wot it well; but I
say it to you that be simple, for ease and comfort: for
we are all one in comfort. For truly it was not shewed
me that God loved me better than the least soul that is
in grace; for I am certain that there be many that never
had Shewing nor sight but of the common teaching of
Holy Church, that love God better than I. For if I
look singularly to myself, I am right nought; but in
[the] general [Body] I am, I hope, in oneness of charity
with all mine even-Christians.

For in this oneness standeth the life of all mankind
that shall be saved. For God is all that is good, as to
my sight, and God hath made all that is made, and
God loveth all that He hath made: and he that loveth
generally all his even-Christians for God, he loveth all
that is. For in mankind that shall be saved is comprehended all: that is to say, all that is made and the
Maker of all. For in man is God, and God is in all.
And I hope by the grace of God he that beholdeth it
thus shall be truly taught and mightily comforted, if he
needeth comfort.

I speak of them that shall be saved, for in this time
God shewed me none other. But in all things I believe
as Holy Church believeth, preacheth, and teacheth. For

---

[1] " sey "=*say* or *tell*.

the Faith of Holy Church, the which I had aforehand understood and, as I hope, by the grace of God earnestly kept in use and custom, stood continually in my sight: [I] willing and meaning never to receive anything that might be contrary thereunto. And with this intent I beheld the Shewing with all my diligence: for in all this blessed Shewing I beheld it as one in God's meaning.[1]

All this was shewed by three [ways]: that is to say, by bodily sight, and by word formed in mine understanding, and by spiritual sight. But the spiritual sight I cannot nor may not shew it as openly nor as fully as I would. But I trust in our Lord God Almighty that He shall of His goodness, and for your love, make you to take it more spiritually and more sweetly than I can or may tell it.

THE SECOND REVELATION

CHAPTER X

"God willeth to be seen and to be sought: to be abided and to be trusted"

AND after this I saw with bodily sight in the face of the crucifix that hung before me, on the which I gazed continually, a part of His Passion: despite, spitting and sullying, and buffetting, and many languoring pains, more than I can tell, and often changing of colour. And one time I saw half the face, beginning at

[1] *i.e.* The teaching of the Faith and the teaching of the special Shewing were both from God and were seen to be at one.

the ear, over-gone with dry blood till it covered to the mid-face. And after that the other half [was] covered on the same wise, the whiles in this [first] part [it vanished] even as it came.

This saw I bodily, troublously and darkly; and I desired more bodily sight, to have seen more clearly. And I was answered in my reason: *If God will shew thee more, He shall be thy light: thee needeth none but Him.* For I saw Him sought.[1]

For we are now so blind and unwise that we never seek God till He of His goodness shew Himself to us. And when we aught see of Him graciously, then are we stirred by the same grace to seek with great desire to see Him more blissfully.

And thus I saw Him, and sought Him; and I had Him, I wanted Him. And this is, and should be, our common working in this [life], as to my sight.

One time mine understanding was led down into the sea-ground, and there I saw hills and dales green, seeming as it were moss-be-grown, with wrack and gravel. Then I understood thus: that if a man or woman were under the broad water, if he might have sight of God so as God is with a man continually, he should be safe in body and soul, and take no harm: and overpassing, he should have more solace and comfort than all this world can tell. For He willeth we should believe that we see Him continually though that to us it seemeth but little [of sight]; and in this belief He maketh us evermore to gain grace. For He will be seen and He will be sought: He will be abided and he will be trusted.

---

[1] In de Cressy's version: "I saw Him and sought Him."

This Second Shewing was so low and so little and so simple, that my spirits were in great travail in the beholding,—mourning, full of dread, and longing: for I was some time in doubt whether it was a Shewing. And then diverse times our good Lord gave me more sight, whereby I understood truly that it was a Shewing. It was a figure and likeness of our foul deeds' shame that our fair, bright, blessed Lord bare for our sins: it made me to think of the Holy Vernacle [1] at Rome, which He hath portrayed with His own blessed face when He was in His hard Passion, with steadfast will going to His death, and often changing of colour. Of the brownness and blackness, the ruefulness and wastedness of this Image many marvel how it might be, since that He portrayed it with His blessed Face who is the fairness of heaven, flower of earth, and the fruit of the Maiden's womb. Then how might this Image be so darkening in colour [2] and so far from fair?—I desire to tell like as I have understood by the grace of God:—

We know in our Faith, and believe by the teaching and preaching of Holy Church, that the blessed Trinity made Mankind to [3] His image and to His likeness. In the same manner-wise we know that when man fell so deep and so wretchedly by sin, there was none other help to restore man but through Him that made man. And He that made man for love, by the same love He would restore man to the same bliss, and overpassing; and like as we were like-made to the Trinity in our first making, our Maker would that we should be like Jesus Christ, Our Saviour, in heaven without end, by the virtue of our again-making.

[1] The Handkerchief of S. Veronica.   [2] "so discolouring."

[3] i.e. according to.

Then atwix these two, He would for love and worship of man make Himself as like to man in this deadly life, in our foulness and our wretchedness, as man might be without guilt. This is that which is meant where it is said afore: it was the image and likeness of our foul black deeds' shame wherein our fair, bright, blessed Lord God was hid. But full certainly I dare say, and we ought to trow it, that so fair a man was never none but He, till what time His fair colour was changed with travail and sorrow and Passion and dying. Of this it is spoken in the Eighth Revelation, where it treateth more of the same likeness. And where it speaketh of the Vernacle of Rome, it meaneth by [reason of] diverse changing of colour and countenance, sometime more comfortably and life-like, sometime more ruefully and death-like, as it may be seen in the Eighth Revelation.

And this [dim] vision was a learning, to mine understanding, that the continual seeking of the soul pleaseth God full greatly: for it may do no more than seek, suffer and trust. And this is wrought in the soul that hath it, by the Holy Ghost; and the clearness of finding, *it* is of His special grace, when it is His will. The seeking, with faith, hope, and charity, pleaseth our Lord, and the finding pleaseth the soul and fulfilleth it with joy. And thus was I learned, to mine understanding, that seeking is as good as beholding, for the time that He will suffer the soul to be in travail. It is God's will that *we seek Him*, to the beholding of Him, for by *that* [1] He shall shew us Himself of His special grace when He will. And how a soul shall have Him in its beholding, He shall

---

[1] " for be that "=*for by* [*means of*] *that*; or possibly the Old English and Scottish 'forbye that'=*besides that.*

teach Himself: and that is most worship to Him and profit to thyself, and [the soul thus] most receiveth of meekness and virtues with the grace and leading of the Holy Ghost. For a soul that only fasteneth it[self] on to God with very trust, either by seeking or in beholding, it is the most worship that it may do to Him, as to my sight.

These are two workings that may be seen in this Vision: the one is seeking, the other is beholding. The seeking is common,—that every soul may have with His grace,—and ought to have that discretion and teaching of the Holy Church. It is God's will that we have three things in our seeking:—The first is that we seek earnestly and diligently, without sloth, and, as it may be through His grace, without unreasonable [1] heaviness and vain sorrow. The second is, that we abide Him steadfastly for His love, without murmuring and striving against Him, to our life's end: for it shall last but awhile. The third is that we trust in Him mightily of full assured faith. For it is His will that we know that He shall appear suddenly and blissfully to all that love Him.

For His working is privy, and He willeth to be perceived; and His appearing shall be swiftly sudden; and He willeth to be trusted. For He is full gracious and homely: Blessed may He be!

---

[1] "onskilful"=without discernment or ability; unpractical. S. de Cressy, "unreasonable."

[2] "hend"=at hand; (handy, dexterous;) courteous, gentle, urbane.

THE THIRD REVELATION

CHAPTER XI

" All thing that is done, it is well done : for our Lord God
doeth all." " Sin is no deed "

AND after this I saw God in a Point,[1] that is to say,
in mine understanding,—by which sight I saw
that He is in all things.

I beheld and considered, seeing and knowing in sight,
with a soft dread, and thought : *What is sin?*

---

[1] See below : " He is in the Mid-point," and lxiii. p. 158, "the blessed
Point from which nature came : that is, God." See also xxi. p. 45,
" Where is now any point of thy pain?" (least part) and xxi. p. 46,
" abiding unto the last point "; and lxiv. p. 161, " set the point of our
thought." These uses of the word may be compared with the following :—From the *Banquet of Dante Alighieri*, tr. by K. Hillard (Kegan
Paul, Trench & Co.), Bk. II. xiv. 12, "*Geometry moves between the point
and the circle*" ; as Euclid says, "the point is the beginning of Geometry,
and according to him, the circle is the most perfect figure, and therefore
may be considered its end. . . . The point by reason of its indivisibility
is immeasurable, and the circle by reason of its arc cannot be exactly
squared, and therefore cannot be measured with precision." Notes by
Miss Hillard : " This is why the Deity is represented by a *point*. *Paradiso*, xxviii. 16 : ' A point beheld I,' ' Heaven and all nature, hangs
upon that point,' etc. Bk. IV. 6, quoting Aristotle's *Physics* : ' *The
circle can be called perfect when it is a true circle*. And this is when
it contains a point which is equally distant from every part of its
circumference.' In the *Vita Nuova* Love appearing, says—' I am as
the centre of a circle, to which all parts of the circumference bear
an equal relation' (' *Amor che muove il sole e l'altre stelle*')." From
Neoplatonism, by C. Bigg, D.D. (S.P.C.K.), p. 122 : " Thus we get
a triplet—Soul, Intelligence, and a higher Intelligence. The last is
spoken of as One, as a point, as neither good nor evil because above
both."

For I saw truly that God doeth all-thing, be it never so little. And I saw truly that nothing is done by hap nor by adventure, but all things by the foreseeing wisdom of God: if it be hap or adventure in the sight of man, our blindness and our unforesight is the cause. For the things that are in the foreseeing wisdom of God from without beginning, (which rightfully and worshipfully and continually He leadeth to the best end,) as they come about fall to us suddenly, ourselves unwitting; and thus by our blindness and our unforesight we say: these be haps and adventures. But to our Lord God they be not so.

Wherefore me behoveth needs to grant that all-thing that is done, it is well-done: for our Lord God doeth all. For in this time the working of creatures was not shewed, but [the working] of our Lord God in the creature: for He is in the Mid-point of all thing, and all He doeth. And I was certain He doeth no sin.

And here I saw verily that sin is no deed: for in all this was not sin shewed. And I would no longer marvel in this, but beheld our Lord, what He would shew.

And thus, as much as it might be for the time, the rightfulness of God's working was shewed to the soul.

Rightfulness hath two fair properties: it is right and it is full. And so are all the works of our Lord God: thereto needeth neither the working of mercy nor grace: for they be all rightful: wherein faileth nought.

But in another time He gave a Shewing for the beholding of sin nakedly, as I shall tell: where He useth working of mercy and grace.

And this vision was shewed, to mine understanding, for that our Lord would have the soul turned truly unto the beholding of Him, and generally of all His works. For they are full good; and all His doings are easy and sweet, and to great ease bringing the soul that is turned from the beholding of the blind Deeming of man unto the fair sweet Deeming of our Lord God. For a man beholdeth some deeds well done and some deeds evil, but our Lord beholdeth them not so: for as all that hath being in nature is of Godly making, so is all that is done, in property of God's doing. For it is easy to understand that the best deed is well done: and so well as the best deed is done—the highest—so well is the least deed done; and all thing in its property and in the order that our Lord hath ordained it to from without beginning. For there is no doer but He.

I saw full surely that he changeth never His purpose in no manner of thing, nor never shall, without end. For there was no thing unknown to Him in His rightful ordinance from without beginning. And therefore all-thing was set in order ere anything was made, as it should stand without end; and no manner of thing shall fail of that point. For He made all things in fulness of goodness, and therefore the blessed Trinity is ever full pleased in all His works.[1]

And all this shewed He full blissfully, signifying thus: *See! I am God: see! I am in all thing: see! I do all thing: see! I lift never mine hands off my works, nor ever shall, without end: see! I lead all thing to the end I ordained it to from without beginning, by the same Might, Wisdom and Love whereby I made it. How should any thing be amiss?*

Thus mightily, wisely, and lovingly was the soul

[1] On this subject, with the "Two Deemings" and "the Godly Will," see xlv., xxxv., xxxvii., lxxxii.

examined in this Vision.   Then saw I soothly that me
behoved, of need, to assent, with great reverence enjoying in God.

THE FOURTH REVELATION

CHAPTER XII

" The dearworthy blood of our Lord Jesus Christ as verily
as it is most precious, so verily it is most plenteous "

AND after this I saw, beholding, the body plenteously
bleeding in seeming of[1] the Scourging, as thus :—
The fair skin was broken full deep into the tender flesh
with sharp smiting all about the sweet body.   So
plenteously the hot blood ran out that there was neither
seen skin nor wound, but as it were all blood.   And
when it came where it should have fallen down, then it
vanished.   Notwithstanding, the bleeding continued
awhile : till it might be seen and considered.[2]   And
this was so plenteous, to my sight, that methought if
it had been so in kind[3] and in substance at that time, it
should have made the bed all one blood, and have passed
over about.

And then came to my mind that God hath made waters
plenteous in earth to our service and to our bodily ease
for tender love that He hath to us, but yet liketh
Him better that we take full homely His blessed blood
to wash us of sin : for there is no water[4] that is made
that He liketh so well to give us.   For it is most plen-

[1] i.e. as it were from.
[2] " sene with avisement," so, p. 26.—" I beheld with avisement."
[3] i.e. Nature, reality.   [4] MS. "licor."

teous as it is most precious : and that by the virtue of His blessed Godhead ; and it is [of] our Kind, and all-blissfully belongeth to us by the virtue of His precious love.

The dearworthy blood of our Lord Jesus Christ as verily as it is most precious, so verily it is most plenteous. Behold and see ! The precious plenty of His dearworthy blood descended down into Hell and burst her bands and delivered all that were there which belonged to the Court of Heaven. The precious plenty of His dearworthy blood overfloweth all Earth, and is ready to wash all creatures of sin, which be of goodwill, have been, and shall be. The precious plenty of His dearworthy blood ascended up into Heaven to the blessed body of our Lord Jesus Christ, and there is in Him, bleeding and praying for us to the Father,—and is, and shall be as long as it needeth ;—and ever shall be as long as it needeth. And evermore it floweth in all Heavens enjoying the salvation of all mankind, that are there, and shall be—fulfilling the number [1] that faileth.

THE FIFTH REVELATION

CHAPTER XIII

" The Enemy is overcome by the blessed Passion and Death of our Lord Jesus Christ "

AND after this, ere God shewed any words, He suffered me for a convenient time to give heed unto Him and all that I had seen, and all intellect [2] that

---

[1] The appointed number of heavenly citizens.

[2] *i.e.* significance, teaching.

was therein, as the simplicity of the soul might take it.[1] Then He, without voice and opening of lips, formed in my soul these words: *Herewith is the Fiend overcome.* These words said our Lord, meaning His blessed Passion as He shewed it afore.

On this shewed our Lord that the Passion of Him is the overcoming of the Fiend. God shewed that the Fiend hath now the same malice that he had afore the Incarnation. And as sore he travaileth, and as continually he seeth that all souls of salvation escape him, worshipfully, by the virtue of Christ's precious Passion. And that is his sorrow, and full evil is he ashamed: for all that God suffereth him to do turneth [for] us to joy and [for] him to shame and woe. And he hath as much sorrow when God giveth him leave to work, as when he worketh not: and that is for that he may never do as ill as he would: for his might is all taken[2] into God's hand.

But in God there may be no wrath, as to my sight: for our good Lord endlessly hath regard to His own worship and to the profit of all that shall be saved. With might and right He withstandeth the Reproved, the which of malice and wickedness busy them to contrive and to do against God's will. Also I saw our Lord scorn his malice and set at nought his unmight; and He willeth that we do so. For this sight I laughed mightily, and that made them to laugh that were about me, and their laughing was a pleasure to me. I thought that I would that all mine even-Christians had seen as I saw,

---

[1] *i.e.* in so far as the simplicity of my soul was able to understand it.—See xxiv.

[2] S. de Cressy has " locked " instead of " taken."

and then would they all laugh with me. But I saw not Christ laugh. For I understood that we may laugh in comforting of ourselves and joying in God for that the devil is overcome. And when I saw Him scorn his malice, it was by leading of mine understanding into our Lord: that is to say, it was an inward shewing of verity, without changing of look.[1] For, as to my sight, it is a worshipful property of God's that [He] is ever the same.

And after this I fell into a graveness,[2] and said: *I see three things: I see game, scorn, and earnest. I see [a] game, in that the Fiend is overcome; I see scorn, in that God scorneth him, and he shall be scorned; and I see earnest, in that he is overcome by the blissful Passion and Death of our Lord Jesus Christ that was done in full earnest and with sober travail.*

When I said, *he is scorned,*—I meant that God scorneth him, that is to say, because He seeth him now as he shall do without end. For in this [word] God shewed that the Fiend is condemned. And this meant I when I said: *he shall be scorned*: [he shall be scorned] at Doomsday, generally of all that shall be saved, to whose consolation he hath great ill-will.[3] For then he shall see that all the woe and tribulation that he hath done to them shall be turned to increase of their joy, without end; and all the pain and tribulation that he would have brought them to shall endlessly go with him to hell.

---

[1] " chere "=expression of countenance.   [2] " sadhede."   [3] " invye."

THE SIXTH REVELATION

CHAPTER XIV

" The age of every man shall be acknowledged before him in Heaven, and every man shall be rewarded for his willing service and for his time "

AFTER this our good Lord said : *I thank thee for thy travail, and especially for thy youth.* By this He Thank His Faith Ser it New

And in this [Shewing] mine understanding was lifted up into Heaven where I saw our Lord as a lord in his own house, which hath called all his dearworthy servants and friends to a stately[1] feast. Then I saw the Lord take no place in His own house, but I saw Him royally reign in His house, fulfilling it with joy and mirth, Himself endlessly to gladden and to solace His dearworthy friends, full homely and full courteously, with marvellous melody of endless love, in His own fair blessed Countenance. Which glorious Countenance of the Godhead fulfilleth the Heavens with joy and bliss.[2]

God shewed three degrees of bliss that every soul shall have in Heaven that willingly hath served God in any degree in earth. The first is the worshipful thanks of our Lord God that he shall receive when he is delivered of pain. This thanking is so high and so worshipful that the soul thinketh it filleth him though there were no more. For methought that all the pain and travail that might be suffered by all living men might not deserve the worshipful thanks that one man shall have that willingly hath served God. The second is

---

[1] MS. "solemne"—ceremonial.   [2] See lxxii. and lxxv.

C

that all the blessed creatures that are in Heaven shall see that worshipful thanking, and He maketh his service known to all that are in Heaven. And here this example was shewed:—A king, if he thank his servants, it is a great worship to them, and if he maketh it known to all the realm, then is the worship greatly increased.—The third is, that as new and as gladdening as it is received in that time, right so shall it last without end.

And I saw that homely and sweetly was this shewed, and that the age of every man shall be [made] known in Heaven, and [he] shall be rewarded for his willing service and for his time. And specially the age of them that willingly and freely offer their youth unto God, passingly is rewarded and wonderfully is thanked.

For I saw that whene'er what time a man or woman is truly turned to God,—for one day's service and for his endless will he shall have all these three decrees of bliss. And the more the loving soul seeth this courtesy of God, the liefer he [1] is to serve him all the days of his life.

THE SEVENTH REVELATION

CHAPTER XV

" It is not God's will that we follow the feeling of pains in sorrow and mourning for them "

AND after this He shewed a sovereign ghostly pleas-ance in my soul. I was fulfilled with the ever-lasting sureness, mightily sustained without any painful

[1] Throughout this MS. *the soul* is referred to generally with the masculine pronoun; the feminine pronoun is never used, in any of its cases; the neuter sometimes occurs.

spiritual

dread. This feeling was so glad and so ghostly that I was in all peace and in rest, that there was nothing in earth that should have grieved me.

This lasted but a while, and I was turned and left to myself in heaviness, and weariness of my life, and irksomeness of myself, that scarcely I could have patience to live. There was no comfort nor none ease to me but faith, hope, and charity; and these I had in truth, but little in feeling.

And anon after this our blessed Lord gave me again the comfort and the rest in soul, in satisfying and sureness so blissful and so mighty that no dread, no sorrow, no pain bodily that might be suffered should have distressed me. And then the pain shewed again to my feeling, and then the joy and the pleasing, and now that one, and now that other, divers times—I suppose about twenty times. And in the time of joy I might have said with Saint Paul : *Nothing shall dispart me from the charity of Christ* ; and in the pain I might have said with Peter : *Lord, save me : I perish!*

This Vision was shewed me, according to mine understanding, [for] that it is speedful to some souls to feel on this wise : sometime to be in comfort, and sometime to fail and to be left to themselves. God willeth that we know that He keepeth us even alike secure in woe and in weal. And for profit of man's soul, a man is sometime left to himself ; although sin is not always the cause : for in this time I sinned not wherefore I should be left to myself—for it was so sudden. Also I deserved not to have this blessed feeling. But freely our Lord giveth when He will ; and suffereth us [to be] in woe sometime. And both is one love.

For it is God's will that we hold us in comfort with all our might: for bliss is lasting without end, and pain is passing and shall be brought to nought for them that shall be saved. And therefore it is not God's will that we follow the feelings of pain in sorrow and mourning for them, but that we suddenly pass over, and hold us in endless enjoyment.

THE EIGHTH REVELATION

CHAPTER XVI

"A Part of His Passion"

AFTER this Christ shewed a part of His Passion near His dying.

I saw His sweet face as it were dry and bloodless with pale dying. And later, more pale, dead, languoring; and then turned more dead unto blue; and then more brown-blue, as the flesh turned more deeply dead. For His Passion shewed to me most specially in His blessed face (and chiefly in His lips): there I saw these four colours, though it were afore fresh, ruddy, and pleasing, to my sight. This was a pitiful change to see, this deep dying. And also the [inward] moisture clotted and dried, to my sight, and the sweet body was brown and black, all turned out of fair, life-like colour of itself, unto dry dying.

For that same time that our Lord and blessed Saviour died upon the Rood, it was a dry, hard wind, and wondrous cold, as to my sight, and what time [all] the precious blood was bled out of the sweet body that might pass therefrom, yet there dwelled a moisture in the sweet flesh of Christ, as it was shewed.

Bloodlessness and pain dried within; and blowing of wind and cold coming from without met together in the sweet body of Christ. And these four,—twain without, and twain within—dried the flesh of Christ by process of time. And though this pain was bitter and sharp, it was full long lasting, as to my sight, and painfully dried up all the lively spirits of Christ's flesh. Thus I saw the sweet flesh dry in seeming by part after part, with marvellous pains. And as long as any spirit had life in Christ's flesh, so long suffered He pain.

This long pining seemed to me as if He had been seven nights dead, dying, at the point of outpassing away, suffering the last pain. And when I said it seemed to me as if He had been seven night dead, it meaneth that the sweet body was so discoloured, so dry, so shrunken, so deathly, and so piteous, as if He had been seven night dead, continually dying. And methought the drying of Christ's flesh was the most pain, and the last, of His Passion.

CHAPTER XVII

"How might any pain be more to me than to see Him that is all my life, and all my bliss, and all my joy suffer?"

AND in this dying was brought to my mind the words of Christ: *I thirst.*

For I saw in Christ a double thirst: one bodily; another spiritual, the which I shall speak of in the Thirty-first Chapter.

For this word was shewed for the bodily thirst: the which I understood was caused by failing of moisture. For the blessed flesh and bones was left all alone without blood and moisture. The blessed body dried alone long time with wringing of the nails and weight of the body. For I understood that for tenderness of the sweet hands and of the sweet feet, by the greatness, hardness, and grievousness of the nails the wounds waxed wide and the body sagged, for weight by long time hanging. And [therewith was] piercing and pressing of the head, and binding of the Crown all baked with dry blood, with the sweet hair clinging, and the dry flesh, to the thorns, and the thorns to the flesh drying; and in the beginning while the flesh was fresh and bleeding, the continual sitting of the thorns made the wounds wide. And furthermore I saw that the sweet skin and the tender flesh, with the hair and the blood, was all raised and loosed about from the bone, with the thorns where-through it were rent in many pieces, as a cloth that were sagging, as if it would hastily have fallen off, for heaviness and looseness, while it had natural moisture. And that was great sorrow and dread to me: for methought I would not for my life have seen it fall. How it was done I saw not; but understood it was with the sharp thorns and the violent and grievous setting on of the Garland of Thorns, unsparingly and without pity. This continued awhile, and soon it began to change, and I beheld and marvelled how it might be. And then I saw it was because it began to dry, and stint a part of the weight, and set about the Garland. And thus it encircled all about, as it were garland upon garland. The Garland of the Thorns was dyed with the blood, and that other garland [of Blood] and the head, all was one colour, as clotted blood when it is dry. The skin of the flesh that shewed (of the face and of the body), was small-rimpled [1] with a tanned colour, like a dry board when it is aged ; and the face more brown than the body.

I saw four manner of dryings : the first was bloodless-ness ; the second was pain following after ; the third, hanging up in the air, as men hang a cloth to dry ; the fourth, that the bodily Kind asked liquid and there was no manner of comfort ministered to Him in all His woe and distress. Ah ! hard and grievous was his pain, but much more hard and grievous it was when the moisture failed and began to dry thus, shrivelling.

These were the pains that shewed in the blessed head : the first wrought to the dying, while it had moisture ; and that other, slow, with shrinking drying, [and] with blowing of the wind from without, that dried and pained Him with cold more than mine heart can think.

And other pains—for which pains I saw that all is too little that I can say : for it may not be told.

The which Shewing of Christ's pains filled me full of pain. For I wist well He suffered but once, but [this was as if] He would shew it me and fill me with mind as I had afore desired. And in all this time of Christ's pains I felt no pain but for Christ's pains. Then thought-me : *I knew but little what pain it was that I asked ;* and, as a wretch, repented me, thinking : *If I had wist what it had been, loth me had been to have prayed it.* For me-thought it passed bodily death, my pains.

I thought : *Is any pain like this ?* And I was answered

---

[1] or *shrivelled.*

in my reason: *Hell is another pain: for there is despair. But of all pains that lead to salvation this is the most pain, to see thy Love suffer. How might any pain be more to me than to see Him that is all my life, all my bliss, and all my joy, suffer?* Here felt I soothfastly[1] that I loved Christ so much above myself that there was no pain that might be suffered like to that sorrow that I had to [see] Him in pain.

CHAPTER XVIII

"When He was in pain, we were in pain"

HERE I saw a part of the compassion of our Lady, Saint Mary: for Christ and she were so oned in love that the greatness of her loving was cause of the greatness of her pain. For in this [Shewing] I saw a Substance of Nature's[2] Love, continued by Grace, that creatures have to Him: which Kind Love was most fully shewed in His sweet Mother, and overpassing; for so much as she loved Him more than all other, her pains passed all other. For ever the higher, the mightier, the sweeter that the love be, the more sorrow it is to the lover to see that body in pain that is loved.

And all His disciples and all His true lovers suffered pains more than their own bodily dying. For I am sure by mine own feeling that the least of them loved Him so far above himself that it passeth all that I can say.

Here saw I a great oneing betwixt Christ and us, to mine understanding: for when He was in pain, we were in pain.

---

[1] in sure verity.   [2] *i.e.* Natural.

And all creatures that might suffer pain, suffered with Him : that is to say, all creatures that God hath made to our service. The firmament, the earth, failed for sorrow in their Nature in the time of Christ's dying. For it belongeth naturally to their property to know Him for their God, in whom all their virtue standeth : when He failed, then behoved it needs to them, because of kindness [between them], to fail with Him, as much as they might, for sorrow of His pains.

And thus they that were His friends suffered pain for love. And, generally, *all* : that is to say, they that knew Him not suffered for failing of all manner of comfort save the mighty, privy keeping of God. I speak of two manner of folk, as they may be understood by two persons : the one was Pilate, the other was Saint Dionyse[1] of France, which was [at] that time a Paynim. For when he saw wondrous and marvellous sorrows and dreads that befell in that time, he said : *Either the world is now at an end, or He that is Maker of Kind suffereth.* Wherefore he did write on an altar : THIS IS THE ALTAR OF UNKNOWN GOD. God that of His goodness maketh the planets and the elements to work of Kind to the blessed man and the cursed, in that time made withdrawing[2] of it from both ; wherefore it was that they that knew Him not were in sorrow that time.

Thus was our Lord Jesus made-naught for us ; and all we stand in this manner made-naught with Him, and shall do till we come to His bliss ; as I shall tell after.

---

[1] Dionysius, "the Areopagite," according to the legend of S. Denis.
[2] MS.—"it was withdrawen from bothe."

CHAPTER XIX

"Thus was I learned to choose Jesus for my Heaven, whom I
saw only in pain at that time"

IN this [time] I would have looked up from the Cross,
but I durst not. For I wist well that while I beheld
in the Cross I was surely-safe; therefore I would not
assent to put my soul in peril: for away from the Cross
was no sureness, for frighting of fiends.

Then had I a proffer in my reason,[1] as if it had been
friendly said to me: *Look up to Heaven to His Father.*
And then saw I well, with the faith that I felt, that
there was nothing betwixt the Cross and Heaven that
might have harmed me. Either me behoved to look up
or else to answer. I answered inwardly with all the
might of my soul, and said: *Nay; I may not: for Thou
art my Heaven.* This I said for that I would not. For
I would liever have been in that pain till Doomsday than
to come to Heaven otherwise than by Him. For I wist
well that He that bound me so sore, He should unbind
me when that He would. Thus was I learned to choose
Jesus to my Heaven, whom I saw only in pain at that
time: meliked no other Heaven than Jesus, which shall
be my bliss when I come there.

And this hath ever been a comfort to me, that I chose
Jesus to my Heaven, by His grace, in all this time of
Passion and sorrow; and that hath been a learning to
me that I should evermore do so: choose only Jesus
to my Heaven in weal and woe.

And though I as a wretched creature had repented me

[1] see xxxv. and lv.

(I said afore if I had wist what pain it would be, I had been loth to have prayed), here saw I truly that it was reluctance and frailty of the flesh without assent of the soul: to which God assigneth no blame. Repenting and willing choice be two contraries which I felt both in one at that time. And these be [of our] two parts: the one outward, the other inward. The outward part is our deadly flesh-hood, which is now in pain and woe, and shall be, in this life: whereof I felt much in this time; and that part it was that repented. The inward part is an high, blissful life, which is all in peace and in love: and this was more inwardly felt; and this part is [that] in which mightily, wisely and with steadfast will I chose Jesus to my Heaven.

And in this I saw verily that the inward part is master and sovereign to the outward, and doth not charge itself with, nor take heed to, the will of that: but all the intent and will is set to be oned unto our Lord Jesus. That the outward part should draw the inward to assent was not shewed to me; but that the inward draweth the outward by grace, and both shall be oned in bliss without end, by the virtue of Christ,—*this* was shewed.

CHAPTER XX

"For every man's sin that shall be saved He suffered, and every man's sorrow and desolation He saw, and sorrowed for Kinship and Love"

AND thus I saw our Lord Jesus languoring long time. For the oneing with the Godhead gave strength to the manhood for love to suffer more than all men might suffer: I mean not only more pain than all men might suffer, but also that He suffered more pain than all men of salvation that ever were from the first beginning unto the last day might tell or fully think, having regard to the worthiness of the highest worshipful King and the shameful, despised, painful death. For He that is highest and worthiest was most fully madenought and most utterly despised.

For the highest point that may be seen in the Passion is to think and know what He is that suffered. And in this [Shewing] He brought in part to mind the height and nobleness of the glorious Godhead, and therewith the preciousness and the tenderness of the blessed Body, which be together united; and also the lothness that is in our Kind to suffer pain. For as much as He was most tender and pure, right so He was most strong and mighty to suffer.

And for every man's sin that shall be saved He suffered: and every man's sorrow and desolation He saw, and sorrowed for Kindness and love. (For in as much as our Lady sorrowed for His pains, in so much He suffered sorrow for her sorrow;—and more, in as greatly as the sweet manhood of Him was worthier in Kind.) For as long as He was passible He suffered for us and sorrowed *for* us; and now He is uprisen and no more passible, yet He suffereth *with* us.

And I, beholding all this by His grace, saw that the Love of Him was so strong which He hath to our soul that willingly He chose it with great desire, and mildly He suffered it with well-pleasing.

For the soul that beholdeth it thus, when it is touched by grace, it shall verily see that the pains of Christ's

Passion pass all pains : [all pains] that is to say, which shall be turned into everlasting, o'erpassing joys by the virtue of Christ's Passion.

CHAPTER XXI

"We be now with Him in His Pains and His Passion, dying. We shall be with Him in Heaven. Through learning in this little pain that we suffer here, we shall have an high endless knowledge of God which we could never have without that"

IT is God's will, as to mine understanding, that we have Three [1] Manners of Beholding His blessed Passion. The First is : *the hard Pain that He suffered,*— [beholding it] with contrition and compassion. And that shewed our Lord in this time, and gave me strength and grace to see it.

And I looked for the departing with all my might, and thought to have seen the body all dead ; but I saw Him not so. And right in the same time that methought, by the seeming, the life might no longer last and the Shewing of the end behoved needs to be,—suddenly (I beholding in the same Cross), He changed [the look of] His blessed Countenance.[2] The changing of His blessed Countenance changed mine, and I was as glad and merry as it was possible. Then brought our Lord merrily to my mind : *Where is now any point of the pain, or of thy grief?* And I was full merry.

I understood that we be now, in our Lord's meaning, in His Cross with Him in His pains and His Passion,

[1] xxii. and xxiii.
[2] His "blisful chere," or blessed Cheer ; lxxii. and Note.

dying; and we, willingly abiding in the same Cross with His help and His grace unto the last point, suddenly He shall change His Cheer to us, and we shall be with Him in Heaven. Betwixt that one and that other shall be no time, and then shall all be brought to joy. And thus said He in this Shewing: *Where is now any point of thy pain, or thy grief?* And we shall be full blessed.

And here saw I verily that if He shewed now [to] us His *Blissful* Cheer, there is no pain in earth or in other place that should aggrieve us; but all things should be to us joy and bliss. But because He sheweth to us time of His Passion, as He bare it in *this* life, and His Cross, therefore we are in distress and travail, with Him, as our frailty asketh. And the cause why He suffereth [it to be so,] is for [that] He will of His goodness make us the higher with Him in His bliss; and for this little pain that we suffer here, we shall have an high endless knowing in God which we could [1] never have without that. And the harder our pains have been with Him in His Cross, the more shall our worship [2] be with Him in His Kingdom.

THE NINTH REVELATION
CHAPTER XXII

"The Love that made Him to suffer passeth so far all His Pains as Heaven is above Earth"

THEN said our good Lord Jesus Christ: *Art thou well pleased that I suffered for thee?* I said: *Yea, good Lord, I thank Thee; Yea, good Lord, blessed mayst Thou be.*

---

[1] "might."　　　　　　　　[2] *i.e.* glory.

Then said Jesus, our kind Lord: *If thou art pleased, I am pleased: it is a joy, a bliss, an endless satisfying to me that ever suffered I Passion for thee; and if I might suffer more, I would suffer more.*

In this feeling my understanding was lifted up into Heaven, and there I saw three heavens: of which sight I marvelled greatly. And though I see three heavens— and all in the blessed manhood of Christ—none is more, none is less, none is higher, none is lower, but [they are] even-like in bliss.

For the First Heaven, Christ shewed me His Father; in no bodily likeness, but in His property and in His working. That is to say, I saw in Christ that the Father is. The working of the Father is this, that He giveth meed to His Son Jesus Christ. This gift and this meed is so blissful to Jesus that His Father might have given Him no meed that might have pleased Him better. The first heaven, that is the pleasing of the Father, shewed to me as one heaven; and it was full blissful: for He is full pleased with all the deeds that Jesus hath done about our salvation. Wherefore we be not only His by His buying, but also by the courteous gift of His Father we be His bliss, we be His meed, we be His worship, we be His crown. (And this was a singular marvel and a full delectable beholding, that we be His crown!) This that I say is so great bliss to Jesus that He setteth at nought all His travail, and His hard Passion, and His cruel and shameful death.

And in these words: *If that I might suffer more, I would suffer more,*—I saw in truth that as often as He *might* die, so often He *would*, and love should never let Him have rest till He had done it. And I beheld with great diligence for to learn how often He would die if He might. And verily the number passed mine understanding and my wits so far that my reason might not, nor could, comprehend it. And when He had thus oft died, or should, yet He would set it at nought, for love : for all seemeth [1] Him but little in regard of His love.

For though the sweet manhood of Christ might suffer but once, the goodness in Him may never cease of proffer : every day He is ready to the same, if it might be. For if He said He would for my love make new Heavens and new Earth, it were but little in comparison ; [2] for this might be done every day if He would, without any travail. But to die for my love so often that the number passeth creature's reason, it is the highest proffer that our Lord God might make to man's soul, as to my sight. Then meaneth He thus : *How should it not be that I should not do for thy love all that I might of deeds which grieve me not, sith I would, for thy love, die so often, having no regard [3] to my hard pains?*

And here saw I, for the Second [4] Beholding in this blessed Passion *the love that made Him to suffer passeth as far all His pains as Heaven is above Earth*. For the pains was a noble, worshipful deed done in a time by the working of love : but [5] Love was without beginning, is, and shall be without ending. For which love He said full sweetly these words : *If I might suffer more, I would suffer more*. He said not, *If it were needful*

---

[1] " ffor al thynketh him but litil in reward of His love " [in comparison with].

[2] and [3] MS. " Reward." See xxi., xxiii.

[5] MS. "and," probably here, as in other places, with something of the force of " but."

to suffer more: for though it were not needful, if He *might* suffer more, He would.

This deed, and this work about our salvation, was ordained as well as God might ordain it. And here I saw a Full Bliss in Christ: for His bliss should not have been full, if it might any better have been done.

CHAPTER XXIII

" The Glad Giver "
" All the Trinity wrought in the Passion of Jesus Christ "

AND in these three words: *It is a joy, a bliss, an endless satisfying to me,* were shewed three heavens, as thus: For the joy, I understood the pleasure of the Father; and for the bliss, the worship of the Son; and for the endless satisfying,[1] the Holy Ghost. The Father is pleased, the Son is worshipped, the Holy Ghost is satisfied.[1]

And here saw I, for the Third Beholding in His blissful Passion: that is to say, *the Joy and the Bliss that make Him to be well-satisfied in it.* For our Courteous Lord shewed His Passion to me in five manners: of which the first is the bleeding of the head; the second is, discolouring of His face; the third is, the plenteous bleeding of the body, in seeming [as] from the scourging; the fourth is, the deep dying:—these four are aforetold for the pains of the Passion. And the fifth is [this] that was shewed for the joy and the bliss of the Passion.

For it is God's will that we have true enjoying with Him in our salvation, and therein He willeth [that] we

[1] " lykyng "; " lykith."

D

be mightily comforted and strengthened; and thus willeth He that merrily with His grace our soul be occupied. For we are His bliss: for in us He enjoyeth without end; and so shall we in Him, with His grace.

And all that He hath done for us, and doeth, and ever shall, was never cost nor charge to Him, nor might be, but only that [which] He did in our manhood, beginning at the sweet Incarnation and lasting to the Blessed Uprise on Easter-morrow:[1] so long dured the cost and the charge about our redemption in *deed*: of [the] which deed He enjoyeth endlessly, as it is aforesaid.

Jesus willeth that we take heed to the bliss that is in the blessed Trinity [because] of our salvation and that *we* desire to have as much spiritual enjoying, with His grace, (as it is aforesaid): that is to say, that the enjoying of our salvation be [as] like to the joy that Christ hath of our salvation as it may be while we are here.

All the Trinity wrought in the Passion of Christ, ministering abundance of virtues and plenty of grace to us by Him: but only the Maiden's Son suffered: whereof all the blessed Trinity endlessly enjoyeth. All this was shewed in these words: *Art thou well pleased?*—and by that other word that Christ said: *If thou art pleased, then am I pleased;*—as if He said: *It is joy and satisfying enough to me, and I ask nought else of thee for my travail but that I might well please thee.*

And in this He brought to mind the property of a glad giver. A glad giver taketh but little heed of the thing that he giveth, but all his desire and all his intent is to please him and solace him to whom

1 " Esterne morrow "=Easter morning.

he giveth it. And if the receiver take the gift highly and thankfully, then the courteous giver setteth at nought all his cost and all his travail, for joy and delight that he hath pleased and solaced him that he loveth. Plenteously and fully was this shewed.

Think also wisely of the greatness of this word "ever." For in it was shewed an high knowing of love [1] that *He* hath in our salvation, with manifold joys that follow of the Passion of Christ. One is that He rejoiceth that He hath done it in deed, and He shall no more suffer; another, that He bought us from endless pains of hell.

THE TENTH REVELATION

CHAPTER XXIV

"Our Lord looked unto His [wounded] Side, and beheld, rejoicing. . . . *Lo! how I loved thee*"

THEN with a glad cheer our Lord looked unto His Side and beheld, rejoicing. With His sweet looking He led forth the understanding of His creature by the same wound into His Side within. And then he shewed a fair, delectable place, and large enough for all mankind that shall be saved to rest in peace and in love.[2] And therewith He brought to mind His dearworthy blood and precious water which he let pour all out for love. And with the sweet beholding He shewed His blessed heart even cloven in two.

And with this sweet enjoying, He shewed unto mine

[1] Experience of loving (?).

[2] See note on the passage in lv., "long and broad, all full of endless heavens"; "He hath, beclosed in Him, all heavens and all joy and bliss."

understanding, in part, *the blessed Godhead*, stirring then the poor soul[1] to understand, as it may be said, that is, to think on,[2] the *endless* Love that was without beginning, and is, and shall be ever. And with this our good Lord said full blissfully: *Lo, how that I loved thee*, as if He had said: *My darling, behold and see thy Lord, thy God that is thy Maker and thine endless joy, see what satisfying and bliss I have in thy salvation; and for my love rejoice [thou] with me.*

And also, for more understanding, this blessed word was said: *Lo, how I loved thee! Behold and see that I loved thee so much ere I died for thee that I would die for thee; and now I have died for thee and suffered willingly that which I may. And now is all my bitter pain and all my hard travail turned to endless joy and bliss to me and to thee. How should it now be that thou shouldst anything pray that pleaseth me but that I should full gladly grant it thee? For my pleasing is thy holiness and thine endless joy and bliss with me.*

This is the understanding, simply as I can say it, of this blessed word: *Lo, how I loved thee.* This shewed our good Lord for to make us glad and merry.

THE ELEVENTH REVELATION

CHAPTER XXV

" I wot well that thou wouldst see my blessed Mother. . . ."
" Wilt thou see in her how thou art loved?"

AND with this same cheer of mirth and joy our good Lord looked down on the right side and brought to my mind where our Lady stood in the time of His

---

[1] See xiii., " the simplicity of the soul."
[2] MS. " that is to mene the endles love."

Passion ; and said : *Wilt thou see her?* And in this sweet word [it was] as if He had said : *I wot well that thou wouldst see my blessed Mother : for, after myself, she is the highest joy that I might shew thee, and most pleasance and worship to me ; and most she is desired to be seen of my blessed creatures.* And for the high, marvellous, singular love that He hath to this sweet Maiden, His blessed Mother, our Lady Saint Mary, He shewed her highly rejoicing, as by the meaning of these sweet words ; as if He said : *Wilt thou see how I love her, that thou mightest joy with me in the love that I have in her and she in me?*

And also (unto more understanding this sweet word) our Lord speaketh to all mankind that shall be saved, as it were all to one person, as if He said : *Wilt thou see in her how thou art loved? For thy love I made her so high, so noble and so worthy ; and this pleaseth me, and so will I that it doeth thee.*

For after Himself she is the most blissful sight.

But hereof am I not learned to long to see her bodily presence while I am here, but the virtues of her blessed soul : her truth, her wisdom, her charity ; whereby I may learn to know myself and reverently dread my God. And when our good Lord had shewed this and said this word : *Wilt thou see her?* I answered and said : *Yea, good Lord, I thank Thee ; yea, good Lord, if it be Thy will.* Oftentimes I prayed this, and I weened to have seen her in bodily presence, but I saw her not so. And Jesus in that word shewed me ghostly sight of her : right as I had seen her afore little and simple, so He shewed her then high and noble and glorious, and pleasing to Him above all creatures.

And He willeth that it be known ; that [so] all those

that please them in Him should please them in her, and in the pleasance that He hath in her and she in Him.[1] And, to more understanding, He shewed this example: *As if a man love a creature singularly, above all creatures*, he willeth to make all creatures to love and to have pleasance in that creature that he loveth so greatly. And in this word that Jesus said: *Wilt thou see her?* methought it was the most pleasing word that He might have given me of her, with that ghostly Shewing that He gave me of her. For our Lord shewed me nothing in special but our Lady Saint Mary; and her He shewed three times.[2] The first was as she was with Child; the second was as she was in her sorrows under the Cross; the third is as she is now in pleasing, worship, and joy.

THE TWELFTH REVELATION

CHAPTER XXVI

"It is I, it is I"

AND after this our Lord shewed Himself more glorified, as to my sight, than I saw Him before [in the Shewing] wherein I was learned that our soul shall never have rest till it cometh to Him, knowing that He is fulness of joy, homely and courteous, blissful and very life.

Our Lord Jesus oftentimes said: *I it am, I it am: I it am that is highest, I it am that thou lovest, I it am that*

---

[1] " And he wil that it be knowen that al those that lyke in him should lyken in hir and in the lykyng that he hath in hir and she in him."

[2] See (1) iv. (referred to in vii.); (2) xviii.

thou enjoyest, I it am that thou servest, I it am that thou longest for, I it am that thou desirest, I it am that thou meanest, I it am that is all. I it am that Holy Church preacheth and teacheth thee, I it am that shewed me here to thee. The number of the words passeth my wit and all my understanding and all my powers. And they are the highest, as to my sight : for therein is comprehended— I cannot tell,—but the joy that I saw in the Shewing of them passeth all that heart may wish for and soul may desire. Therefore the words be not declared here ; but every man after the grace that God giveth him in understanding and loving, receive them in our Lord's meaning.

THE THIRTEENTH REVELATION

CHAPTER XXVII

" Often I wondered why by the great foreseeing wisdom of God the beginning of sin was not hindered : for then, methought, all should have been well." " Sin is behovable— [playeth a needful part]— ; but all shall be well "

AFTER this the Lord brought to my mind the longing that I had to Him afore. And I saw that nothing letted me but sin. And so I looked, generally, upon us all, and methought : *If sin had not been, we should all have been clean and like to our Lord, as He made us.*

And thus, in my folly, afore this time often I wondered why by the great foreseeing wisdom of God the beginning of sin was not letted : for then, methought, all should have been well. This stirring [of mind] was much to be forsaken, but nevertheless mourning and sorrow I made therefor, without reason and discretion.

But Jesus, who in this Vision informed me of all that is needful to me, answered by this word and said : *It behoved that there should be sin ;* [1] *but all shall be well, and all shall be well, and all manner of thing shall be well.*

In this naked word *sin,* our Lord brought to my mind, generally, *all that is not good,* and the shameful despite and the utter noughting [2] that He bare for us in this life, and His dying ; and all the pains and passions of all His creatures, ghostly and bodily ; (for we be all partly noughted, and we shall be noughted following our Master, Jesus, till we be full purged, that is to say, till we be fully noughted of our deadly flesh and of all our inward affections which are not very good ;) and the beholding of this, with all pains that ever were or ever shall be,—and with all these I understand the Passion of Christ for most pain, and overpassing. All this was shewed in a touch and quickly passed over into comfort : for our good Lord would not that the soul were affeared of this terrible sight.

But I saw not *sin* : for I believe it hath no manner of substance nor no part of being, nor could it be known but by the pain it is cause of.

And thus [1] pain, *it* is something, as to my sight, for a time ; for it purgeth, and maketh us to know ourselves and to ask mercy. For the Passion of our Lord is comfort to us against all this, and so is His blessed will.

---

[1] " Synne is behovabil, but al shal be wel & al shal be wel & al manner of thyng shal be wele."

[2] Being made as nothing, set at nought.

[3] S. de Cressy has " this " instead of *thus*.

And for the tender love that our good Lord hath to all that shall be saved, He comforteth readily and sweetly, signifying thus: *It is sooth[1] that sin is cause of all this pain; but all shall be well, and all shall be well, and all manner [of] thing shall be well.*

These words were said full tenderly, showing no manner of blame to me nor to any that shall be saved. Then were it a great unkindness[2] to blame or wonder on God for my sin, since He blameth not me for sin.

And in these words I saw a marvellous high mystery hid in God, which mystery He shall openly make known to us in Heaven: in which knowing we shall verily see the cause why He suffered sin to come. In which sight we shall endlessly joy in our Lord God.[3]

---

[1] *i.e.* truth, an actual reality. See lxxxii.

[2] As it were, an unreasonable contravention of natural, filial trust.

[3] See also chap. lxi. From the *Enchiridion* of Saint Augustine:—
"All things that exist, therefore, seeing that the Creator of them all is supremely good, are themselves good. But because they are not like their Creator, supremely and unchangeably good, their good may be diminished and increased. But for good to be diminished is an evil, although, however much it may be diminished, it is necessary, if the being is to continue, that some good should remain to constitute the being. For however small or of whatever kind the being may be, the good which makes it a being cannot be destroyed without destroying the being itself. . . . So long as a being is in process of corruption, there is in it some good of which it is being deprived; and if a part of the being should remain which cannot be corrupted, this will certainly be an incorruptible being, and accordingly the process of corruption will result in the manifestation of this great good. But if it do not cease to be corrupted, neither can it cease to possess good of which corruption may deprive it. But if it should be thoroughly and completely consumed by corruption, there will then be no good left, because there will be no being. Wherefore corruption can consume the good only by consuming the being. Every being, therefore, is a good; a great good, if it cannot be corrupted; a little good, if it can:

CHAPTER XXVIII

" Each brotherly compassion that man hath on his fellow Christians, with charity, it is Christ in him "

THUS I saw how Christ hath compassion on us for the cause of sin. And right as I was afore in the [Shewing of the] Passion of Christ fulfilled with pain and compassion, like so in this [sight] I was fulfilled, in part, with compassion of all mine even-Christians—for that well, well beloved people that shall be saved. For God's servants, Holy Church, shall be shaken in sorrow and anguish, tribulation in this world, as men shake a cloth in the wind.

And as to this our Lord answered in this manner : *A great thing shall I make hereof in Heaven of endless worship and everlasting joys.*

Yea, so far forth I saw, that our Lord joyeth of the tribulations of His servants, with ruth and compassion. On each person that He loveth, to His bliss for to bring [them], He layeth something that is no blame in His sight, whereby they are blamed and despised in this

but in any case, only the foolish or ignorant will deny that it is a good. And if it be wholly consumed by corruption, then the corruption itself must cease to exist, as there is no being left in which it can dwell."

Chap. x. "By the Trinity, thus supremely and equally and unchangeably good, all things were created ; and these are not supremely and equally and unchangeably good, but yet they are good, even taken separately. Taken as a whole, however, they are very good, because their *ensemble* constitutes the universe in all its wonderful order and beauty."—*The Works of Aurelius Augustine, Bishop of Hippo*, (Edited by the Rev. Marcus Dods, D.D.), vol. ix.

world, scorned, mocked,[1] and outcasted. And this He
doeth for to hinder the harm that they should take
from the pomp and the vain-glory of this wretched life,
and make their way ready to come to Heaven, and
up-raise them in His bliss everlasting. For He saith:
*I shall wholly break you of your vain affections and your vicious
pride; and after that I shall together gather you, and make you
mild and meek, clean and holy, by oneing to me.*

And then I saw that each kind compassion that man
hath on his even-Christians with charity, it is Christ in
him.

That same noughting that was shewed in His Passion,
it was shewed again here in this Compassion. Wherein
were two manner of understandings in our Lord's meaning. The one was the bliss that we are brought to,
wherein He willeth that we rejoice. The other is for
comfort in our pain: for He willeth that we perceive
that it shall all be turned to worship and profit by virtue
of His passion, that we perceive that we suffer not alone
but with Him, and see Him to be our Ground, and that
we see His pains and His noughting passeth so far all
that we may suffer, that it may not be fully thought.

The beholding of this will save us from murmuring[1]
and despair in the feeling of our pains. And if we see
soothly that our sin deserveth it, yet His love excuseth
us, and of His great courtesy He doeth away all our
blame, and beholdeth us with ruth and pity as children
innocent and unloathful.

---

[1] "Something that is no lak in his syte, whereby thei are lakid &
dispisyd in thys world, scornyd" (a word like "rapyd"—probably
"mokyd," as in S. de C.) "& outcasten."

[2] "gruching."

CHAPTER XXIX

" How could all be well, for the great harm that is come
by sin to the creature ? "

BUT in this I stood beholding things general, troublously and mourning, saying thus to our Lord in
my meaning, with full great dread : *Ah! good Lord, how
might all be well, for the great hurt that is come, by sin, to
the creature?* And here I desired, as far as I durst, to
have some more open declaring wherewith I might be
eased in this matter.

And to this our blessed Lord answered full meekly
and with full lovely cheer, and shewed that Adam's sin
was the most harm that ever was done, or ever shall be,
to the world's end; and also He shewed that this [sin]
is openly known in all Holy Church on earth. Furthermore He taught that I should behold the glorious
Satisfaction [1]: for this Amends-making [2] is more pleasing
to God and more worshipful, without comparison, than
ever was the sin of Adam harmful. Then signifieth our
blessed Lord thus in this teaching, that we should take
heed to this : *For since I have made well the most harm,
then it is my will that thou know thereby that I shall make well
all that is less.*

[1] and [2] "asyeth"; "asyeth making" = *asseth.*, Satisfying, Fulfilment.
See p. 2.

CHAPTER XXX

"Two parts of Truth: the part that is open: our Saviour and our salvation;—and the part that is hid and shut up from us: all beside our salvation"

HE gave me understanding of two parts [of truth]. The one part is our Saviour and our salvation. This blessed part is open and clear and fair and light, and plenteous,—for all mankind that is of good will, and shall be, is comprehended in this part. Hereto are we bounden of God, and drawn and counselled and taught inwardly by the Holy Ghost and outwardly by Holy Church in the same grace. In this willeth our Lord that we be occupied, joying in Him; for He enjoyeth in us. The more plenteously that we take of this, with reverence and meekness, the more thanks we earn of Him and the more speed[1] to ourselves, thus—may we say— enjoying *our* part of our Lord. The other [part] is hid and shut up from us: that is to say, all that is beside our salvation. For it is our Lord's privy counsel, and it belongeth to the royal lordship of God to have His privy counsel in peace, and it belongeth to His servant, for obedience and reverence, not to learn[2] wholly His counsel. Our Lord hath pity and compassion on us for that some creatures make themselves so busy therein; and I am sure if we knew how much we should please Him and ease ourselves by leaving it, we would. The

[1] *i.e.* profit.
[2] "It longyth to the ryal Lordship of God to have his privy councell in pece, and it longyth to his servant for obedience and reverens not to wel wetyn his counselye."

saints that be in Heaven, they will to know nothing but that which our Lord willeth to shew them : and also their charity and their desire is ruled after the will of our Lord : and thus ought we to will, like to them. Then shall we nothing will nor desire but the will of our Lord, as they do : for we are all one in God's seeing.

And here was I learned that we shall trust and rejoice only in our Saviour, blessed Jesus, for all thing.

CHAPTER XXXI

"The Spiritual Thirst (which was in Him from without beginning) is desire in Him as long as we be in need, drawing us up to His Bliss"

AND thus our good Lord answered to all the questions and doubts that I might make, saying full comfortably : *I may make all thing well, I can make all thing well, I will make all thing well, and I shall make all thing well ; and thou shalt see thyself that all manner of thing shall be well.*

In that He saith, *I may*, I understand [it] for the Father ; and in that He saith, *I can*, I understand [it] for the Son ; and where He saith, *I will*, I understand [it] for the Holy Ghost ; and where He saith, *I shall*, I understand [it] for the unity of the blessed Trinity : three Persons and one Truth ; and where He saith, *Thou shalt see thyself*, I understand the oneing of all mankind that shall be saved unto the blessed Trinity. And in these five words God willeth we be enclosed in rest and in peace.

Thus shall the Spiritual Thirst of Christ have an end. For this is the Spiritual Thirst of Christ: the love-longing that lasteth, and ever shall, till we see that sight on Doomsday. For we that shall be saved and shall be Christ's joy and His bliss, some be yet here and some be to come, and so shall some be, unto that day. Therefore this is His thirst and love-longing, to have us altogether whole in Him, to His bliss,—as to my sight. For we be not now as fully whole in Him as we shall be then.

For we know in our Faith, and also it was shewed in all [the Revelations] that Christ Jesus is both God and man. And anent the Godhead, He is Himself highest bliss, and was, from without beginning, and shall be, without end: which endless bliss may never be heightened nor lowered in itself. For this was plenteously seen in every Shewing, and specially in the Twelfth, where He saith: *I am that [which] is highest.* And anent Christ's Manhood, it is known in our Faith, and also [it was] shewed, that He, with the virtue of Godhead, for love, to bring us to His bliss suffered pains and passions, and died. And these be the works of Christ's Manhood wherein He rejoiceth; and that shewed He in the Ninth Revelation, where He saith: *It is a joy and bliss and endless pleasing to me that ever I suffered Passion for thee.* And this is the bliss of Christ's *works,* and thus he signifieth where He saith in that same Shewing: we be His bliss, we be His meed, we be His worship, we be His crown.

For anent that Christ is our Head, He is glorified and impassible; and anent His Body in which all His members are knit, He is not yet fully glorified nor all impassible. Therefore the same desire and thirst that

He had upon the Cross (which desire, longing, and thirst, as to my sight, was in Him from without beginning) the same hath He yet, and shall [have] unto the time that the last soul that shall be saved is come up to His bliss.

For as verily as there is a property in God of ruth and pity, so verily there is a property in God of thirst and longing. (And of the virtue of this longing in Christ, *we* have to long again to Him : without which no soul cometh to Heaven.) And this property of longing and thirst cometh of the endless Goodness of God, even as the property of pity cometh of His endless Goodness. And though longing and pity are two sundry properties, as to my sight, in this standeth the point of the Spiritual Thirst : which is *desire in Him as long as we be in need*, drawing us up to His bliss. And all this was seen in the Shewing of Compassion : for that shall cease on Doomsday.

Thus He hath ruth and compassion on us, and He hath longing to have us ; but His wisdom and His love suffereth not the end to come till the best time.

CHAPTER XXXII

" There be deeds evil done in our sight, and so great harms taken, that it seemeth to us that it were impossible that ever it should come to good end." " That Great Deed ordained . . . by which our Lord God shall make all things well "

ONE time our good Lord said : *All thing shall be well* ; and another time he said : *Thou shalt see thyself that all* MANNER [*of*] *thing shall be well* ; and in these two [sayings] the soul took sundry understandings.

One was that He willeth we know that not only He taketh heed to noble things and to great, but also to little and to small, to low and to simple, to one and to other. And so meaneth He in that He saith: ALL MANNER OF THINGS *shall be well*. For He willeth we know that the least thing shall not be forgotten.

Another understanding is this, that there be deeds evil done in our sight, and so great harms taken, that it seemeth to us that it were impossible that ever it should come to good end. And upon this we look, sorrowing and mourning therefor, so that we cannot resign us unto the blissful beholding of God as we should do. And the cause of this is that the use of our reason is now so blind, so low, and so simple, that we cannot know that high marvellous Wisdom, the Might and the Goodness of the blissful Trinity. And thus signifieth He when He saith: THOU SHALT SEE THYSELF *if*[1] *all manner of things shall be well*. As if He said: *Take now heed faithfully and trustingly, and at the last end thou shalt verily see it in fulness of joy*.

And thus in these same five words aforesaid: *I may make all things well*, etc., I understand a mighty comfort of all the works of our Lord God that are yet to come. There is a Deed the which the blessed Trinity shall do in the last Day, as to my sight, and when the Deed shall be, and how it shall be done, is unknown of all creatures that are beneath Christ, and shall be till when it is done.

[" [2] The Goodness and the Love of our Lord God " will that we wit [know] that it shall be; And the " Might and the Wisdom of him by the same Love will

---

[1] " if " = " that." (Acts xxvi. 8.)
[2] Inserted from Serenus de Cressy's version.

E

" hill [conceal] it, and hide it from us what it shall be,
" and how it shall be done."]

And the cause why He willeth that we know [this Deed shall be], is for that He would have us the more eased in our soul and [the more] set at peace in love [1]— leaving the beholding of all troublous things that might keep us back from true enjoying of Him. This is that Great Deed ordained of our Lord God from without beginning, treasured and hid in His blessed breast, only known to Himself: by which He shall make all things well.

For like as the blissful Trinity made all things of nought, right so the same blessed Trinity shall make well all that is not well.

And in this sight I marvelled greatly and beheld our Faith, marvelling thus: Our Faith is grounded in God's word, and it belongeth to our Faith that we believe that God's word shall be saved in all things; and one point of our Faith is that many creatures shall be condemned: as angels that fell out of Heaven for pride, which be now fiends; and man [2] in earth that dieth out of the Faith of Holy Church: that is to say, they that be heathen men; and also man [2] that hath received christendom and liveth unchristian life and so dieth out of charity: all these shall be condemned to hell without end, as Holy Church teacheth me to believe. And all this [so] standing,[3] methought it was impossible that all manner of things should be well, as our Lord shewed in the same time.

---

1 " pecid in love—levyng the beholdyng of al tempests that might letten us of trew enjoyeng in hym." S. de C.: " let us of true enjoying in him."   2 S. de C., " many."   3 " stondyng al this."

And as to this I had no other answer in Shewing of our Lord God but this: *That which is impossible to thee is not impossible to me: I shall save my word in all things and I shall make all things well.* Thus I was taught, by the grace of God, that I should steadfastly hold me in the Faith as I had aforehand understood, [and] therewith that I should firmly believe that all things shall be well, as our Lord shewed in the same time.

For this is the Great Deed that our Lord shall do, in which Deed He shall save His word and He shall make all well that is not well. How it shall be done there is no creature beneath Christ that knoweth it, nor shall know it till it is done; according to the understanding that I took of our Lord's meaning in this time.

CHAPTER XXXIII

" It is God's will that we have great regard to all His deeds that He hath done, but evermore it needeth us to leave the beholding what the Deed shall be "

AND yet in this I desired, as [far] as I durst, that I might have full sight of Hell and Purgatory. But it was not my meaning to make proof of anything that belongeth to the Faith: for I believed soothfastly that Hell and Purgatory is for the same end that Holy Church teacheth, but my meaning was that I might have seen, for learning in all things that belong to my Faith: whereby I might live the more to God's worship and to my profit.

But for [all] my desire, I could [1] [see] of this right nought, save as it is aforesaid in the First Shewing, where I saw that the devil is reproved of God and endlessly condemned. In which sight I understood as to all creatures that are of the devil's condition in this life, and therein end, that there is no more mention made of them afore God and all His Holy than of the devil,—notwithstanding that they be of mankind —whether they be christened or not.

For though the Revelation was made of goodness in which was made little mention of evil, yet I was not drawn thereby from any point of the Faith that Holy Church teacheth me to believe. For I had sight of the Passion of Christ in diverse Shewings,—the First, the Second, the Fifth, and the Eighth,—wherein I had in part a feeling of the sorrow of our Lady, and of His true friends that saw Him in pain; but I saw not so properly specified the Jews that did Him to death. Notwithstanding I knew in my Faith that they were accursed and condemned without end, saving those that converted, by grace. And I was strengthened and taught generally to keep me in the Faith in every point, and in all as I had before understood: hoping that I was therein with the mercy and the grace of God; desiring and praying in my purpose that I might continue therein unto my life's end.

And it is God's will that we have great regard to all His deeds that He hath done, but evermore it needeth us to leave the beholding what the Deed shall be. And let us desire to be like our brethren which be saints in Heaven, that will right nought but God's will and are

1 " I coude of this right nowte."

well pleased both with hiding and with shewing. For I saw soothly in our Lord's teaching, the more we busy us to know His secret counsels in this or any other thing, the farther shall we be from the knowing thereof.

CHAPTER XXXIV

" All that is speedful for us to learn and to know, full courteously will our Lord shew us "

OUR Lord God shewed two manner of secret things. One is this great Secret [Counsel] with all the privy points that belong thereto: and these secret things He willeth we should know [as *being*, but as] *hid* until the time that He will clearly shew them to us. The other are the secret things that He willeth to make open and known to us ; for He would have us understand that it is His will that we should know them. They are secrets to us not only for that He willeth that they be secrets to us, but they are secrets to us for our blindness and our ignorance ; and thereof He hath great ruth, and therefore He will Himself make them more open to us, whereby we may know Him and love Him and cleave to Him. For all that is speedful for us to learn and to know, full courteously will our Lord shew us : and [of] that is this [Shewing], with all the preaching and teaching of Holy Church.

God shewed full great pleasance that He hath in all men and women that mightily and meekly and with all their will take the preaching and teaching of Holy Church. For it is His Holy Church : He is the Ground,

He is the Substance, He is the Teaching, He is the Teacher, He is the End, He is the Meed for which every kind soul travaileth.

And *this* [of the Shewing] is [made] known, and shall be known to every soul to which the Holy Ghost declareth it. And I hope truly that all those that seek this, He shall speed : for they seek God.

All this that I have now told, and more that I shall tell after, is comforting against sin. For in the Third Shewing when I saw that God doeth all that is done, I saw no sin : and then I saw that all *is* well. But when God shewed me for sin, then said He : *All* SHALL *be well.*

CHAPTER XXXV

" I desired to learn assuredly as to a certain creature that I loved. . . . It is more worship to God to behold Him in *all* than in any special thing "

AND when God Almighty had shewed so plenteously and joyfully of His Goodness, I desired to learn assuredly as to a certain creature that I loved, if it should continue in good living, which I hoped by the grace of God was begun. And in this desire for a *singular* Shewing, it seemed that I hindered myself : for I was not taught in this time. And then was I answered in my reason, as it were by a friendly intervenor [1] : *Take it* GENERALLY, *and behold the graciousness of the Lord God as He sheweth to thee : for it is more worship to God to behold Him*

---

1 " A friendful mene "=intermediary (person or thing), medium : compare chaps. xix., lv.

in all than in any special thing. And therewith I learned that it is more worship to God to know all-thing in general, than to take pleasure in any special thing. And if I should do wisely according to this teaching, I should not only be glad for nothing in special, but I should not be greatly distressed for no manner of thing[1]: for ALL *shall be well.* For the fulness of joy is to behold God in *all :* for by the same blessed Might, Wisdom, and Love, that He made all-thing, to the same end our good Lord leadeth it continually, and thereto Himself shall bring it; and when it is time we shall see it. And the ground of this was shewed in the First [Revelation], and more openly in the Third, where it saith: *I saw God in a point.*

All that our Lord doeth is rightful, and that which He suffereth[2] is worshipful: and in these two is comprehended good and ill: for all that is good our Lord doeth, and that which is evil our Lord suffereth. I say not that any evil is worshipful, but I say the sufferance of our Lord God is worshipful: whereby His Goodness shall be known, without end, in His marvellous meekness and mildness, by the working of mercy and grace.

Rightfulness is that thing that is so good that [it] may not be better than it is. For God Himself is very Rightfulness, and all His works are done rightfully as they are ordained from without beginning by His high Might, His high Wisdom, His high Goodness. And right as He ordained unto the best, right so He worketh continually, and leadeth it to the same end; and He is ever full-pleased with Himself and with all His works.

---

[1] See xxxvi. 74.   [2] *i.e.* alloweth.

And the beholding of this blissful accord is full sweet to the soul that seeth by grace. All the souls that shall be saved in Heaven without end be made rightful in the sight of God, and by His own goodness: in which rightfulness we are endlessly kept, and marvellously, above all creatures.

And *Mercy* is a working that cometh of the goodness of God, and it shall last in working all along, as sin is suffered to pursue rightful souls. And when sin hath no longer leave to pursue, then shall the working of mercy cease, and then shall all be brought to rightfulness and therein stand without end.

And by His sufferance we fall; and in His blissful Love with His Might and His Wisdom we are kept; and by mercy and grace we are raised to manifold more joys.

Thus in Rightfulness and Mercy He willeth to be known and loved, now and without end. And the soul that wisely beholdeth it in grace, it is well pleased with both, and endlessly enjoyeth.

CHAPTER XXXVI

" My sin shall not hinder His Goodness working. . . . A deed shall be done—as we come to Heaven—and it may be known here in part ;—though it be truly taken for the general Man, yet it excludeth not the special. For what our good Lord will do by His poor creatures, it is now unknown to me "

OUR Lord God shewed that a deed shall be done, and Himself shall do it, and I shall do nothing but sin, and my sin shall not hinder [1] His Goodness working.

" lettyn his goodnes werkyng."

And I saw that the beholding of this is a heavenly joy in a fearing soul which evermore kindly by grace desireth God's will. This deed shall be begun here, and it shall be worshipful to God and plenteously profitable to His lovers in earth; and ever as we come to Heaven we shall see it in marvellous joy, and it shall last thus in working unto the last Day; and the worship and the bliss of it shall last in Heaven afore God and all His Holy [ones] for ever.

Thus was this deed seen and understood in our Lord's signifying: and the cause why He shewed it is to make us rejoice in Him and in all His works. When I saw His Shewing continued, I understood that it was shewed for a great thing that was for to come, which thing God shewed that He Himself should do it: which deed hath these properties aforesaid. And this shewed He well blissfully, signifying that I should take it myself faithfully and trustingly.

But what this deed should be was kept secret from me.

And in this I saw that He willeth not that we dread to know the things that He sheweth: He sheweth them because He would have us know them; by which knowing He would have us love Him and have pleasure and endlessly enjoy in Him. For the great love that He hath to us He sheweth us all that is worshipful and profitable for the time. And the things that He will now have privy, yet of His great goodness He sheweth them *close*: in which shewing He willeth that we believe and understand that we shall see the same verily in His endless bliss. Then ought we to rejoice in Him for all that He sheweth and all that He hideth; and if we steadily[1] and meekly do thus, we shall find therein great ease ; and endless thanks we shall have of Him therefor.

And this is the understanding of this word :—That it shall be done for me, meaneth that it shall be done for the general Man : that is to say, all that shall be saved. It shall be worshipful and marvellous and plenteous, and God Himself shall do it ; and this shall be the highest joy that may be, to behold the deed that God Himself shall do, and man shall do right nought but sin. Then signifieth our Lord God thus, as if He said : *Behold and see! Here hast thou matter of meekness, here hast thou matter of love, here hast thou matter to make nought of[2] thyself, here hast thou matter to enjoy in me ;—and, for my love, enjoy [thou] in me : for of all things, therewith mightest thou please me most.*

And as long as we are in this life, what time that we by our folly turn us to the beholding of the reproved, tenderly our Lord God toucheth us and blissfully calleth us, saying in our soul : *Let be all thy love, my dearworthy child : turn thee to me—I am enough to thee—and enjoy in thy Saviour and in thy salvation.* And that this is our Lord's working in us, I am sure the soul that hath understanding[3] therein by grace shall see it and feel it.

And though it be so that this deed be truly taken for the general Man, yet it excludeth not the special. For what our good Lord will do by His poor creatures, it is now unknown to me.

But this deed and that other aforesaid, they are not both one but two sundry. This deed shall be done

---

1 "wilfully." 2 "to nowten."
3 "is a perceyvid" (S. de Cressy, "pearced" ; Collins, "pierced";)= has perception.

sooner (and that [time] shall be as we come to Heaven), and to whom our Lord giveth it, it may be known here in part. But that Great Deed aforesaid shall neither be known in Heaven nor earth till it is done.

And moreover He gave special understanding and teaching of working of miracles, as thus :—*It is known that I have done miracles here afore, many and diverse, high and marvellous, worshipful and great. And so as I have done, I do now continually, and shall do in coming of time.*

It is known that afore miracles come sorrow and anguish and tribulation [1]; and that is for that we should know our own feebleness and our mischiefs that we are fallen in by sin, to meeken us and make us to dread God and cry for help and grace. Miracles come after that, and they come of the high Might, Wisdom, and Goodness of God, shewing His virtue and the joys of Heaven so far at it may be in this passing life: and that to strengthen our faith and to increase our hope, in charity. Wherefore it pleaseth Him to be known and worshipped in miracles. Then signifieth He thus: He willeth that we be not borne over low for sorrow and tempests that fall to us: for it hath ever so been afore miracle-coming.

CHAPTER XXXVII

"In every soul that shall be saved is a Godly Will that never assented to sin, nor ever shall."—"For failing of Love on our part, therefore is all our travail"

GOD brought to my mind that I should sin. And for pleasance that I had in beholding of Him, I attended not readily to that shewing ; and our Lord full

[1] See v., xlviii., lix., lxi.

mercifully abode, and gave me grace to attend. And this shewing I took singularly to myself; but by all the gracious comfort that followeth, as ye shall see, I was learned to take it for all mine even-Christians: *all in general and nothing in special*: though our Lord shewed me that I should sin, by me alone is understood all.

And therein I conceived a soft dread. And to this our Lord answered: *I keep thee full surely.* This word was said with more love and secureness and spiritual keeping than I can or may tell. For as it was shewed that [I][1] should sin, right so was the comfort shewed: secureness and keeping for all mine even-Christians.

What may make me more to love mine even-Christians than to see in God that He loveth all that shall be saved as it were all one soul?

For in every soul that shall be saved is a Godly Will that never assented to sin, nor ever shall. Right as there is a beastly will in the lower part that may will no good, right so there is a Godly Will in the higher part, which will is so good that it may never will evil, but ever good. And therefore we are that which He loveth and endlessly we do that which Him pleaseth.

This shewed our Lord in [shewing] the wholeness of love that we stand in, in His sight: yea, that He loveth us now as well while we are here, as He shall do while we are there afore His blessed face. But for failing of love on our part, therefore is all our travail.

---

[1] Perhaps the omitted word is 'all'; but de Cressy has "I" as above: "that I should sin."

CHAPTER XXXVIII

In Heaven "the token of sin is turned to worship."—
Examples thereof

ALSO God shewed that sin shall be no shame to man, but worship. For right as to every sin is answering a pain by truth, right so for every sin, to the same soul is given a bliss by love: right as diverse sins are punished with diverse pains according as they be grievous, right so shall they be rewarded with diverse joys in Heaven according as they have been painful and sorrowful to the soul in earth. For the soul that shall come to Heaven is precious to God, and the place so worshipful that the goodness of God suffereth never that soul to sin that shall come there without that the which sin shall be rewarded; and it is made known without end, and blissfully restored by overpassing worship.

For in this Sight mine understanding was lifted up into Heaven, and then God brought merrily to my mind David, and others in the Old Law without number; and in the New Law He brought to my mind first Mary Magdalene, Peter and Paul, and those of Inde;[1] and Saint John of Beverley[2]; and others also without

[1] S. Thomas and S. Jude. According to tradition the Gospel was carried to India by these Apostles.

[2] S. John of Beverley was consecrated Bishop of Hexham in 687, and was afterwards Archbishop of York. "He founded the monastery of Beverley in the midst of the wood called Deira, among the ruins of the deserted Roman settlement of Pentuaria. This monastery, like so many others of the Anglo-Saxons, was a double community of monks

number: how they are known in the Church in earth with their sins, and it is to them no shame, but all is turned for them to worship. And therefore our courteous Lord sheweth [it thus] for them here in part like as it is there in fulness: for there the token of sin is turned to worship.

And Saint John of Beverley, our Lord shewed him full highly, in comfort to us for homeliness; and brought to my mind how he is a dear neighbour,[1] and of our knowing. And God called him *Saint John of Beverley* plainly as we do, and that with a most glad sweet cheer, shewing that he is a full high saint in Heaven in His sight, and a blissful. And with this he made mention that in his youth and in his tender age he was a dearworthy servant to God, greatly God loving and dreading, and yet God suffered him to fall, mercifully keeping him that he perished not, nor lost no time. And afterward God raised him to manifold more grace, and by the contrition and meekness that he had in his living, God hath given him in Heaven manifold joys, overpassing

and nuns. In 718 John retired for the remaining years of his life to Beverley, where he died in 721 on the 7th of May. . . . He was canonised in 1037. Henschenius the Bollandist, in the second tome of May, has published books of the miracles wrought at the relicks of St John of Beverley written by eye-witnesses. His sacred bones were honourably translated into the church of Alfric, Archbishop of York, in 1037. A feast in honour of his translation was kept on the 25th of October."—Alban Butler's *Lives of the Saints*, etc.

Perhaps the fact that the Saint's original Feast Day of the 7th of May occurred on the second day of Julian's illness, had something to do with his being brought to her mind a few days after with so much vividness.

1 "and browte to mynd how he is an hende neybor and of our knowyng"—*i.e.* he was a countryman of our own. "hende"=near, urbane, gentle.

that [which] he should have had if he had not fallen. And that this is sooth, God sheweth in earth with plenteous miracles doing about his body continually.

And all this was to make us glad and merry in love.

CHAPTER XXXIX

" Sin is the sharpest scourge. . . . By contrition we are made clean, by compassion we are made ready, and by true longing towards God we are made worthy "

SIN is the sharpest scourge that any chosen soul may be smitten with : which scourge thoroughly beateth [1] man and woman, and maketh him hateful in his own sight, so far forth that afterwhile [2] he thinketh himself he is not worthy but as to sink in hell,—till [that time] when contrition taketh him by touching of the Holy Ghost, and turneth the bitterness into hopes of God's mercy. And then He beginneth his wounds to heal, and the soul to quicken [as it is] turned unto the life of Holy Church. The Holy Ghost leadeth him to confession, with all his will to shew his sins nakedly and truly, with great sorrow and great shame that he hath defouled the fair image of God. Then receiveth he penance for every sin [as] enjoined by his doomsman [3] that is grounded in Holy Church by the teaching of the Holy Ghost. And this is one meekness that greatly pleaseth God ; and also bodily sickness of God's sending, and also sorrow and shame from without, and

[1] "al forbetyth." S. de Cressy : "all to beateth," Judges ix. 53.
[2] "otherwhile."
[3] S. de C. : "Dome's-man, i.e. Confessarius."

reproof, and despite of this world, with all manner of grievance and temptations that we be cast in,[1] bodily and ghostly.

Full preciously our Lord keepeth us when it seemeth to us that we are near forsaken and cast away for our sin and because we have deserved it. And because of meekness that we get hereby, we are raised well-high in God's sight by His grace, with so great contrition, and also compassion, and true longing to God. Then they be suddenly delivered from sin and from pain, and taken up to bliss, and made even high saints.

By contrition we are made clean, by compassion we are made ready, and by true longing toward God we are made worthy. These are three means, as I understand, whereby that all souls come to heaven: that is to say, that have been sinners in earth and shall be saved: for by these three medicines it behoveth that every soul be healed. Though the soul be healed, his wounds are seen afore God,—not as wounds but as worships. And so on the contrary-wise, as we be punished here with sorrow and penance, we shall be rewarded in heaven by the courteous love of our Lord God Almighty, who willeth that none that come there lose his travail in any degree. For He [be]holdeth sin as sorrow and pain to His lovers, to whom He assigneth no blame, for love. The meed that we shall receive shall not be little, but it shall be high, glorious, and worshipful. And so shall shame be turned to worship and more joy.

But our courteous Lord willeth not that His servants despair, for often nor for grievous falling: for our falling hindereth [2] not Him to love us. Peace and love are ever

---

[1] MS. "will be cast in."   [2] letteth not Him to love us.

in us, being and working; but we be not alway in peace and in love. But He willeth that we take heed thus that He is Ground of all our whole life in love; and furthermore that He is our everlasting Keeper and mightily defendeth us against our enemies, that be full fell and fierce upon us;—and so much our need is the more for [that] we give them occasion by our falling.[1]

CHAPTER XL

"True love teacheth us that we should hate sin only for love." "To me was shewed no harder hell than sin." "God willeth that we endlessly hate the sin and endlessly love the soul, as God loveth it"

THIS is a sovereign friendship of our courteous Lord that He keepeth us so tenderly while we be in sin; and furthermore He toucheth us full privily and sheweth us our sin by the sweet light of mercy and grace. But

[1] See chap. lxviii. In both passages the Brit. Mus. MS. seems to have "him," not "hem"=them. The reading here might be: "For we give *Him* occasion by our falling"—occasion to keep and defend us: and so in lxxviii.: "He keepeth us mightily and mercifully in the time that we are in our sin and among all our enemies that are full fell upon us;—and so much we are in the more peril. For we give Him occasion thereto and know not our own need." Or possibly the sense is (1): He defendeth us "so much [as] our need is the more" [so much more as]; and (2) "so much [more as] we are in the more peril." But S. de Cressy's version has in both passages "them," and this reading agrees with chap. lxxvi.: "We have this [fear] by the stirring of our enemy and by our own folly and blindness"—we who "fall often into sin."

when we see our self so foul, then ween we that God were wroth with us for our sin, and then are we stirred of the Holy Ghost by contrition unto prayer and desire for the amending of our life with all our mights, to slacken the wrath of God, unto the time we find a rest in soul and a softness in conscience. Then hope we that God hath forgiven us our sins: and it is truth. And then sheweth our courteous Lord Himself to the soul— well-merrily and with glad cheer—with friendly welcoming as if it [1] had been in pain and in prison, saying sweetly thus: *My darling I am glad thou art come to me: in all thy wo I have ever been with thee; and now seest thou my loving and we be oned in bliss.* Thus are sins forgiven by mercy and grace, and our soul is worshipfully received in joy like as it shall be when it cometh to Heaven, as oftentimes as it cometh by the gracious working of the Holy Ghost and the virtue of Christ's Passion.

Here understand I in truth that all manner of things are made ready for us by the great goodness of God, so far forth that what time we be ourselves in peace and charity, we be verily saved. But because we may not have this in fulness while we are here, therefore it falleth to us evermore to live in sweet prayer and lovely longing with our Lord Jesus. For He longeth ever to bring us to the fulness of joy; as it is aforesaid, where He sheweth the Spiritual Thirst.

But now if any man or woman because of all this spiritual comfort that is aforesaid, be stirred by folly to say or to think: *If this be true, then were it good to sin* [*so as*] *to have the more meed,*—or else to charge the less [guilt] to sin,—beware of this stirring: for verily if it

1 " he," that is, the soul.

come it is untrue, and of the enemy of the same true love that teacheth us that we should hate sin only for love. I am sure by mine own feeling, the more that any kind[1] soul seeth this in the courteous love of our Lord God, the lother he is to sin and the more he is ashamed. For if afore us were laid [together] all the pains in Hell and in Purgatory and in Earth—death and other—, and [by itself] sin, we should rather choose all that pain than sin. For sin is so vile and so greatly to be hated that it may be likened to no pain which is not sin. And to me was shewed no harder hell than sin. For a kind[1] soul hath no hell but sin.

And [when] we give our intent to love and meekness, by the working of mercy and grace we are made all fair and clean. As mighty and as wise as God is to save men, so willing He is. For Christ Himself is [the] ground of all the laws of Christian men, and He taught us to do good against ill: here may we see that He is Himself this charity, and doeth to us as He teacheth us to do. For He willeth that we be like Him in wholeness of endless love to ourself and to our even-Christians: no more than His love is broken to us for our sin, no more willeth He that our love be broken to ourself and to our even-Christians: but [that we] endlessly hate the sin and endlessly love the soul, as God loveth it. Then shall we hate sin like as God hateth it, and love the soul as God loveth it. And this word that He said is an endless comfort: *I keep thee securely.*

---

[1] A naturally-loving, filial human soul.

THE FOURTEENTH REVELATION.

CHAPTER XLI

" *I am the Ground of thy beseeching.*"   " Also to prayer
belongeth thanking "

AFTER this our Lord shewed concerning Prayer. In
which Shewing I see two conditions in our Lord's
signifying : one is rightfulness, another is sure trust.

But yet oftentimes our trust is not full : for we are
not sure that God heareth us, as we think because of
our unworthiness, and because we feel right nought,
(for we are as barren and dry oftentimes after our
prayers as we were afore) ; and this, in our feeling our
folly, is cause of our weakness.[1]   For thus have I felt
in myself.

And all this brought our Lord suddenly to my mind,
and shewed these words, and said : *I am Ground of thy
beseeching : first it is my will that thou have it ; and after, I make
thee to will it ; and after, I make thee to beseech it and thou beseechest it.   How should it then be that thou shouldst not have
thy beseeching ?*

And thus in the first reason, with the three that
follow, our good Lord sheweth a mighty comfort, as
it may be seen in the same words.   And in the first
reason,—where He saith : *And thou beseechest it*, there
He sheweth [His] full great pleasance, and endless meed
that He will give us for our beseeching.   And in the
second reason, where He saith : *How should it then be ?*

[1] MS. : " *And this in our felyng our foly is cause of our wekenes.*"   S. de
Cressy : " And thus in our feelings our folly is cause of our weakness."

etc., this was said for an impossible [thing]. For it is most impossible that we should beseech mercy and grace, and not have it. For everything that our good Lord maketh us to beseech, Himself hath ordained it to us from without beginning. Here may we see that our beseeching is not cause of God's goodness; and that shewed He soothfastly in all these sweet words when He saith: *I am [the] Ground.*—And our good Lord willeth that this be known of His lovers in earth; and the more that we know [it] the more should we beseech, if it be wisely taken; and so is our Lord's meaning.

Beseeching is a true, gracious, lasting will of the soul, oned and fastened into the will of our Lord by the sweet inward work of the Holy Ghost. Our Lord Himself, He is the first receiver of our prayer, as to my sight, and taketh it full thankfully and highly enjoying; and He sendeth it up above and setteth it in the Treasure, where it shall never perish. It is there afore God with all His Holy continually received, ever speeding [the help of] our needs; and when we shall receive our bliss it shall be given us for a degree of joy, with endless worshipful thanking from [1] Him.

Full glad and merry is our Lord of our prayer; and He looketh thereafter and He willeth to have it because with His grace He maketh us like to Himself in condition as we are in kind: and so is His blissful will. Therefore He saith thus: *Pray inwardly,[2] though thee thinketh it savour thee not: for it is profitable, though thou feel not, though thou see nought; yea, though thou think thou canst not. For in dryness and in barrenness, in sickness and in*

---

[1] " of "=by, from.

[2] " inderly "=inwardly—or from the heart: heartily, as in lxvi.

feebleness, then is thy prayer well-pleasant to me, though thee thinketh it savour thee nought but little. And so is all thy believing prayer in my sight. For the meed and the endless thanks that He will give us, *therefor* He is covetous to have us pray continually in His sight. God accepteth the goodwill and the travail of His servant, howsoever we feel: wherefore it pleaseth Him that we work both in our prayers and in good living, by His help and His grace, reasonably with discretion keeping our powers [1] [turned] to Him, till when that we have Him that we seek, in fulness of joy: that is, Jesus. And that shewed He in the Fifteenth [Revelation], farther on, in this word: *Thou shalt have me to thy meed.*

And also to prayer belongeth thanking. Thanking is a true inward knowing, with great reverence and lovely dread turning ourselves with all our mights unto the working that our good Lord stirreth us to, enjoying and thanking inwardly. And sometimes, for plenteousness it breaketh out with voice, and saith: *Good Lord, I thank Thee!* [2] *Blessed mayst Thou be!* And sometime when the heart is dry and feeleth not, or else by temptation of our enemy,—then it is driven by reason and by grace to cry upon our Lord with voice, rehearing His blessed Passion and His great Goodness; and the virtue of our Lord's word turneth into the soul and quickeneth the heart and entereth [3] it by His grace into true working, and maketh it pray right blissfully. And truly to enjoy our Lord, it is a full blissful thanking in His sight.

---

[1] *i.e.* Faculties.—MS. "Mights."
[2] "Grante mercy"=*grand-merci*.
[3] "entrith," leadeth.

CHAPTER XLII

"Prayer is a right understanding of that fulness of joy that is
to come, with accordant longing and sure trust"

OUR Lord God willeth that we have true understanding, and specially in three things that belong to
our prayer. The first is: *by whom and how that our prayer
springeth*. *By whom*, He sheweth when He saith: *I am
[the] Ground*; and *how*, by His Goodness: for He saith
first: *It is my will*. The second is: *in what manner and
how we should use our prayer*; and that is that our will be
turned unto the will of our Lord, enjoying: and so
meaneth He when He saith: *I make thee to will it*. The
third is that we should know *the fruit and the end of our
prayers*: that is, that we be oned and like to our Lord in
all things; and to this intent and for this end was all this
lovely lesson shewed. And He will help us, and we
shall make it so as He saith Himself;—Blessed may
He be!

For this is our Lord's will, that our prayer and our
trust be both alike large. For if we trust not as much
as we pray, we do not full worship to our Lord in our
prayer, and also we tarry [1] and pain our self. The cause
is, as I believe, that we know not truly that our Lord is
[the] Ground on whom our prayer springeth; and also
that we know not that it is given us by the grace of His
love. For if we knew this, it would make us to trust
to have, of our Lord's gift, all that we desire. For I
am sure that no man asketh mercy and grace with true
meaning, but if mercy and grace be first given to him.

[1] *i.e.* torment, tire, hinder.

But sometimes it cometh to our mind that we have prayed long time, and yet we think to ourselves that we have not our asking. But herefor should we not be in heaviness. For I am sure, by our Lord's signifying, that either we abide a better time, or more grace, or a better gift. He willeth that we have true knowing in Himself that He is Being; and in this knowing He willeth that our understanding be grounded, with all our mights and all our intent and all our meaning; and in this ground He willeth that we take our place and our dwelling, and by the gracious light of Himself He willeth that we have understanding of the things that follow. The first is our noble and excellent making; the second, our precious and dearworthy again-buying; the third, all-thing that He hath made beneath us, [He hath made] to serve us, and for our love keepeth it. Then signifieth He thus, as if He said: *Behold and see that I have done all this before thy prayers; and now thou art, and prayest me.* And thus He signifieth that it belongeth to us to learn that the greatest deeds be [already] done, as Holy Church teacheth; and in the beholding of this, with thanking, we ought to pray for the deed that is now in doing: and that is, that He rule and guide us, to His worship, in this life, and bring us to His bliss. And therefor He hath done all.

Then signifieth He thus: that we [should] see that He doeth it, and that we [should] pray therefor. For the one is not enough. For if we pray and see not that He doeth it, it maketh us heavy and doubtful; and that is not His worship. And if we see that He doeth, and we pray not, we do not our debt, and so may it not be: that is to say, so is it not [the thing that is] in His beholding.

But to see that He doeth it, and to pray forthwithal,—so is he worshiped and we sped. All-thing that our Lord hath ordained to do, it is His will that we pray therefor, either in special or in general. And the joy and the bliss that it is to Him, and the thanks and the worship that we shall have therefor, it passeth the understanding of creatures, as to my sight.

For prayer is a right[1] understanding of that fulness of joy that is to come, with well-longing and sure trust. Failing of our bliss that we be kindly ordained to, maketh us to long; true understanding and love, with sweet mind in our Saviour, graciously maketh us to trust. And in these two workings our Lord beholdeth us continually[2]: for it is our due part, and His Goodness may no less assign to us.

Thus it belongeth to us to do our diligence; and when we have done it, then shall us yet think that [it] is nought,—and sooth it is. But if we do as we can, and ask, in truth, for mercy and grace, all that faileth us we shall find in Him. And thus signifieth He where He saith: *I am Ground of thy beseeching.* And thus in this blessed word, with the Shewing, I saw a full over-coming against all our weakness and all our doubtful dreads.

---

[1] " rythwis "=right manner of.

[2] Or: 'And for these two workings our Lord looketh to us con-tinually.' See above: " so is it not in His beholding," and chap. xliii. " for He beholdeth us in love and would make us partners of His good deed."

CHAPTER XLIII

" Prayer uniteth the soul to God "

PRAYER oneth the soul to God. For though the soul be ever like to God in kind and substance, restored by grace, it is often unlike in condition, by sin on man's part. Then is prayer a witness that the soul willeth as God willeth; and it comforteth the conscience and enableth man to grace. And thus He teacheth us to pray, and mightily to trust that we shall have it. For He beholdeth us in love and would make us partners of His good deed, and therefore He stirreth us to pray for that which it pleaseth him to do. For which prayer and good will, that we have of His gift, He will reward us and give us endless meed.

And this was shewed in this word : *And thou beseechest it*. In this word God shewed so great pleasance and so great content, as though He were much beholden to us for every good deed that we do (and yet it is *He* that doeth it) because that we beseech Him mightily to do all things that seem to Him good : as if He said : *What might then please me more than to beseech me, mightily, wisely, and earnestly, to do that thing that I shall do?*

And thus the soul by prayer accordeth to God.

But when our courteous Lord of His grace sheweth Himself to our soul, we have that [which] we desire. And then we see not, for the time, what we should more pray, but all our intent with all our might is set wholly to the beholding of Him. And this is an high unperceivable prayer, as to my sight : for all the cause wherefor we pray it, is oned into the sight and beholding of

Him to whom we pray; marvellously enjoying with reverent dread, and with so great sweetness and delight in Him that we can pray right nought but as He stirreth us, for the time. And well I wot, the more the soul seeth of God, the more it desireth Him by His grace.

But when we see Him not so, then feel we need and cause to pray, because of failing, for enabling of our self, to Jesus. For when the soul is tempested, troubled, and left to itself by unrest, then it is time to pray, for to make itself pliable and obedient [1] to God. (But the soul by no manner of prayer maketh God pliant to it: for He is ever alike in love.)

And this I saw: that what time we see needs wherefor we pray, then our *good Lord followeth us*, helping our desire; and when we of His special grace plainly behold Him, seeing none other needs, then *we follow Him* and He draweth us unto Him by love. For I saw and felt that His marvellous and plentiful Goodness fulfilleth all our powers; and therewith I saw that His continuant working in all manner of things is done so goodly, so wisely, and so mightily, that it overpasseth all our imagining, and all that we can ween and think; and then we can do no more but behold Him, enjoying, with an high, mighty desire to be all oned unto Him,—centred to His dwelling,—and enjoy in His loving and delight in His goodness.

And then shall we, with His sweet grace, in our own meek continuant prayer come unto Him now in this life by many privy touchings of sweet spiritual sights and feeling, measured to us as our simpleness may bear it. And this is wrought, and shall be, by the grace of the

[1] " supple and buxum."

Holy Ghost, so long till we shall die in longing, for love. And then shall we all come into our Lord, our Self clearly knowing, and God fully having; and we shall endlessly be all had in God: Him verily seeing and fully feeling, Him spiritually hearing, and Him delectably in-breathing, and [of] Him sweetly drinking.[1]

And then shall we see God face to face, homely and fully. The creature that is made shall see and endlessly behold God which is the Maker. For thus may no man see God and live after, that is to say, in this deadly life. But when He of His special grace will shew Himself here, He strengtheneth the creature above its self, and He measureth the Shewing, after His own will, as it is profitable for the time.

[1] To express the fulness of spiritual perception the mystic seizes on all the five sense-perceptions as symbols. For the last word S. de Cressy gives again the word " smelling " (rendered here, above, by " in-breathing "). Collins reads the Brit. Mus. MS. as "following"; but the word there is " swelowyng " = swallowing.

ANENT CERTAIN POINTS IN THE FORE-GOING FOURTEEN REVELATIONS

CHAPTER XLIV

" God is endless, sovereign Truth,—Wisdom,—Love, not-made ; and man's Soul is a creature in God which hath the same properties made "

GOD shewed in all the Revelations, oftentimes, that man worketh evermore His will and His worship lastingly without any stinting. And *what* this work is, was shewed in the First, and that in a marvellous example : for it was shewed in the working of the soul of our blissful Lady, Saint Mary : [that is, the working of] Truth and Wisdom.[1] And *how* [it is done] I hope by the grace of the Holy Ghost I shall tell, as I saw.

Truth seeth God, and Wisdom beholdeth God, and of these two cometh the third : that is, a holy marvellous[2] delight in God ; which is Love. Where Truth and Wisdom are verily, there is Love verily, coming of them both. And all of God's making : for He is endless sovereign Truth, endless sovereign Wisdom, endless sovereign Love, unmade ; and man's Soul is a creature in God which hath the same properties *made*,[3] and evermore it doeth that it was made for : it seeth God, it beholdeth God, and it loveth God. Whereof God enjoyeth in the creature ; and the creature in God, endlessly marvelling.

In which marvelling he seeth his God, his Lord, his Maker so high, so great, and so good, in comparison

[1] See chap. iv.   [2] *i.e. marvelling.*   [3] chaps. liv., lv.

with him that is made, that scarcely the creature seemeth ought to the self. But the clarity and the clearness of Truth and Wisdom maketh him to see and to bear witness[1] that he is made for Love: in which God endlessly keepeth him.

CHAPTER XLV

" All heavenly things and all earthly things that belong to Heaven are comprehended in these two judgments "

GOD deemeth us [looking] upon our Nature-Substance, which is ever kept one in Him, whole and safe without end : and *this* doom is [because] of His rightfulness [in the which it is made and kept]. And man judgeth [looking] upon our changeable Sense-soul, which seemeth now one [thing], now other,—according as it taketh of the [higher or lower] parts,—and [is that which] showeth outward. And *this* wisdom [of man's judgment] is *mingled* [because of the diverse things it beholdeth]. For sometimes it is good and easy, and sometimes it is hard and grievous. And in as much as it is good and easy it belongeth to the rightfulness ; and in as much as it is hard and grievous [by reason of the sin beheld, which sheweth in our Sense-soul,] our good Lord Jesus reformeth it by [the working in our Sense-soul of] mercy and grace through the virtue of His blessed Passion, and so bringeth it to the rightfulness.

And though these two [judgments] be thus accorded and oned, yet both shall be known in Heaven without end. The first doom, which is of God's rightfulness, is

1 " beknowen."

[because] of His high endless life [in our Substance]; and this is that fair sweet doom that was shewed in all the fair Revelation, in which I saw Him assign to us no manner of blame. But though this was sweet and delectable, yet in the beholding only of this, I could not be fully eased: and that was because of the doom of Holy Church, which I had afore understood and which was continually in my sight. And therefore by *this* doom methought I understood that sinners are worthy sometime of blame and wrath; but these two could I not see in God; and therefore my desire was more than I can or may tell. For the higher doom was shewed by God Himself in that same time, and therefore me behoved needs to take it; and the lower doom was learned me afore in Holy Church, and therefore I might in no way leave the lower doom. Then was this my desire: that I might see in God in what manner that which the doom of Holy Church teacheth is true in His sight, and how it belongeth to me verily to know it; whereby the two dooms might both be saved, so as it were worshipful to God and right way to me.

And to all this I had none other answer but a marvellous example of a lord and of a servant, as I shall tell after: and that full mistily shewed.[1] And yet I stand desiring, and will unto my end, that I might by grace know these two dooms as it belongeth to me. For all heavenly, and all earthly things that belong to Heaven, are comprehended in these two dooms. And the more understanding, by the gracious leading of the Holy Ghost, that we have of these two dooms, the more we shall see and know our failings. And ever the more

[1] Chap. li.

that we see them, the more, of nature, by grace, we shall long to be fulfilled of endless joy and bliss. For we are made thereto, and our Nature-Substance is now blissful in God, and hath been since it was made, and shall be without end.

CHAPTER XLVI

" It is needful to see and to know that we are sinners: wherefore we deserve pain and wrath." "He is God: Good, Life, Truth, Love, Peace: His Clarity and His Unity suffereth Him not to be wroth "

BUT our passing life that we have here in our sense-soul knoweth not what our Self is. [And when we verily and clearly see and know what our Self is][1] then shall we verily and clearly see and know our Lord God in fulness of joy. And therefore it behoveth needs to be that the nearer we be to our bliss, the more we shall long [after it]: and that both by nature and by grace. We may have knowing of our Self in this life by continuant help and virtue of our high Nature. In which knowing we may exercise and grow, by forwarding and speeding of mercy and grace; but we may never fully know our Self until the last point: in which point this passing life and manner of pain and woe shall have an end. And therefore it belongeth properly to us, both by nature and by grace, to long and desire with all our mights to know our Self in fulness of endless joy.

[1] So S. de Cressy has it. There is evidently an omission in the MS. of part of this sentence. See lvi., lxxii. The dim sight of God comes before the dim sight of the Self, but the clear sight of God comes after the clear sight of the Self.

And yet in all this time, from the beginning to the end, I had two manner of beholdings. The one was endless continuant love, with secureness of keeping, and blissful salvation,—for of this was all *the Shewing*. The other was of the common teaching of Holy Church, in which I was afore informed and grounded—and with all my will having in use and understanding. And the beholding of *this* went not from me: for by the Shewing I was not stirred nor led therefrom in no manner of point, but I had therein teaching to love it and find it good[1]: whereby I might, by the help of our Lord and His grace, increase and rise to more heavenly knowing and higher loving.

And thus in all the Beholding methought it was needful to see and to know that we are sinners, and do many evils that we ought to leave, and leave many good deeds undone that we ought to do: wherefore we deserve pain and wrath. And notwithstanding all this, I saw soothfastly that our Lord was never wroth, nor ever shall be. For He is God: Good, Life, Truth, Love, Peace; His Clarity[2] and His Unity suffereth Him not to be wroth. For I saw truly that it is against the property of His Might to be wroth, and against the property of His Wisdom, and against the property of His Goodness. God is the Goodness that may not be wroth, for He is not [other] but Goodness: our soul is oned to Him, unchangeable Goodness, and between God and our soul is neither wrath nor forgiveness in His sight. For our soul is so fully oned to God of His own Goodness that between God and our soul may be right nought.

---

[1] "like it."

[2] Cressy has: "He is Peace; and His Might, His Wisdom, His Charity, and His Unity," etc.

G

And to this understanding was the soul led by love and drawn by might in every Shewing: *that it is thus our good Lord shewed*, and *how it is thus in truth of His great Goodness*. And He willeth that we desire to learn it—that is to say, as far as it belongeth to His creature to learn it. For all things that the simple soul [1] understood, God willeth that they be shewed and [made] known. For the things that He will have privy, mightily and wisely Himself He hideth them, for love. For I saw in the same Shewing that much privity is hid, which may never be known until the time that God of His goodness hath made us worthy to see it; and therewith I am well-content, abiding our Lord's will in this high marvel. And now I yield me to my Mother, Holy Church, as a simple child oweth.

CHAPTER XLVII

"We fail oftentimes of the sight of Him, and anon we fall into our self, and then find we no feeling of right,—nought but contrariness that is in our self"

TWO things belong to our soul as duty: the one is that we reverently marvel, the other that we meekly suffer, ever enjoying in God. For He would have us understand that we shall in short time see clearly in Himself all that we desire.

And notwithstanding all this, I beheld and marvelled greatly: *What is the mercy and forgiveness of God?* For by the teaching that I had afore, I understood that the mercy of God should be the forgiveness of His wrath

[1] Chap. ii. "a simple creature"; "the soul," xxiv., xiii., etc., and xxxii. p. 64.

after the time that we have sinned. For methought that to a soul whose meaning and desire is to love, the wrath of God was harder than any other pain, and therefore I took [1] that the forgiveness of His wrath should be one of the principal points of His mercy. But howsoever I might behold and desire, I could in no wise see this point in all the Shewing. [2]

But how I understood and saw of the work of mercy, I shall tell somewhat, as God will give me grace. I understood this : Man is changeable in this life, and by frailty and overcoming falleth into sin : he is weak and unwise of himself, and also his will is overlaid. And in this time he is in tempest and in sorrow and woe ; and the cause is blindness : for he seeth not God. For if he saw God continually, he should have no mischievous feeling, nor any manner of motion or yearning that serveth to sin. [3]

Thus saw I, and felt in the same time ; and methought that the sight and the feeling was high and plenteous and gracious in comparison with that which our common feeling is in this life ; but yet I thought it was but small and low in comparison with the great desire that the soul hath to see God.

For I felt in me five manner of workings, which be these : Enjoying, mourning, desire, dread, and sure hope. Enjoying : for God gave me understanding and knowing that it was Himself that I saw ; mourning : and that was for failing ; desire : and that was I might see Him ever more and more, understanding and knowing that we shall never

[1] understood—took it.
[2] " But for nowte that I myte beholden and desyrin I could not se."
[3] "ne no manner steryng ne [or y^e = the] yernyng."

have full rest till we see Him verily and clearly in heaven; dread was: for it seemed to me in all that time that that sight should fail, and I be left to myself; sure hope was in the endless love: that I saw I should be kept by His mercy and brought to His bliss. And the joying in His sight with this sure hope of His merciful keeping made me to have feeling and comfort so that mourning and dread were not greatly painful. And yet in all this I beheld in the Shewing of God that this manner of sight may not be continuant in this life,—and that for His own worship and for increase of our endless joy. And therefore we fail oftentimes of the sight of Him, and anon we fall into our self, and then find we no feeling of right,—naught but contrariness that is in our self; and that of the elder root of our first sin,[1] with all the sins that follow, of our contrivance. And in this we are in travail and tempest[2] with feeling of sins, and of pain in many divers manners, spiritual and bodily, as it is known to us in this life.

CHAPTER XLVIII

" I beheld the property of Mercy, and I beheld the property of Grace : which have two manners of working in one love "

BUT our good Lord the Holy Ghost, which is endless life dwelling in our soul, full securely keepeth us; and worketh therein a peace and bringeth it to ease by grace, and accordeth it to God and maketh it pliant.[3]

[1] *i.e.* contrariness, springing from the beginning of sin in the first fall of man.

[2] " traveylid and tempested."   [3] " buxum "=ready to bend or obey.

And this is the mercy and the way that our Lord continually leadeth us in as long as we be here in this life which is changeable.

For I saw no wrath but on man's part; and that forgiveth He in us. For wrath is not else but a forwardness and a contrariness to peace and love; and either it cometh of failing of might, or of failing of wisdom, or of failing of goodness: which failing is not in God, but is on our part. For we by sin and wretchedness have in us a wretched and continuant contrariness to peace and to love. And that shewed He full often in His lovely Regard of Ruth and Pity.[1] For the ground of mercy is love, and the working of mercy is our keeping in love. And this was shewed in such manner that I could[2] not have perceived of the part of mercy but as it were alone in love; that is to say, as to my sight.

Mercy is a sweet gracious working in love, mingled with plenteous pity: for mercy worketh in keeping us, and mercy worketh turning to us all things to good. Mercy, by love, suffereth us to fail in measure and in as much as we fail, in so much we fall; and in as much as we fall, in so much we die: for it needs must be that we die in so much as we fail of the sight and feeling of God that is our life. Our failing is dreadful, our falling is shameful, and our dying is sorrowful: but in all this the sweet eye of pity and love is lifted never off us, nor the working of mercy ceaseth.[3]

For I beheld the property of mercy, and I beheld the

---

[1] "lovely chere," loving Look. See li., lxxi., etc.

[2] "I cowth not a perceyven of."

[3] "But in all this the swete eye of pite and love cumith never of us ne the werkyng of mercy cesyth not."

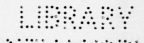

property of grace : which have two manners of working in one love. Mercy is a pitiful property which
belongeth to the Motherhood in tender love ; and grace
is a worshipful property which belongeth to the
royal Lordship in the same love. Mercy worketh :
keeping, suffering, quickening, and healing ; and all is
tenderness of love. And grace worketh : raising, rewarding, endlessly overpassing that which our longing
and our travail deserveth, spreading abroad and shewing
the high plenteous largess[1] of God's royal Lordship in
His marvellous courtesy ; and this is of the abundance
of love. For grace worketh our dreadful failing into
plenteous, endless solace ; and grace worketh our shameful falling into high, worshipful rising ; and grace
worketh our sorrowful dying into holy, blissful life.

For I saw full surely that ever as our contrariness
worketh to us here in earth pain, shame, and sorrow,
right so, on the contrary wise, grace worketh to us in
heaven solace, worship, and bliss ; and overpassing.
And so far forth, that when we come up and receive
the sweet reward which grace hath wrought for us, then
we shall thank and bless our Lord, endlessly rejoicing
that ever we suffered woe. And that shall be for a
property of blessed love that we shall know in God
which we could never have known without woe going
before.

And when I saw all this, it behoved me needs to grant
that the mercy of God and the forgiveness is to slacken
and waste *our* wrath.

[1] or largeness.

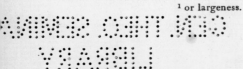

CHAPTER XLIX

" Where our Lord appeareth, peace is taken, and wrath hath
no place." " Immediately is the soul made at one with God
when it is truly set at peace in itself "

FOR this was an high marvel to the soul which was
continually shewed in all the Revelations, and was
with great diligence beholden, that our Lord God, anent
Himself may not forgive, for He may not be wroth : it
were impossible. For this was shewed : that our life is
all grounded and rooted in love, and without love we
may not live ; and therefore to the soul that of His
special grace seeth so far into the high, marvellous
Goodness of God, and seeth that we are endlessly oned
to Him in love, it is the most impossible that may be,
that God should be wroth. For wrath and friendship
be two contraries. For He that wasteth and destroyeth
our wrath and maketh us meek and mild,—it behoveth
needs to be that He [Himself] be ever one in love, meek
and mild : which is contrary to wrath.

For I saw full surely that where our Lord appeareth,
peace is taken and wrath hath no place. For I saw no
manner of wrath in God, neither for short time nor for
long ;—for in sooth, as to my sight, if God might be
wroth for an instant,[1] we should never have life nor
place nor being. For as verily as we have our being
of the endless Might of God and of the endless Wisdom
and of the endless Goodness, so verily we have our
keeping in the endless Might of God, in the endless

---

[1] " a touch."

Wisdom, and in the endless Goodness. For though we feel in ourselves, [frail] wretches, debates and strifes, yet are we all-mannerful enclosed in the mildness of God and in His meekness, in His benignity and in His graciousness.[1] For I saw full surely that all our endless friendship, our place, our life and our being, is in God.

For that same endless Goodness that keepeth us when we sin, that we perish not, the same endless Goodness continually treateth in us a peace against our wrath and our contrarious falling, and maketh us to see our need with a true dread, and mightily to seek unto God to have forgiveness, with a gracious desire of our salvation. And though we, by the wrath and the contrariness that is in us, be now in tribulation, distress, and woe, as falleth to our blindness and frailty, yet are we *securely* safe by the merciful keeping of God, that we perish not. But we are not *blissfully* safe, in having of our endless joy, till we be all in peace and in love : that is to say, full pleased with God and with all His works, and with all His judgments, and loving and peaceable with our self and with our even-Christians and with all that God loveth, as love beseemeth.[2] And this doeth God's Goodness in us.

Thus saw I that God is our very Peace, and He is our sure Keeper when we are ourselves in unpeace, and He continually worketh to bring us into endless peace. And thus when we, by the working of mercy and grace, be made meek and mild, we are fully safe ; suddenly is the soul oned to God when it is truly peaced in itself : for in Him is found no wrath. And thus I saw when

---

[1] " buxumhede."   [2] " liketh."

we are all in peace and in love, we find no contrariness, nor no manner of letting through that contrariness which is now in us; [nay], our Lord of His Goodness maketh it to us full profitable. For that contrariness is cause of our tribulations and all our woe, and our Lord Jesus taketh them and sendeth them up to Heaven, and there are they made more sweet and delectable than heart may think or tongue may tell. And when we come thither we shall find them ready, all turned into very fair and endless worships. Thus is God our steadfast Ground: and He shall be our full bliss and make us unchangeable, as He is, when we are there.

CHAPTER L

"The blame of our sin continually hangeth upon us." "In the sight of God the soul that shall be saved was never dead, nor ever shall be dead"

A<small>ND</small> in this life mercy and forgiveness is our way and evermore leadeth us to grace. And by the tempest and the sorrow that we fall into on our part, we be often dead as to man's doom in earth; but in the sight of God the soul that shall be saved was never dead, nor ever shall be.

But yet here I wondered and marvelled with all the diligence of my soul, saying thus within me: *Good Lord, I see Thee that art very Truth; and I know in truth*[1] *that we sin grievously every day and be much blameworthy; and I may neither leave the knowing of Thy truth,*[2] *nor do I see Thee shew to us any manner of blame. How may this be?*

[1] and [2] "sothly," "sothe."

For I knew by the common teaching of Holy Church and by mine own feeling, that the blame of our sin continually hangeth upon us, from the first man unto the time that we come up unto heaven: then was this my marvel that I saw our Lord God shewing to us no more blame than if we were as clean and as holy as Angels be in heaven. And between these two contraries my reason was greatly travailed through my blindness, and could have no rest for dread that His blessed presence should pass from my sight and I be left in unknowing [of] how He beholdeth us in our sin. For either [it] behoved me to see in God that sin was all done away, or else me behoved to see in God how He seeth it, whereby I might truly know how it belongeth to me to see sin, and the manner of our blame. My longing endured, Him continually beholding;—and yet I could have no patience for great straits [1] and perplexity, thinking: *If I take it thus that we be no sinners and not blameworthy, it seemeth as I should err and fail of knowing of this truth [2]; and if it be so that we be sinners and blameworthy,—Good Lord, how may it then be that I cannot see this true thing [2] in Thee, which art my God, my Maker, in whom I desire to see all truths? [3]*

For three points make me hardy to ask it. The first is, because it is so low a thing: for if it were an high thing I should be a-dread. The second is, that it is so common: for if it were special and privy, also I should be a-dread. The third is, that it needeth me to know it (as methinketh) if I shall live here for knowing of good and evil, whereby I may, by reason and grace, the more dispart them asunder, and love goodness and hate evil,

[1] "awer," p. 127.   [2] "soth" and "sothnes."   [3] "trueths."

as Holy Church teacheth.   I cried inwardly, with all my might seeking unto God for help, saying thus: *Ah! Lord Jesus, King of bliss, how shall I be eased? Who shall teach me and tell me that [thing] me needeth to know, if I may not at this time see it in Thee?*

CHAPTER LI

" He is the Head, and we be His members."   "Therefore our Father nor may nor will more blame assign to us than to His own Son, precious and worthy Christ "

AND then our Courteous Lord answered in shewing full mistily a wonderful example of a Lord that hath a Servant: and He gave me sight to my understanding of both.   Which sight was shewed doubly in the Lord and doubly in the Servant: the one part was shewed spiritually in bodily likeness, and the other part was shewed more spiritually, without bodily likeness.

For the first [sight], thus, I saw two persons in bodily likeness: that is to say, a Lord and a Servant; and therewith God gave me spiritual understanding.   The Lord sitteth stately in rest and in peace; the Servant standeth by afore his Lord reverently, ready to do his Lord's will.   The Lord looketh upon his Servant full lovingly and sweetly, and meekly he sendeth him to a certain place to do his will.   The Servant not only he goeth, but suddenly he starteth, and runneth in great haste, for love to do his Lord's will.   And anon he falleth into a slade,[1] and taketh full great hurt.   And

---

[1] *i.e.* a steep hollow place; a ravine.

then he groaneth and moaneth and waileth and struggleth, but he neither may rise nor help himself by no manner of way.

And of all this the most mischief[1] that I saw him in, was failing of comfort: for he could not turn his face to look upon his loving Lord, which was to him full near, —in Whom is full comfort;—but as a man that was feeble and unwise for the time, he turned his mind[2] to his feeling and endured in woe.

In which woe he suffered seven great pains. The first was the sore bruising that he took in his falling, which was to him feelable pain; the second was the heaviness of his body; the third was feebleness following from these two; the fourth, that he was blinded in his reason and stunned in his mind, so far forth that almost he had forgotten his own love; the fifth was that he might not rise; the sixth was most marvellous to me, and that was that he lay all alone: I looked all about and beheld, and far nor near, high nor low, I saw to him no help; the seventh was that the place which he lay on was a long, hard, and grievous [place].

I marvelled how this Servant might meekly suffer there all this woe, and I beheld with carefulness to learn if I could perceive in him any fault, or if the Lord should assign to him any blame. And in sooth there was none seen: for only his goodwill and his great desire was cause of his falling; and he was unlothful, and as good inwardly as when he stood afore his Lord, ready to do his will. And right thus continually his loving Lord full tenderly beholdeth him. But now with a *double* manner of Regard: one outward, full meekly

[1] *i.e.* injury, harm.   [2] "entended."

and mildly, with great ruth and pity,—and this was of the first [sight], another *inward*, more spiritually,—and this was shewed with a leading of mine understanding into the Lord, [in the] which I saw Him highly rejoicing for the worshipful restoring that He will and shall bring His Servant to by His plenteous grace; and this was of that other shewing.

And now [was] my understanding led again into the first [sight]; both keeping in mind. Then saith this courteous Lord in his meaning: *Lo, lo, my loved Servant, what harm and distress he hath taken in my service for my love,—yea, and for his goodwill. Is it not fitting that I award him [for] his affright and his dread, his hurt and his maim and all his woe? And not only this, but falleth it not to me to give a gift that [shall] be better to him, and more worshipful, than his own wholeness should have been?—or else methinketh I should do him no grace.*

And in this an inward spiritual Shewing of the Lord's meaning descended into my soul: in which I saw that it behoveth needs to be, by virtue of His great [Goodness] and His own worship, that His dearworthy Servant, which He loved so much, should be verily and blissfully rewarded, above that he should have been if he had not fallen. Yea, and so far forth, that his falling and his woe, that he hath taken thereby, shall be turned into high and overpassing worship and endless bliss.

And at this point the shewing of the example vanished, and our good Lord led forth mine understanding in sight and in shewing of the Revelation to the end. But notwithstanding all this forth-leading, the marvelling over the example went never from me: for methought it was given me for an answer to my desire, and yet could I not take therein full understanding to mine ease at that time. For in the Servant that was shewed for Adam, as I shall tell, I saw many diverse properties that might in no manner of way be assigned [1] to single Adam. And thus in that time I stood for much part in unknowing : for the full understanding of this marvellous example was not given me in that time. In which mighty example three properties of the Revelation be yet greatly hid ; and notwithstanding this [further forthleading], I saw and understood that every Shewing is full of secret things [left hid].

And therefore me behoveth now to tell three properties in which I am somewhat eased. The first is the beginning of teaching that I understood therein, in the same time ; the second is the inward teaching that I have understood therein afterward ; the third, all the whole Revelation from the beginning to the end (that is to say of this Book) which our Lord God of His goodness bringeth oftentimes freely to the sight of mine understanding. And these three are so oned, as to my understanding, that I cannot, nor may, dispart them. And by these three, as one, I have teaching whereby I ought to believe and trust in our Lord God, that of the same goodness of which He shewed it, and for the same end, right so, of the same goodness and for the same end He shall declare it to us when it is His will.

For, twenty years after the time of the Shewing, save three months, I had teaching inwardly, as I shall tell : *It belongeth to thee to take heed to all the properties and conditions that were shewed in the example, though thou think that they be misty and indifferent [2] to thy sight.* I assented willingly, with great desire, and inwardly [beheld] with

---

[1] " aret "=reckoned.   [2] *i.e.* not of definite purport, indistinct.

heedfulness [1] all the points and properties that were shewed in the same time, as far forth as my wits and understanding would serve: beginning my beholding at the Lord and at the Servant, and the manner of sitting of the Lord, and the place that he sat on, and the colour of his clothing and the manner of shape, and his countenance without, and his nobleness and his goodness within; at the manner of standing of the Servant, and the place where, and how; at his manner of clothing, the colour and the shape; at his outward having and at his inward goodness and his unloathfulness.

The Lord that sat stately in rest and in peace, I understood that He is God. The Servant that stood afore the Lord, I understood that it was shewed for Adam: that is to say, one man was shewed, that time, and his falling, to make it thereby understood how God beholdeth All-Man and his falling. For in the sight of God all man is one man, and one man is all man. This man was hurt in his might and made full feeble; and he was stunned in his understanding so that he [was] turned from the beholding of his Lord. But his will was kept whole in God's sight;—for his will I saw our Lord commend and approve. But himself was letted and blinded from the knowing of this will; and this is to him great sorrow and grievous distress: for neither doth he see clearly his loving Lord, which is to him full meek and mild, nor doth he see truly what himself is in the sight of his loving Lord. And well I wot when these two are wisely and truly seen, we shall get rest and peace here in part, and the fulness of the bliss of Heaven, by His plenteous grace.

1 " avisement."

And this was a beginning of teaching which I saw in the same time, whereby I might come to know in what manner He beholdeth us in our sin. And then I saw that only Pain blameth and punisheth, and our courteous Lord comforteth and sorroweth; and ever He is to the soul in glad Cheer, loving, and longing to bring us to His bliss.

The place that the Lord sat on was simple, on the earth, barren and desert, alone in wilderness; his clothing was ample and full seemly, as falleth to a Lord; the colour of his cloth was blue as azure, most sad and fair. his cheer was merciful; the colour of his face was fair-brown,—with full seemly features; his eyes were black, most fair and seemly, shewing [*outward*] full of lovely *pity*, and [shewing], *within* him, an high Regard,[1] long and broad, all full of endless heavens. And the lovely looking wherewith He looked upon His Servant continually,—and especially in his falling,—methought it might melt our hearts for love and burst them in two for joy. The fair looking shewed [itself] of a seemly mingledness which was marvellous to behold: the one [part] was Ruth and Pity, the other was Joy and Bliss. The Joy and Bliss passeth as far Ruth and Pity as Heaven is above earth: the Pity was earthly and the Bliss was heavenly: the Ruth and Pity of the Father was [in regard] of the falling of Adam, which is His most loved creature; the Joy and Bliss was [in regard] of His dear-

---

[1] MS. "within him an *heyward* long and brode, all full of endless hevyns." Cressy and Collins transcribe this word without explanation, but give "heavenliness" for "heavens." It seems most likely that "hey" has been written as if affixed to "ward" (*i.e.* "regard," "deeming," or "reward"), or else to "reward," meaning, as usual, *regard* ("Beholding"). See pp. 108 and 113. *Cf.* note at the end of this chapter.

worthy Son, which is even with the Father. The Merciful
Beholding of His Countenance[1] of love fulfilled all earth
and descended down with Adam into hell, with which
continuant pity Adam was kept from endless death. And
thus Mercy and Pity dwelleth with mankind unto the
time we come up into Heaven.

But man is blinded in this life and therefore we may
not see our Father, God, as He is. And what time that
He of His goodness willeth to shew Himself to man, He
sheweth Himself homely, as man. Notwithstanding, I
reason, in verity[2] we ought to know and believe that the
Father is not man.

But his sitting on the earth barren and desert, is to
signify this:—He made man's soul to be His own City
and His dwelling-place: which is most pleasing to Him
of all His works. And what time that man was fallen
into sorrow and pain, he was not all seemly to serve in
that noble office; and therefore our Lord Father would
prepare Himself no other place, but would sit upon the
earth abiding mankind, which is mingled with earth, till
what time by His grace His dearworthy Son had brought
again His City into the noble fairness with His hard
travail. The blueness of the clothing betokeneth His
steadfastness; the brownness of his fair face, with the
seemly blackness of the eyes, was most accordant to
shew His holy soberness. The length and breadth of
his garments, which were fair, flaming about, betokeneth
that He hath, beclosed in Him, all Heavens, and all Joy
and Bliss:[3] and this was shewed in a touch [of time],
where I have said: *Mine understanding was led into the*

---

[1] "lofly cher."   [2] "I reson sothly we owen."
[3] See p. 112, the "high reward"

H

Lord; in which [inward shewing] I saw Him highly *rejoice* for the worshipful restoring that He will and shall bring His servant to by His plenteous grace.

And yet I marvelled, beholding the Lord and the Servant aforesaid. I saw the Lord sit stately, and the Servant standing reverently afore his Lord. In which Servant there is double understanding, one *without*, another *within*. *Outwardly* :—he was clad simply, as a labourer which were got ready for his toil;[1] and he stood full near the Lord—not evenly in front[2] of him, but in part to one side, on the left. His clothing was a white kirtle, single, old, and all defaced, dyed with sweat of his body, strait-fitting to him, and short —as it were an handful beneath the knee; [thread]bare, seeming as it should soon be worn out, ready to be ragged and rent. And of this I marvelled greatly, thinking : this is now an unseemly clothing for the Servant that is so greatly loved to stand in afore so worshipful a Lord. And *inwardly* in him was shewed a ground of love : which love that he had to the Lord was even-like[3] to the love that the Lord had to him.

The wisdom of the Servant saw inwardly that there was one thing to do which should be to the worship of the Lord. And the Servant, for love, having no regard to himself nor to nothing that might befall him, hastily he started and ran at the sending of his Lord, to do that thing which was his will and his worship. For it seemed by his outward clothing as he had been a continuant labourer of long time, and by the *inward sight*

---

[1] "which wer disposed to travel."
[2] "even fornempts "=strait opposite.
[3] *i.e.* equal (MS. "even like").

that I had both of the Lord and the Servant it seemed that he was a[1] new [one], that is to say, new beginning to travail: which Servant was never sent out afore.

There was a treasure in the earth which the Lord loved. I marvelled and thought what it might be, and I was answered in mine understanding: *It is a food which is delectable and pleasant to the Lord.* For I saw the Lord sit as a man, and I saw neither meat nor drink wherewith to serve him. This was one marvel. Another marvel was that this majestic Lord had no servant but one, and him he sent out. I beheld, thinking what manner of labour it might be that the Servant should do. And then I understood that he should do the greatest labour and hardest travail: that is, he should be a gardener, delve and dyke, toil and sweat, and turn the earth upside-down, and seek the deepness, and water the plants in time. And in this he should continue his travail and make sweet floods to run, and noble and plenteous fruits to spring, which he should bring afore the Lord to serve him therewith to his desire. And he should never turn again till he had prepared this food all ready as he knew that it pleased the Lord. And then he should take this food, with the drink in the food, and bear it full worshipfully afore the Lord. And all this time the Lord should sit in the same place, abiding his Servant whom he sent out.

And yet I marvelled from whence the Servant came. For I saw in the Lord that HE hath within Himself endless life, and all manner of goodness, save that treasure that was in the earth. And [also] *that* [treasure] was grounded in the Lord in marvellous deepness of endless

---

[1] S. de Cressy: "anaved"; MS. "anew."

love, but it was not all to His worship till the Servant had thus nobly prepared it, and brought it before Him in himself present. And without the Lord was nothing but wilderness. And I understood not all what this example meant, and therefore I marvelled whence the Servant came.

In the Servant is comprehended the Second Person in the Trinity ; and in the Servant is comprehended Adam : that is to say, All-Man. And therefore when I say the *Son*, it meaneth the Godhead which is even with the Father ; and when I say the *Servant*, it meaneth Christ's Manhood, which is rightful Adam. By the nearness of the Servant is understood the Son, and by the standing on the left side is understood Adam. The Lord is the Father, God ; the Servant is the Son, Christ Jesus ; the Holy Ghost is Even [1] Love which is in them both.

When Adam fell, God's Son fell : because of the rightful oneing which had been made in heaven, God's Son might not [be disparted] from Adam. (For by Adam I understand All-Man.) Adam fell from life to death, into the deep [2] of this wretched world, and after that into hell : God's Son fell with Adam, into the deep [3] of the Maiden's womb, who was the fairest daughter of Adam ; and for this end : to excuse Adam from blame in heaven and in earth ; and mightily He fetched him out of hell.

By the wisdom and goodness that was in the Servant is understood God's Son ; by the poor clothing as a

---

[1] *i.e.* equal—see p. 114. "All of the Charity of God," the mutual love that also embraces created souls, p. 118.

[2] and [3] "the slade."

labourer standing near the left side, is understood the Manhood and Adam, with all the scathe[1] and feebleness that followeth. For in all this our good Lord shewed His own Son and Adam but *one* Man. The virtue and the goodness that we have is of Jesus Christ, the feebleness and the blindness that we have is of Adam : which two were shewed in the Servant.

And thus hath our good Lord Jesus taken upon Him all our blame, and therefore our Father nor may nor will more blame assign to us than to His own Son, dearworthy Christ. Thus was He, the Servant, afore His coming into earth standing ready afore the Father in purpose, till what time He would send Him to do that worshipful deed by which mankind was brought again into heaven ;— that is to say, notwithstanding that He is God, even with the Father as anent the Godhead. But in His foreseeing purpose that He would be Man, to save man in fulfilling of His Father's will, so He stood afore His Father as a Servant, willingly[2] taking upon Him all our charge. And then He started full readily at the Father's will, and anon He fell full low, into the Maiden's womb, having no regard to Himself nor to His hard pains.

The white kirtle is the flesh ; the singleness is that there was right nought atwix the Godhead and Manhood ; the straitness is poverty ; the eld is of Adam's wearing ; the defacing, of sweat of Adam's travail ; the shortness sheweth the Servant's labour.

And thus I saw the Son saying in His meaning[3]: *Lo! my dear Father, I stand before Thee in Adam's kirtle, all*

---

[1] " mischief."
[2] " wilfully "=voluntarily, of His own Will as God.
[3] purpose, intent, thought or speech.

ready to start and to run: I would be in the earth to do Thy worship when it is Thy will to send me. How long shall I desire? Full soothfastly wist the Son when it would be the Father's will and how long He should desire: that is to say, [He wist it] anent the Godhead: for He is the Wisdom of the Father; wherefore this question was shewed with understanding of the *Manhood* of Christ. For all mankind that shall be saved by the sweet Incarnation and blissful Passion of Christ, all is the Manhood of Christ: for He is the Head and we be His members. To which members the day and the time is unknown when every passing woe and sorrow shall have an end, and the everlasting joy and bliss shall be fulfilled; which day and time for to see, all the Company of Heaven longeth. And all that shall be under heaven that shall come thither, their way is by longing and desire. Which desire and longing was shewed in the Servant's standing afore the Lord,—or else thus in the Son's standing afore the Father in Adam's kirtle. For the longing[1] and desire of all Mankind that shall be saved appeared in Jesus: for Jesus is All that shall be saved, and All that shall be saved is Jesus. And all of the Charity of God; with obedience, meekness, and patience, and virtues that belong to us.

Also in this marvellous example I have teaching with me as it were the beginning of an A.B.C., whereby I have some understanding of our Lord's meaning. For the secret things of the Revelation be hid therein;—notwithstanding that *all* the Shewings are full of secret things. The *sitting* of the Father betokeneth His Godhead: that is to say, by shewing of rest and peace: for

[1] " langor."

in the Godhead may be no travail.[1] And that He shewed Himself as *Lord*, betokeneth His [governance] to our manhood. The *standing* of the Servant betokeneth travail ; *on one side*, and on the *left*, betokeneth that he was not all worthy to stand even-right afore the Lord ; his *starting* was the Godhead, and the *running* was the Manhood : for the Godhead started from the Father into the Maiden's womb, falling into the taking of our Kind. And in this falling he took great sore : the *sore* that He took was our flesh, in which He had also swiftly feeling of deadly pains. That he stood *adread* before the Lord and not even-right, betokeneth that His clothing was not seemly[2] to stand in even-right afore the Lord, nor *that* might not, nor should not, be His office while He was a labourer ; nor also He might not sit in rest and peace with the Lord till He had won His peace rightfully with His hard travail ; and that he stood by the *left* side [betokeneth] that the Father left His own Son, willingly,[3] in the Manhood to suffer all man's pains, without sparing of Him. By that *his kirtle was in point to be ragged and rent*, is understood the blows, the scourgings, the thorns and the nails, the drawing and the dragging, His tender flesh rending. (As I saw in some part [before] how the flesh was rent from the skull, falling in pieces until the time when the bleeding ceased, and then it began to dry again, cleaving to the bone.) And by the *struggling and writhing, groaning and moaning*, is understood that He might never rise almightily from the time that He was fallen into the Maiden's womb, till his

---

[1] *i.e.* painful toil. " He sitteth . . . in peace and rest. And the God- head ruleth and careth for heaven and earth and all that is " (lxvii.).
   [2] " honest."   [3] " wilfully."

body was slain and dead, He yielding the soul into the Father's hands with all Mankind for whom He was sent.

And at this point He began first to shew His might: for He went into Hell, and when He was there He raised up the great Root out of the deep deepness which rightfully was knit to Him in high Heaven. The body was in the grave till Easter-morrow, and from that time He lay nevermore. For then was rightfully ended the struggling and the writhing, the groaning and the moaning. And our foul deadly flesh that God's Son took on Him, which was Adam's old kirtle, strait, [worn]-bare, and short, was then by our Saviour made fair, new, white and bright and of endless cleanness; loose and long [1]; fairer and richer than was then the clothing which [before] I saw on the Father: for that clothing was blue, but Christ's clothing is [coloured] now of a fair seemly medlour, which is so marvellous that I can it not describe: for it is all of very worships.

Now sitteth not the Son on earth in wilderness, but He sitteth in His noblest Seat, which He made in Heaven most to His pleasing. Now standeth not the Son afore the Father as a Servant afore the Lord dreadingly, meanly clad, in part naked; but He standeth afore the Father even-right, richly clad in blissful largeness, with a Crown upon His head of precious richness. For it was shewed that *we be His Crown*: which Crown is the Joy of the Father, the Worship of the Son, the Satisfying of the Holy Ghost, and endless marvellous Bliss to all that be in Heaven. Now standeth not the Son afore the Father on the left side, as a labourer, but He sitteth on His Father's right hand, in endless

[1] "wyde and syde" = wide and long.

rest and peace.[1] (But it is not meant that the Son sitteth on the right hand, side by side, as one man sitteth by another in this life,—for there is no such sitting, as to my sight, in the Trinity,—but He sitteth on His Father's right hand,—that is to say: in the highest nobleness of the Father's joys.) Now is the Spouse, God's Son, in peace with His loved Wife, which is the Fair Maiden of endless Joy. Now sitteth the Son, Very God and Man, in His City in rest and peace: which [City] His Father hath adight to Him of His endless purpose; and the Father in the Son; and the Holy Ghost in the Father and in the Son.

[1] But see also xxxix. p. 81, lxxx. p. 194.

Note :—If "*an heyward*"—"long and brode all full of endless hevyns," p. 112,—were to be rendered as "an high reward," revealed for the future along with, though less clearly than, the divine pity for the pains of the present, reference might be made to Revelation ix. pp. 47, 50 : "It is a joy, a bliss, an endless satisfying to me that ever suffered I Passion for thee." . . . "In this feeling mine understanding was lifted up into Heaven : and there I saw three heavens"; and to Rev. x. p. 51 : "then with a glad Cheer our Lord looked into His Side and beheld, rejoicing. With His sweet looking He led forth the understanding of His creature by the same wound into His Side within. And then He shewed a fair delectable place, and large enough for all mankind that shall be saved to rest in peace and in love."

But "Regard" (scope of true, continuing, divine Sight, Insight, All-comprehending sight) seems more likely to be the true rendering. "Long and broad" go strangely with the word, but on p. 113 the *length and breadth* of the garments is interpreted immediately after the colour of the eyes, and is said to betoken that "He hath in Him, all Heavens, and all Joy and Bliss," and indeed these words but fill out the idea of the more frequently used "high" to signify the "enclosing" of "endless heavens : " that Sphere of "fulness" which is infinite. With this passage may be compared one below, on p. 113 : "The Merciful Beholding of His loving Cheer fulfilled all earth and descended down with Adam into hell, . . . and thus Mercy and Pity dwelleth with mankind unto the time we come up into Heaven." The

CHAPTER LII

"We have now matter of mourning: for our sin is cause of Christ's pains; and we have, lastingly, matter of joy: for endless love made Him to suffer"

AND thus I saw that God rejoiceth that He is our Father, and God rejoiceth that He is our Mother, and God rejoiceth that He is our Very Spouse and our soul is His loved Wife. And Christ rejoiceth that He is our Brother, and Jesus rejoiceth that He is our Saviour. These are five high joys, as I understand, in which He willeth that we enjoy; Him praising, Him thanking, Him loving, Him endlessly blessing.

All that shall be saved, we have in us, for the time of this life, a marvellous mingling [1] both of weal and woe: we have in us our Lord Jesus uprisen, we have in us the wretchedness and the mischief of Adam's falling, dying. By Christ we are steadfastly kept, and by His grace touching us we are raised into sure trust of salvation. And by Adam's falling we are so broken, in our feeling, in diverse manners by sins and by sundry pains, in which we are made dark, that scarsely we can take any comfort.

---

other, the Inward, the *high* Beholding or Regard is not said to "fill" Heaven, but to be "full of" endless Heavens. So elsewhere it is said that in our *Sense-soul*, the lower part of human nature, *God dwells*, but that our *Substance*, the higher part, *dwells in God*. (The regard of Mercy and Pity is with the Sense-soul; the high Regard of Joy and Bliss is with the Substance.) P. 132, chap. lv.: "I saw that our Substance is in God, and also I saw that in our Sense-soul God is." lvi. p. 135: "The worshipful City that our Lord Jesus sitteth in, it is our Sense-part, in which He is enclosed; and our Nature-Substance is beclosed in Jesus, with the blessed Soul of Christ sitting in rest in the Godhead."

1 "medlour," "medle."

But in our intent[1] we abide in God, and faithfully trust to have mercy and grace; and this is His own working in us. And of His goodness He openeth the eye of our understanding, by which we have sight, sometime more and sometime less, according as God giveth ability to receive. And now we are raised into the one, and now we are suffered to fall into the other.

And thus is this medley so marvellous in us that scarsely we know of our self or of our even-Christian in what way we stand, for the marvellousness of this sundry feeling. But that same Holy Assent, *that* we assent to God when we feel Him, truly setting our will to be with Him, with all our heart, and with all our soul, and with all our might. And then we hate and despise our evil stirrings and all that might be occasion of sin, spiritual and bodily.[2] And yet nevertheless when this sweetness is hid, we fall again into blindness, and so into woe and tribulation in diverse manners. But then is this our comfort, that we *know in our faith* that by virtue of Christ which is our Keeper, we assent never thereto, but we groan there-against, and dure on, in pain and woe, praying, unto that time that He sheweth Him again to us.

And thus we stand in this medley all the days of our life. But He willeth that we trust that He is lastingly

---

[1] "menyng."

[2] "And thus is this medle so mervelous in us that onethys we knowen of our selfe or of our evyn Cristen in what way we stonden for the marveloushede of this sundry felyng. But that ilke holy assent that we assenten to God when we feel hym truly willand to be with him with al our herte, with al our soule and with al our myte, and than we haten and dispisen our evil sterings and al that myte be occasion of synne gostly and bodily."

with us. And that in three manner.—He is with us in Heaven, very Man, in His own Person, us updrawing; and that was shewed in [the Shewing of] the Spiritual Thirst. And He is with us in earth, us leading; and that was shewed in the Third [Shewing], where I saw God in a Point. And He is with us in our soul, endlessly dwelling, us ruling and keeping; and that was shewed in the Sixteenth [Shewing], as I shall tell.

And thus in the Servant was shewed the scathe and blindness of Adam's falling; and in the Servant was shewed the wisdom and goodness of God's Son. And in the Lord was shewed the ruth and pity of Adam's woe, and in the Lord was shewed the high nobility and the endless worship that Mankind is come to by the virtue of the Passion and death of His dearworthy Son. And therefore mightily He joyeth in his falling for the high raising and fulness of bliss that Mankind is come to, overpassing that we should have had if he had not fallen.—And thus to see this overpassing nobleness was mine understanding led into God in the same time that I saw the Servant fall.

And thus we have, now, matter of mourning: for our sin is cause of Christ's pains; and we have, lastingly, matter of joy: for endless love made Him to suffer. And therefore the creature that seeth and feeleth the working of love by grace, hateth nought but sin: for of all things, to my sight, love and hate are [the] hardest and most unmeasureable contraries. And notwithstanding all this, I saw and understood in our Lord's meaning that we may not in this life keep us from sin as wholly in full cleanness as we shall be in Heaven. But we may well by grace keep us from the sins which would lead us to endless pains, as Holy Church teacheth us; and eschew venial [ones] reasonably up to our might. And if we by our blindness and our wretchedness any time fall, we should readily rise, knowing the sweet touching of grace, and with all our will amend us upon the teaching of Holy Church, according as the sin is grievous, and go forthwith to God in love; and neither, on the one side, fall over low, inclining to despair, nor, on the other side, be over-reckless, as if we made no matter of it [1]; but nakedly acknowledge our feebleness, finding that we may not stand a twinkling of an eye but by Keeping of grace, and reverently cleave to God, on Him only trusting.

For after one wise is the Beholding by [2] God, and after another wise is the Beholding by [2] man. For it belongeth to man meekly to accuse himself, and it belongeth to the proper Goodness of our Lord God courteously to excuse man. And these be two parts that were shewed in the double Manner of Regard with which the Lord beheld the falling of His loved Servant. The one was shewed outward, very meekly and mildly, with great ruth and pity; and that of endless Love. And right thus willeth our Lord that we accuse our self, earnestly and truly seeing and knowing our falling and all the harms that come thereof; seeing and learning [3] that we can never restore it; and therewith that we earnestly and truly see and know His everlasting love that He hath to us, and His plenteous mercy. And thus graciously to see and know both together is the meek accusing that our Lord asketh of us, and Himself worketh it where it is. And this is the lower part of man's life, and it was

---

[1] "gove no fors"=gave it no force.　　"of."
[3] "witand"=witting.

shewed in the [Lord's] *outward* manner of Regard. In which shewing I saw *two* parts : the one is the rueful falling of man, the other is the worshipful Satisfaction [1] that our Lord hath made for man.

The other manner of Regard was shewed *inward*: and that was more highly and all [fully] *one*.[2] For the life and the virtue that we have in the lower part is of the higher, and it cometh down to us [from out] of the Natural love of the [high] Self, by [the working of] grace. Atwix [the life of] the one and [the life of] the other there is right nought : for it is all one love. Which one blessed love hath now, in us, double working : for in the lower part are pains and passions, mercies and forgiveness, and such other that are profitable ; but in the higher part are none of these, but all one high love and marvellous joy : in [3] which joy all pains are highly restored. And in this [time] our Lord showed not only our Excusing [4] [from blame, in His beholding of our higher part], but the worshipful nobility that He shall bring us to [by the working of grace in our lower part], turning all our blame [that is therein, from our falling] into endless worship [when we be oned to the high Self above].[5]

1 " Asseth."

2 " and al on "—perhaps for *all is one.*

3 " in "=*in, into,* or *unto.*

4 *i.e. Exculpating*—as in Romans ii. 15.

5 " Man,—seeing he is not a simple nature—in one aspect of his being, which is the better, and that I may speak more openly what I ought to speak, his very self, is immortal ; but on the other side, which is weak and fallen, and which alone is known to those who have no faith except in sensible things, he is obnoxious to mortality and mutability."—From the *Didascolon* of Hugo of St Victor, as quoted in F. D. Maurice's *Mediæval Philosophy*, p. 147.

CHAPTER LIII

"In every soul that shall be saved is a Godly Will that never assented to sin, nor ever shall." "Ere that He made us He loved us, and when we were made we loved Him"

AND I saw that He willeth that we understand He taketh not harder the falling of any creature that shall be saved than He took the falling of Adam, which, we know, was endlessly loved and securely kept in the time of all his need, and now is blissfully restored in high overpassing joy. For our Lord is so good, so gentle, and so courteous, that He may never assign default [in those] in whom He shall ever be blessed and praised.

And in this that I have now told was my desire in part answered, and my great difficulty [1] some deal eased, by the lovely, gracious Shewing of our good Lord. In which Shewing I saw and understood full surely that in every soul that shall be saved is a Godly Will that never assented to sin, nor ever shall: which Will is so good that it may never will evil, but evermore continually it willeth good; and worketh good in the sight of God. Therefore our Lord willeth that we know this in the Faith and the belief; and especially that we have all this blessed Will whole and safe in our Lord Jesus Christ. For that same Kind [2] that Heaven shall be filled with behoveth needs, of God's rightfulness, so to have been knit and oned to Him, that therein was kept a Sub-

[1] "awer"=awe, travail of perplexity, dilemma—see p. 106.
[2] Man's nature.

stance which might never, nor should, be parted from Him; and *that* through His own Good Will in His endless foreseeing purpose.

But notwithstanding this rightful knitting and this endless oneing, yet the redemption and the again-buying of mankind is needful and speedful in everything, as it is done for the same intent and to the same end that Holy Church in our Faith us teacheth.

For I saw that God *began* never to love mankind: for right the same that mankind shall be in endless bliss, fulfilling the joy of God as anent His works, right so the same, mankind hath been in the foresight of God: known and loved from without beginning in his [1] rightful intent. By the endless assent of the full accord of all the Trinity, the Mid-Person willed to be Ground and Head of this fair Kind: out of Whom we be all come, in Whom we be all enclosed, into Whom we shall all wend,[2] in Him finding our full Heaven in everlasting joy, by the foreseeing purpose of all the blessed Trinity from without beginning.

For ere that He made us He loved us, and when we were made we loved Him. And this is a Love that is *made*, [to our Kindly Substance], [by virtue] of the Kindly Substantial *Goodness* of the Holy Ghost; Mighty, in Reason, [by virtue] of the *Might* of the Father; and Wise, in Mind, [by virtue] of the *Wisdom* of the Son. And thus is Man's Soul made by God and in the same point knit to God.

And thus I understand that man's Soul is made of nought: that is to say, it is made, but of nought that is

---

[1] Or (it may be): "In His Rightful Intent . . . the Mid-Person willed. . . ."   [2] "wynden."

made. And thus :—When God should make man's body He took the clay of earth, which is a matter mingled and gathered of all bodily things ; and thereof He made man's body. But to the making of man's Soul He would take right nought, but made it. And thus is the Nature-made rightfully oned to the Maker, which is Substantial Nature not-made : that is, God. And therefore it is that there may nor shall be right nought atwix God and man's Soul.

And in this endless Love man's Soul is kept whole, as the matter of the Revelations signifieth and sheweth : in which endless Love we be led and kept of God and never shall be lost. For He willeth we [1] be aware that our Soul is a life, which life of His Goodness and His Grace shall last in Heaven without end, Him loving, Him thanking, Him praising. And right the same that we shall be without end, the same we were treasured in God and hid, known and loved from without beginning.

Wherefore He would have us understand that the noblest thing that ever He made is mankind : and the fullest Substance and the highest Virtue is the blessed Soul of Christ. And furthermore He would have us understand that His[2] dearworthy Soul [of Manhood] was preciously knit to Him in the making [by Him of Manhood's Substantial Nature] which knot is so subtle and so mighty that (it)[3]—[man's soul]—is oned into God : in

---

[1] " wetyn " = wit.

[2] S. de Cressy has " this " ; the word in the MS. is more like " his."

[3] The pronoun " it " given by S. de Cressy is omitted in the MS. The meaning is, perhaps, that the Manhood-Substance, or Soul of Christ, was in its making, by the Second Person in the Trinity, so united to Himself that Man's Substance and each man's soul (in salvation), being one with it, are one with God the Son. See li. p. 117.

I

which oneing it is made endlessly holy. Furthermore He would have us know that all the souls that shall be saved in Heaven without end, are knit and oned in this oneing and made holy in this holiness.

CHAPTER LIV

" Faith is nought else but a right understanding, with true belief and sure trust, of our Being: that we are in God, and God is in us: Whom we see not "

AND because of this great, endless love that God hath to all Mankind, He maketh no disparting in love between the blessed Soul of Christ and the least soul that shall be saved. For it is full easy to believe and to trust that the dwelling of the blessed Soul of Christ is full high in the glorious Godhead, and verily, as I understand in our Lord's signifying, where the blessed Soul of Christ is, there is the Substance of all the souls that shall be saved by Christ.

Highly ought we to rejoice that God dwelleth in our soul, and much more highly ought we to rejoice that our soul dwelleth in God. Our soul is *made* to be God's dwelling-place; and the dwelling-place of the soul is God, Which is *unmade*. And high understanding it is, inwardly to see and know that God, which is our Maker, dwelleth in our soul; and an higher understanding it is, inwardly to see and to know that our soul, that is made, dwelleth in God's Substance: of which Substance, God, we are that we are.

And I saw no difference between God and our Sub-

stance: but as it were all God; and yet mine understanding took that our Substance is in God: that is to
say, that God is God, and our Substance is a creature in
God. For the Almighty Truth of the Trinity is our
Father: for He made us and keepeth us in Him; and
the deep Wisdom of the Trinity is our Mother, in Whom
we are all enclosed; the high Goodness of the Trinity
is our Lord, and in Him we are enclosed, and He in us.
We are enclosed in the Father, and we are enclosed in
the Son, and we are enclosed in the Holy Ghost. And
the Father is enclosed in us, and the Son is enclosed in
us, and the Holy Ghost is enclosed in us: Almightiness,
All-Wisdom, All-Goodness: one God, one Lord.

And our faith is a Virtue that cometh of our Nature-
Substance into our Sense-soul by the Holy Ghost; in
which all our virtues come to us: for without that, no
man may receive virtue. For it is nought else but a
right understanding, with true belief, and sure trust, of
our Being: that we are in God, and God in us, Whom
we see not. And this virtue, with all other that God
hath ordained to us coming therein, worketh in us great
things. For Christ's merciful working is in us, and we
graciously accord to Him through the gifts and the
virtues of the Holy Ghost. This working maketh that
we are Christ's children, and Christian in living.

CHAPTER LV

*"Christ is our Way "—" Mankind shall be restored
from double death "*

AND thus Christ is our Way, us surely leading in His
laws, and Christ in His body mightily beareth us
up into heaven. For I saw that Christ, us all having in
Him that shall be saved by Him, worshipfully presenteth
His Father in heaven with us; which present full thankfully His Father receiveth, and courteously giveth it to
His Son, Jesus Christ : which gift and working is joy to
the Father, and bliss to the Son, and pleasing to the
Holy Ghost. And of all things that belong to us [to do],
it is most pleasing to our Lord that we enjoy in this joy
which is in the blessed Trinity [in virtue] of our salvation. (And this was seen in the Ninth Shewing, where
it speaketh more of this matter.) And notwithstanding
all our feeling of woe or weal, God willeth that we
should understand and hold[1] by faith that we are more
verily in heaven than in earth.

Our Faith cometh of the natural Love of our soul, and
of the clear light of our Reason, and of the steadfast
Mind which we have from[2] God in our first making.
And what time that our soul is inspired into our body,
in which we are made sensual, so soon mercy and grace
begin to work, having of us care and keeping with pity
and love : in which working the Holy Ghost formeth, in
our Faith, *Hope* that we shall come again up above to our

---

[1] "feythyn."   [2] "of."

Substance, into the Virtue of Christ, increased and fulfilled through the Holy Ghost. Thus I understood that
the sense-soul is grounded in Nature, in Mercy, and in
Grace: which Ground enableth us to receive gifts that
lead us to endless life.

For I saw full assuredly that our Substance is in God,
and also I saw that in our sense-soul[1] God is: for in the
self-[same] point that our Soul is made sensual, in the
self-[same] point is the City of God ordained to Him
from without beginning; into which seat He cometh, and
never shall remove [from] it. For God is never out of
the soul: in which He dwelleth blissfully without end.
And this was seen in the Sixteenth Shewing where it
saith: *The place that Jesus taketh in our soul, He shall never
remove [from] it.* And all the gifts that God may give
to creatures, He hath given to His Son Jesus for us:
which gifts He, dwelling in us, hath enclosed in Him
unto the time that we be waxen and grown,—our soul
with our body and our body with our soul, either of
them taking help of other,—till we be brought up unto
stature, as nature worketh. And then, in the ground of
nature, with working of mercy, the Holy Ghost graciously
inspireth into us gifts leading to endless life.

And thus was my understanding led of God to see in
Him and to understand, to perceive and to know, that
our soul is *made-trinity*,[2] like to the unmade blissful
Trinity,[2] known and loved from without beginning, and
in the making oned to the Maker, as it is aforesaid.
This sight was full sweet and marvellous to behold,
peaceable, restful, sure, and delectable.

And because of the worshipful oneing that was

---

[1] " sensualite."   [2] Wisdom, Truth, Love or Goodness, p. 93.

thus made by God betwixt the soul and body, it behoveth needs to be that mankind shall be restored from double death: which restoring might never be until the time that the Second Person in the Trinity had taken the lower [1] part of man's nature; to Whom the highest [2] [part] was oned in the First-making. And these two parts were in Christ, the higher and the lower: which is but one Soul; the higher part was one in peace with God, in full joy and bliss; the lower part, which is sense-nature, [3] suffered for the salvation of mankind.

And these two parts [in Christ] were seen and felt in the Eighth Shewing, in which my body was fulfilled with feeling and mind of Christ's Passion and His death, and furthermore with this was a subtile feeling and privy inward sight of the High Part which I was shewed in the same time when I could not, [even] for the friendly [4] proffer [made to me], look up into Heaven: and that was because of that mighty beholding [that I had] of the Inward Life. Which Inward Life is that High Substance, that precious Soul, [of Christ], which is endlessly rejoicing in the Godhead.

---

[1] the Sense-soul.   [2] the Substance.   [3] "sensualite."

[4] "wher I myte not for the mene profir lokyn up on to hevyn." "mene"=medium, is perhaps a sub. in the gen.=intervenor's, intermediary's. See xix. p. 42 and xxxv. p. 70, S. de Cressy has: "Where I might not for the mean profer look up"; Collins: "for the meanwhile."

CHAPTER LVI

" God is nearer to us than our own soul "
" We can never come to full knowing of God till we know first clearly our own Soul "

AND thus I saw full surely that it is readier to us to come to the knowing of God than to know our own Soul. For our Soul is so deep-grounded in God, and so endlessly treasured, that we may not come to the knowing thereof till we have first knowing of God, which is the Maker, to whom it is oned. But, notwithstanding, I saw that we have, for fulness, to desire wisely and truly to know our own Soul : whereby we are learned to seek it where it is, and that is, in God. And thus by gracious leading of the Holy Ghost, we should know them both in one : whether we be stirred to know God or our Soul, both [these stirrings] are good and true.

God is nearer to us than our own Soul : for He is [the] Ground in whom our Soul standeth, and He is [the] Mean that keepeth the Substance and the Sense-nature together so that they shall never dispart. For our soul sitteth in God in very rest, and our soul standeth in God in very strength, and our Soul is kindly rooted in God in endless love : and therefore if we will have knowledge of our Soul, and communing and dalliance therewith, it behoveth to seek unto our Lord God in whom it is enclosed. (And of this enclosement I saw and understood more in the Sixteenth Shewing, as I shall tell.)

And as anent our Substance and our Sense-part, both

together may rightly be called our Soul:[1] and that is because of the oneing that they have in God. The worshipful City that our Lord Jesus sitteth in is our Sense-soul, in which He is enclosed: and our Kindly Substance is enclosed in Jesus with the blessed Soul of Christ sitting in rest in the Godhead.

And I saw full surely that it behoveth needs to be that we should be in longing and in penance unto the time that we be led so deep into God that we verily and truly know our own Soul. And truly I saw that into this high deepness our good Lord Himself leadeth us in the same love that He made us, and in the same love that He bought us by Mercy and Grace through virtue of His blessed Passion. And notwithstanding all this, we may never come to full knowing of God till we know first clearly our own Soul. For until the time that our Soul is in its full powers[2] we cannot be all fully holy: and that is [until the time] that our Sense-soul by the virtue of Christ's Passion be brought up to the Substance, with all the profits of our tribulation that our Lord shall make us to get by Mercy and Grace.

I[3] had, in part, [experience of the] Touching [of God in the soul], and it is grounded in Nature. That is to say, our Reason is grounded in God, which is Substantial Naturehood.[3] [Out] of this Substantial Naturehood Mercy and Grace springeth and spreadeth into us, working all things in fulfilling of our joy: these are

[1] "& anempts our substance and sensualite it may rytely be clepid our soule."

[2] "the full myts."

[3] "I had in partie touching and it is grounded in kynd: that is to sey, our reson is groundid in God, which is substantial kyndhede."

our Ground in which we have our Increase and our Fulfilling.

These be three properties in one Goodness: and where one worketh, all work in the things which be *now* belonging to us. God willeth that we understand [this], desiring with all our heart to have knowing of them more and more unto the time that we be fulfilled: for fully to know them is nought else but endless joy and bliss that we shall have in Heaven, which God willeth should be begun here in knowing of His love.

For only by our Reason we may not profit, but if we have evenly therewith Mind and Love: nor only in our Nature-Ground that we have in God we may not be saved but if we have, coming of the same Ground, Mercy and Grace. For of these three working all together we receive all our Goodness. Of the which the first [gifts] are goods of Nature: for in our First making God gave us as full goods as we might receive in our spirit alone,[1]—and also greater goods; but His foreseeing purpose in His endless wisdom willed that we should be double.

CHAPTER LVII

"In Christ our two natures are united"

AND anent our Substance He made us noble, and so rich that evermore we work His will and His worship. (Where I say "we," it meaneth Man that shall

---

[1] "ffor in our first makyng God gaf us as ful goods and also greter godes as we myte receivin only in our spirite." In the MS. the word "spirit" is used only here, where it means "the Substance."

be saved.) For soothly I saw that we are that which He loveth, and do that which Him pleaseth, lastingly without any stinting: and [that by virtue] of the great riches and of the high noble virtues by measure come to our soul what time it is knit to our body: in which knitting we are made Sensual.

And thus in our Substance we are full, and in our Sense-soul we fail: which failing God will restore and fulfil by working of Mercy and Grace plenteously flowing into us out of His own Nature-Goodness.[1] And thus His Nature-Goodness maketh that Mercy and Grace work in us, and the Nature-goodness that we have of Him enableth us to receive the working of Mercy and Grace.

I saw that our nature is in God whole: in which [whole nature of Manhood] He maketh diversities flowing out of Him to work His will: whom Nature keepeth, and Mercy and Grace restoreth and fulfilleth. And of these none shall perish: for our nature that is the higher part is knit to God, in the making; and God is knit to our nature that is the lower part, in our flesh-taking: and thus in Christ our two natures are oned. For the Trinity is comprehended in Christ, in whom our higher part is grounded and rooted; and our lower part the Second Person hath taken: which nature first to Him was made-ready.[2] For I saw full surely that all the works that God hath done, or ever shall, were fully known to Him and aforeseen from without beginning. And for Love He made Mankind, and for the same Love would be Man.

The next[3] Good that we receive is our Faith, in which our profiting beginneth. And it cometh [out] of

---

[1] " kynde godhede."   [2] " adyte."   [3] or the *first*.

the high riches of our nature-Substance into our Sensual soul, and it is grounded in us through the Nature-Goodness of God, by the working of Mercy and Grace. And thereof come all other goods by which we are led and saved. For the Commandments of God come therein: in which we ought to have two manners of understanding: [the one is that we ought to understand and know] which are His biddings, to love and to keep them; the other is that we ought to know His forbiddings, to hate and to refuse them. For in these two is all our working comprehended. Also in our faith come the Seven Sacraments, each following other in order as God hath ordained them to us: and all manner of virtues.

For the same virtues that we have received of our Substance, given to us in Nature by the Goodness of God,—the same virtues by the working of Mercy are given to us in Grace through the Holy Ghost, *renewed*: which virtues and gifts are treasured to us in Jesus Christ. For in that same [1] time that God knitted Himself to our body in the Virgin's womb, He took our Sensual soul: [2] in which taking He, us all having enclosed in Him, oned it to our Substance: in which oneing He was perfect Man. For Christ having knit in Him each [3] man that shall be saved, is perfect Man. Thus our Lady is our Mother in whom we are all enclosed and of her born, [4] in Christ: (for she that is

[1] " ilk " = " same."

[2] Here, as above, the *MS.* term for the " *Sensual soul* " is the " *Sensualite.* "

[3] " ilk " = " each."

[4] The MS. word is in both cases " borne," which may mean either *born* or *borne.* S. de Cressy gives " born " both for the first word and the second. See lx. " He sustaineth us within Himself in love," etc.; and lxiii. " In the taking of our nature He quickened us," etc.

Mother of our Saviour is Mother of all that shall be saved in our Saviour;) and our Saviour is our Very Mother in whom we be endlessly borne,[1] and never shall come out of Him.

Plenteously and fully and sweetly was this shewed, and it is spoken of in the First, where it saith: *We are all in Him enclosed and He is enclosed in us.* And that [enclosing of Him in us] is spoken of in the Sixteenth Shewing, where it saith: *He sitteth in our soul.*

For it is His good-pleasure to reign in our Understanding blissfully, and sit in our Soul restfully, and to dwell in our Soul endlessly, us all working into Him: in which working He willeth that we be His helpers, giving to Him all our attending, learning His lores, keeping His laws, desiring that all be done that He doeth; truly trusting in Him.

For soothly I saw that our Substance is in God.[2]

[1] See foot-note 4, p. 139.

[2] From *The Scale [or Ladder] of Perfection*, by Walter Hilton (Fourteenth century), edition of 1659, Part III. ch. ii. :—

"The soule of a man is a life consisting of three powers, *Memory*, *Understanding*, and *Will*, after the image and likeness of the blessed Trinity. . . . Whereby you may see, that man's soule (which may be called a created Trinity) was in its natural state replenished in its three powers, with the remembrance, sight, and love of the most blessed uncreated Trinity, which is God. . . . But when Adam sinned, choosing love and delight in himselfe, and in the creatures, he lost all his excellency and dignity, and thou also in him."

Ch. III. Sec. i. "And though we should prove not to be able to recover it fully here in this life, yet should we desire and endeavour to recover the image and likeness of the dignity we had, so that our soul might be reformed as it were in a shadow by grace to the image of the Trinity which we had by nature, and hereafter shall have fully in bliss. . . ." Sec. ii. "Seeke then that which thou hast lost, that thou mayest finde it; for well I wote, whosoever once hath an inward sight, but a little of that dignity and that spirituall fairness which a soule hath

CHAPTER LVIII

"All our life is in three: 'Nature, Mercy, Grace.' The high Might of the Trinity is our Father, and the deep Wisdom of the Trinity is our Mother, and the great Love of the Trinity is our Lord"

GOD, the blessed Trinity, which is everlasting Being, right as He is endless from without beginning, right so it was in His purpose endless, to make Mankind.

by creation, and shall have again by grace, he will loath in his heart all the blisse, the liking, and the fairnesse of this world. . . . Nevertheless as thou hast not as yet seen what it is fully, for thy spiritual eye is not yet opened, I shall tell thee one word for all, in the which thou shalt seeke, desire, and finde it; for in that one word is all that thou hast lost. This word is Jesus. . . . If thou feelest in thy heart a great desire to Jesus . . . then seekest thou well thy Lord Jesus. And when thou feelest this desire to God, or to Jesus (for it is all one) holpen and comforted by a ghostly might, insomuch that it is turned into love, affection, and spiritual fervour and sweetnesse, into light and knowing of truth, so that for the time the point of thy thought is set upon no other created thing, nor feeleth any stirring of vain-glory, nor of selfe-love, nor any other evill affection (for they cannot appear at that time) but this thy desire is onely enclosed, rested, softened, suppled, and annoynted in Jesus, then hast thou found somewhat of Jesus; I mean not him as he is, but a shadow of him; for the better that thou findest him, the more shalt thou desire him. Then observe by what manner of Prayer or Meditation or exercise of Devotion thou findest greatest and purest desire stirred up in thee to him, and most feeling of him, by that kind of prayer, exercise, or worke seekest thou him best, and shalt best finde him. . . .

"See then the mercy and courtesie of Jesus. Thou hast lost him, but where? soothly in thy house, that is to say, in thy soul, that if thou hadst lost all thy reason of thy soule, by its first sinne, thou shouldst never have found him again; but he left thee thy reason, and so he is still in thy soule, and never is quite lost out of it.

Which fair Kind first was prepared [1] to His own Son, the Second Person. And when He would, by full accord of all the Trinity, He made us all at once; and in our making He knit us and oned us to Himself: by which oneing we are kept as clear and as noble as we were made. By the virtue of the same precious oneing, we love our Maker and seek Him, praise Him and thank Him, and endlessly enjoy Him. And this is the work which is wrought continually in every soul that shall be saved: which is the Godly Will aforesaid. And thus in

---

"Nevertheless, thou art never the nearer him, till thou hast found him. He is in thee, though he be lost from thee; but thou art not in him, till thou hast found him. This is his mercy also, that he would suffer himself to be lost onely where he may be found, so that thou needest not run to *Rome*, nor to *Jerusalem* to seeke him there, but turne thy thoughts into thy owne soule, where he is hid, as the Prophet saith; *Truly thou art the hidden God*, hid in thy soule, and seek him there. Thus saith he himselfe in the Gospel; *The kingdome of heaven is likened to a treasure hid in the field, the which when a man findeth, for joy thereof, he goeth and selleth all that he hath, and buyeth that field.* Jesus is a treasure hid in the soule. . . .

"As long as Jesus findeth not his image reformed in thee, he is strange, and the farther from thee: therefore frame and shape thyself to be arrayed in his likenesse, that is in humility and charity, which are his liveries, and then will he know thee, and familiarly come to thee, and acquaint thee with his secrets. Thus saith he to his Disciples; *Who so loveth me, he shall be loved of my Father, and I will manifest my selfe unto him.* There is not any vertue nor any good work that can make thee like to our Lord, without Humility and Charity, for these two above all other are most acceptable ('most leyf') to him, which appeareth plainly in the Gospel, where our Lord speaketh of humility thus; *Learn of me, for I am meeke and humble in heart.* He saith not, learn of me to go barefoot, or to go into the desart, and there to fast forty dayes, nor yet to choose to your selves Disciples (as I did) but learne of me meeknesse, for I am meek and lowly in heart. Also of charity he saith thus; *This is my Commandment, that ye love one another as I*

[1] MS. "adyte to"=ordained to, made ready for.

our making, God, Almighty, is our Nature's Father; and God, All-Wisdom, is our Nature's Mother; with the Love and the Goodness of the Holy Ghost : which is all one God, one Lord. And in the knitting and the oneing He is our Very, True Spouse, and we His loved Wife, His Fair Maiden : with which Wife He is never displeased. For He saith : I love thee and thou lovest me, and our love shall never be disparted in two.

---

loved you, for by that shall men know you for my Disciples. Not that you worke miracles, or cast out Devills, or preach, or teach, but that each one of you love one another in charity. If therefore thou wilt be like him, have humility and charity. Now thou knowest what charity is, *viz.* To love thy neighbour as thy selfe."

Chap. IV. Sec. i. . . . "Now I shall tell thee (according to my feeble ability) how thou mayest enter into thy selfe to see the ground of sin, and destroy it as much as thou canst, and so recover a part of thy souls dignity. . . . Draw in thy thoughts . . . and set thy intent and full purpose, as if thou wouldst not seek nor find any thing but onely the grace and spiritual presence of Jesus."

"This will be painful; for vaine thoughts will presse into thy heart very thick, to draw thy minde down to them. And in doing thus, thou shalt find somewhat, but not Jesus whom thou seekest, but onely a naked remembrance of his name. But what then shalt thou finde? Surely this; A darke and ill-favoured image of thy owne soule, which hath neither light of knowledge nor feeling of love of God. . . . This is not the image of Jesus, but the image of sin, which St Paul calleth a *body of sinne and of death.* . . . Peradventure now thou beginnest to thinke with thy selfe what this image is like, and that thou shouldst not study much upon it, I will tell thee. It is like no bodily thing; What is it then saist thou? Verily it is *nought,* or no reall thing, as thou shalt finde, if thou try by doing as I have spoken; that is, draw in thy thoughts into thy selfe from all bodily things, and then shalt thou find right *nought* wherein thy soule may rest.

"This *nothing* is nought else but darknesse of conscience, and a lacking of the love of God and of light; as sin is nought but a want of good, if it were so that the ground of sin was much abated and dryed up in thee, and thy soule was reformed right as the image of Jesus; then if thou

I beheld the working of all the blessed Trinity: in which beholding I saw and understood these three properties: the property of the Fatherhood, the property of the Motherhood, and the property of the Lordhood, in one God. In our Father Almighty we have our keeping and our bliss as anent our natural Substance, which is to us by our making, without beginning. And in the Second Person in skill[1] and wisdom we have our keeping as anent our Sense-soul: our restoring and our

---

didst draw into thy selfe thy heart, thou shouldst not find this *Nought*, but thou shouldst find Jesus; not only the naked remembrance of this name, but Jesus Christ in thy soule readily teaching thee, thou shouldst there find light of understanding, and no darknesse of ignorance, a love and liking of him; and no pain of bitternesse, heavinesse, or tediousenesse of him. . . .

"And here also thou must beware that thou take Jesus Christ into thy thoughts against this darknesse in thy mind, by busie prayer and fervent desire to God, not setting the point of thy thoughts on that foresaid *Nought*, but on Jesus Christ whom thou desirest. Think stifly on his passion, and on his Humility, and through his might thou shalt arise. Do as if thou wouldst beate downe this darke image, and go through-stitch with it. Thou shalt hate ('agryse') and loath this darknesse and this *Nought*, just as the Devill, and thou shalt despise and all to break it ('brest it').

"For within this Nought is Jesus hid in his joy, whom thou shalt not finde with all thy seeking, unlesse thou passe this darknesse of conscience.

"This is the ghostly travel I spake of, and the cause of all this writing is to stir thee thereto, if thou have grace. This darknesse of conscience, and this *Nought* is the image of the first *Adam*: St Paul knew it well, for he said thus of it; As we have before borne the *image of the earthly man*, that is the first *Adam, right so that we might now beare the image of the heavenly man*, which is Jesus, the second *Adam*. St *Paul* bare this image oft full heavily, for it was so cumbersome to him, that he cryed out of it, saying thus; *O who shall deliver me from this body and this image of death*. And then he comforted himselfe and others also thus: *The grace* of God through Jesus Christ."

[1] MS. "Witt."

saving; for He is our Mother, Brother, and Saviour. And in our good Lord, the Holy Ghost, we have our rewarding and our meed-giving for our living and our travail, and endless overpassing of all that we desire, in His marvellous courtesy, of His high plenteous grace.

For all our life is in *three*: in the first we have our Being, in the second we have our Increasing, and in the third we have our Fulfilling: the first is Nature, the second is Mercy, and the third is Grace.

For the first, I understood that the high Might of the Trinity is our Father, and the deep Wisdom of the Trinity is our Mother, and the great Love of the Trinity is our Lord: and all this have we in Nature and in the making of our Substance.[1]

And furthermore I saw that the Second Person, which is our Mother as anent the Substance, that same dear-worthy Person is become our Mother as anent the Sense-soul. For we are double by God's making: that is to say, Substantial and Sensual. Our Substance is the higher part, which we have in our Father, God Almighty; and the Second Person of the Trinity is our Mother in Nature, in making of our Substance: in whom we are grounded and rooted. And He is our Mother in Mercy, in taking of our Sense-part. And thus our Mother is to us in diverse manners working: in whom our parts are kept undisparted. For in our Mother Christ we profit and increase, and in Mercy He reformeth us and restoreth, and, by the virtue of His Passion and His Death and Up-rising, oneth us to our Substance. Thus worketh our Mother in Mercy to all His children which are to Him yielding[2] and obedient.

[1] " in our substantiall makyng."   [2] " buxum."

K

And Grace worketh with Mercy, and specially in two properties, as it was shewed : which working belongeth to the Third Person, the Holy Ghost. He worketh *rewarding* and *giving*. Rewarding is a large giving-of-truth that the Lord doeth to him that hath travailed ; and giving is a courteous working which He doeth freely of Grace, fulfilling and overpassing all that is deserved of creatures.

Thus in our Father, God Almighty, we have our being ; and in our Mother of Mercy we have our reforming and restoring : in whom our Parts are oned and all made perfect Man ; and by [reward]-yielding and giving in Grace of the Holy Ghost, we are fulfilled.

And our Substance is [in] [1] our Father, God Almighty, and our Substance is [in] [1] our Mother, God, All-wisdom; and our Substance is in our Lord the Holy Ghost, God All-goodness. For our Substance is whole in each Person of the Trinity, which is one God. And our Sense-soul is only in the Second Person Christ Jesus ; in whom is the Father and the Holy Ghost: and in Him and by Him we are mightily taken out of Hell, and out of the wretchedness in Earth worshipfully brought up into Heaven and blissfully oned to our Substance: increased in riches and in nobleness by all the virtues of Christ, and by the grace and working of the Holy Ghost.

[1] S. de Cressy gives the " in " twice missed in the Brit. Mus. MS.

CHAPTER LIX

"Jesus Christ that doeth Good against evil is our Very Mother: we have our Being of Him where the Ground of Motherhood beginneth,—with all the sweet Keeping by Love, that endlessly followeth."

AND all this bliss we have by Mercy and Grace: which manner of bliss we might never have had nor known but if that property of Goodness which is God had been contraried: whereby we have this bliss. For wickedness hath been suffered to rise contrary to the Goodness, and the Goodness of Mercy and Grace contraried against the wickedness and turned all to goodness and to worship, to all these that shall be saved. For it is the property in God which doeth good against evil. Thus Jesus Christ that doeth good against evil is our Very Mother: we have our Being of Him,—where the Ground of Motherhood beginneth,—with all the sweet Keeping of Love that endlessly followeth. As verily as God is our Father, so verily God is our Mother; and that shewed He in all, and especially in these sweet words where He saith: *I it am.*[1] That is to say, *I it am, the Might and the Goodness of the Fatherhood; I it am, the Wisdom of the Motherhood; I it am, the Light and the Grace that is all blessed Love: I it am, the Trinity, I it am, the Unity: I am the sovereign Goodness of all manner of things. I am that maketh thee to love: I am that maketh thee to long: I it am, the endless fulfilling of all true desires.*

For there the soul is highest, noblest, and worthiest,

[1] It is I.

where it is lowest, meekest, and mildest: and [out] of this *Substantial Ground* we have all our virtues in our Sense-part by gift of Nature, by helping and speeding of Mercy and Grace: without the which we may not profit.

Our high Father, God Almighty, which is Being, He knew and loved us from afore any time: of which knowing, in His marvellous deep charity and the foreseeing counsel of all the blessed Trinity, He willed that the Second Person should become our Mother. Our Father [willeth], our Mother worketh, our good Lord the Holy Ghost confirmeth: and therefore it belongeth to us to love our God in whom we have our being: Him reverently thanking and praising for [1] our making, mightily praying to our Mother for [1] mercy and pity, and to our Lord the Holy Ghost for [1] help and grace.

For in these three is all our life: Nature, Mercy, Grace: whereof we have meekness and mildness; patience and pity; and hating of sin and of wickedness,— for it belongeth properly to virtue to hate sin and wickedness. And thus is Jesus our Very Mother in Nature [by virtue] of our first making; and He is our Very Mother in Grace, by taking our nature made. All the fair working, and all the sweet natural office of dearworthy Motherhood is impropriated [2] to the Second Person: for in Him we have this Godly Will whole and safe without end, both in Nature and in Grace, of His own proper Goodness. I understood three manners of beholding of Motherhood in God: the first is grounded in our Nature's *making*; the second is *taking* of our nature,—

---

[1] MS. "of."

[2] Or "appropriated to"; MS. "impropried"=made to be the property of; assigned and consigned to.

and there beginneth the Motherhood of Grace; the third is Motherhood of *working*,—and therein is a forth-spreading by the same Grace, of length and breadth and height and of deepness without end.   And all is one Love.

CHAPTER LX

"The Kind, loving, Mother"

BUT now behoveth to say a little more of this forth-spreading, as I understand in the meaning of our Lord: how that we be brought again by the Mother-hood of Mercy and Grace into our Nature's place, where that we were made by the Motherhood of Nature-Love: which Kindly-love, it never leaveth us.

Our Kind Mother, our Gracious Mother,[1] for that He would all wholly become our Mother in all things, He took the Ground of His Works full low and full mildly in the Maiden's womb.   (And that He shewed in the First [Shewing] where He brought that meek Maid afore the eye of mine understanding in the simple stature as she was when she conceived.)   That is to say: our high God is sovereign Wisdom of all: in this low place He arrayed and dight Him full ready in our poor flesh, Himself to do the service and the office of Motherhood in all things.

The Mother's service is nearest, readiest, and surest: [nearest, for it is most of nature; readiest, for it is most of love; and surest[2]] for it is most of truth.   This office none might, nor could, nor ever should do to the

[1] Our Mother by Nature, our Mother in Grace.

[2] These clauses, probably omitted by mistake, are in S. de Cressy's version.

full, but He alone. We know that all our mothers'
bearing is [bearing of] us to pain and to dying: and
what is this but that our Very Mother, Jesus, He—
All-Love—beareth us to joy and to endless living?—
blessed may He be! Thus He sustaineth[1] us within
Himself in love; and travailed, unto the full time that
He would suffer the sharpest throes and the most
grievous pains that ever were or ever shall be; and
died at the last. And when He had finished, and so
borne us to bliss, yet might not all this make full content to His marvellous love; and that sheweth He in
these high overpassing words of love: *If I might suffer
more, I would suffer more.*

He might no more die, but He would not stint of
working: wherefore then it behoveth Him to feed us;
for the dearworthy love of Motherhood hath made Him
debtor to us. The mother may give her child suck of
her milk, but our precious Mother, Jesus, He may feed
us with Himself, and doeth it, full courteously and full
tenderly, with the Blessed Sacrament that is precious
food of my life; and with all the sweet Sacraments He
sustaineth us full mercifully and graciously. And so
meant He in this blessed word where that He said:
It is I[2] *that Holy Church preacheth thee and teacheth thee.*
That is to say: *All the health and life of Sacraments, all the
virtue and grace of my Word, all the Goodness that is ordained
in Holy Church for thee, it is I.* The Mother may lay the
child tenderly to her breast, but our tender Mother,
Jesus, He may homely lead us into His blessed breast,
by His sweet open side, and shew therein part of the
Godhead and the joys of Heaven, with spiritual sureness

---

[1] S. de Cressy has "sustained." See lvii. p. 139.   [2] "I it am."

of endless bliss. And that shewed He in the Tenth [Shewing], giving the same understanding in this sweet word where He saith: *Lo! how I loved thee;* looking unto [the Wound in] His side, rejoicing.

This fair lovely word *Mother*, it is so sweet and so close in Nature of itself[1] that it may not verily be said of none but of *Him;* and to her that is very Mother of Him and of all. To the property of Motherhood belongeth natural love, wisdom, and knowing; and it is good: for though it be so that our bodily forthbringing be but little, low, and simple in regard of our spiritual forthbringing, yet it is He that doeth it in the creatures by whom that it is done. The Kindly,[2] loving Mother that witteth and knoweth the need of her child, she keepeth it full tenderly, as the nature[2] and condition of Motherhood will. And as it waxeth in age, she changeth her working, but not her love. And when it is waxen of more age, she suffereth that it be beaten[3] in breaking down of vices, to make the child receive virtues and graces. This working, with all that be fair and good, our Lord doeth it in them by whom it is done: thus He is our Mother in Nature by the working of Grace in the lower part for love of the higher part. And He willeth that we know this: for He will have all our love fastened to Him. And in this I saw that all our duty that we owe, by God's bidding, to Fatherhood and Motherhood, for [reason of] God's Fatherhood and Motherhood is fulfilled in true loving of God; which blessed love Christ worketh in us. And this was shewed in all [the Revelations] and especially in the high plenteous words where He saith: *It is I that thou lovest.*

---

[1] "so kynd of the self."   [2] "kynde," "kind."   [3] "bristinid."

CHAPTER LXI

" By the assay of this falling we shall have an high marvellous knowing of Love in God, without end. For strong and marvellous is that love which may not, nor will not, be broken for trespass "

AND in our spiritual forthbringing He useth more tenderness of keeping, without any likeness : by as much as our soul is of more price in His sight. He kindleth our understanding, He directeth our ways, He easeth our conscience, He comforteth our soul, He lighteneth our heart, and giveth us, in part, knowing and believing in His blissful Godhead, with gracious mind in His sweet Manhood and His blessed Passion, with reverent marvelling in His high, overpassing Goodness ; and maketh us to love all that He loveth, for His love, and to be well-pleased with Him and all His works. And when we fall, hastily He raiseth us by His lovely calling [1] [2] and gracious touching. And when we be

[1] "clepyng."

[2] From the *Ancren Riwle* (Camden Society's version, edited by J. Morton, D.D.), p. 231 : " The sixth comfort is, that our Lord, when He suffereth us to be tempted, playeth with us, as the mother with her young darling : she flies from him, and hides herself, and lets him sit alone, and look anxiously around, and call *Dame ! Dame !* and weep awhile ; and then she leapeth forth laughing, with outspread arms, and embraceth and kisseth him, and wipeth his eyes. In like manner, our Lord sometimes leaveth us alone, and withdraweth His grace, His comfort, and His support, so that we feel no delight in any good that we do, nor any satisfaction of heart ; and yet, at that very time, our dear Father loveth us never the less, but doth it for the great love that He hath to us."

p. 235 : " The fourth reason why our Lord hideth Himself is, that thou mayest seek him more earnestly, and call, and weep after Him, as the little baby doth after his mother " (" ase deth thet lutel baban "—in another manuscript 'lite barn '—" efter his moder ").

thus strengthened by His sweet working, then we with all our will choose Him, by His sweet grace, to be His servants and His lovers lastingly without end.

And after this He suffereth some of us to fall more hard and more grievously than ever we did afore, as us thinketh. And then ween we (who be not all wise) that all were nought that we have begun. But this is not so. For it needeth us to fall, and it needeth us to see it. For if we never fell, we should not know how feeble and how wretched we are of our self, and also we should not fully know that marvellous love of our Maker. For we shall see verily in heaven, without end, that we have grievously sinned in this life, and notwithstanding this, we shall see that we were never hurt in His love, we were never the less of price in His sight. And by the assay of this falling we shall have an high, marvellous knowing of love in God, without end. For strong and marvellous is that love which may not, nor will not, be broken for trespass. And this is one understanding of [our] profit. Another is the lowness and meekness that we shall get by the sight of our falling: for thereby we shall highly be raised in heaven; to which raising we might[1] never have come without that meekness. And therefore it needeth us to see it; and if we see it not, though we fell it should not profit us. And commonly, first we fall and later we see it: and both of the Mercy of God.

The mother may suffer the child to fall sometimes, and to be hurt in diverse manners for its own profit, but she may never suffer that any manner of peril come to the child, for love. And though our earthly mother may

[1] *i.e.* could.

suffer her child to perish, our heavenly Mother, Jesus, may not suffer us that are His children to perish: for He is All-mighty, All-wisdom, and All-love; and so is none but He,—blessed may He be!

But oftentimes when our falling and our wretchedness is shewed us, we are so sore adread, and so greatly ashamed of our self, that scarcely we find where we may hold us. But then willeth not our courteous Mother that we flee away, for Him were nothing lother. But He willeth then that we use the condition of a child: for when it is hurt, or adread, it runneth hastily to the mother for help, with all its might. So willeth He that we do, as a meek child saying thus: *My kind Mother, my Gracious Mother, my dearworthy Mother, have mercy on me: I have made myself foul and unlike to Thee, and I nor may nor can amend it but with thine help and grace.* And if we feel us not then eased forthwith, be we sure that He useth the condition of a wise mother. For if He see that it be more profit to us to mourn and to weep, He suffereth it, with ruth and pity, unto the best time, for love. And He willeth then that we use the property of a child, that evermore of nature trusteth to the love of the mother in weal and in woe.

And He willeth that we take us mightily to the Faith of Holy Church and find there our dearworthy Mother, in solace of true Understanding, with all the blessed Common. For one single person may oftentimes be broken, as it seemeth to himself, but the whole Body of Holy Church was never broken, nor never shall be, without end. And therefore a sure thing it is, a good and a gracious, to will meekly and mightily to be fastened and oned to our Mother, Holy Church, that is,

Christ Jesus. For the food of mercy that is His dear-worthy blood and precious water is plenteous to make us fair and clean ; the blessed wounds of our Saviour be open and enjoy to heal us ; the sweet, gracious hands of our Mother be ready and diligently about us. For He in all this working useth the office of a kind nurse that hath nought else to do but to give heed about [1] the salvation of her child.

It is His office to save us : it is His worship to do [for] us,[2] and it is His will [that] we know it : for He willeth that we love Him sweetly and trust in Him meekly and mightily. And this shewed He in these gracious words : *I keep thee full surely.*

CHAPTER LXII

" God is Very Father and Very Mother of Nature : and all natures that He hath made to flow out of Him to work His will shall be restored and brought again into Him by the salvation of Mankind through the working of Grace "

FOR in that time He shewed our frailty and our fall-ings, our afflictings and our settings at nought,[3] our despites and our outcastings, and all our woe so far forth as methought it might befall in this life. And therewith

---

[1] " entend about."

[2] S. de Cressy has here " to do it." This MS. seems to have : " to don us," possibly for to work at us, carry out our salvation to perfection, or, to take in hand for us, " to *do* for us." See *The Paston Letters*, vol. ii. (Letter 472), *May* 1463, " he prayid hym that he wold don for hym in hys mater, and gaf hym a reward ; and withinne ryth short tym after, his mater sped."

[3] " our brekyngs and our nowtyngs."

He shewed His blessed Might, His blessed Wisdom, His blessed Love: that He keepeth us in this time as tenderly and as sweetly to His worship, and as surely to our salvation, as He doeth when we are in most solace and comfort. And thereto He raiseth us spiritually and highly in heaven, and turneth it all to His worship and to our joy, without end. For His love suffereth us never to lose time.

And all this is of the Nature-Goodness of God, by the working of Grace. God is Nature[1] in His being: that is to say, that Goodness that is Nature, it is God. He is the ground, He is the substance, He is the same thing that is Nature-hood.[2] And He is very Father and very Mother of Nature: and all natures that He hath made to flow out of Him to work His will shall be restored and brought again into Him by the salvation of man through the working of Grace.

For of all natures[3] that He hath set in diverse creatures by part, in man is all the whole; in fulness and in virtue, in fairness and in goodness, in royalty and nobleness, in all manner of majesty, of preciousness and worship. Here may we see that we are all beholden to God for nature, and we are all beholden to God for grace. Here may we see us needeth not greatly to seek far out to know sundry natures, but to Holy Church, unto our Mother's breast: that is to say, unto our own soul where our Lord dwelleth ; and there shall we find all now in faith and in understanding. And afterward verily in Himself clearly, in bliss.

But let no man nor woman take this singularly to himself: for it is not so, it is general: for it is [of] our

---

[1] " kynde."   [2] " kindhede."   [3] " kyndes."

precious Christ, and to Him was this fair nature adight[1]
for the worship and nobility of man's making, and for
the joy and the bliss of man's salvation; even as He saw,
wist, and knew from without beginning.

CHAPTER LXIII

"As verily as sin is unclean, so verily is it unkind"—a
disease or monstrous thing against nature. "He shall heal us
full fair."

HERE may we see that we have verily of Nature to
hate sin, and we have verily of Grace to hate sin.
For Nature is all good and fair in itself, and Grace was
sent out to save Nature and destroy sin, and bring again
fair nature to the blessed point from whence it came:
that is God; with more nobleness and worship by the
virtuous working of Grace. For it shall be seen afore
God by all His Holy in joy without end that Nature
hath been assayed in the fire of tribulation and therein
hath been found no flaw, no fault.[2] Thus are Nature
and Grace of one accord: for Grace is God, as Nature
is God: He is two in manner of working and one in
love; and neither of these worketh without other: they
be not disparted.

And when we by Mercy of God and with His help
accord us to Nature and Grace, we shall see verily that
sin is in sooth viler and more painful than hell, without
likeness: for it is contrary to our fair nature. For as
verily as sin is unclean, so verily is it unnatural,[3] and

---

[1] *i.e.* made ready, prepared, appointed.

[2] "no lak (blame), no defaute."

[3] "as sothly as sin is onclene as sothly is it onkinde."

thus an horrible thing to see for the loved [1] soul that would be all fair and shining in the sight of God, as Nature and Grace teacheth.

Yet be we not adread of this, save inasmuch as dread may speed us : but meekly make we our moan to our dearworthy Mother, and He shall besprinkle us in His precious blood and make our soul full soft and full mild, and heal us full fair by process of time, right as it is most worship to Him and joy to us without end. And of this sweet fair working He shall never cease nor stint till all His dearworthy children be born and forth-brought. (And that shewed He where He shewed [me] understanding of the ghostly Thirst, that is the love-longing that shall last till Doomsday.)

Thus in [our] Very Mother, Jesus, our life is grounded, in the foreseeing Wisdom of Himself from without beginning, with the high Might of the Father, the high sovereign Goodness of the Holy Ghost. And in the taking of our nature He quickened us ; in His blessed dying upon the Cross He bare us to endless life ; and from that time, and now, and evermore unto Doomsday, He feedeth us and furthereth us : even as that high sovereign Kindness of Motherhood, and as Kindly need of Childhood asketh.

Fair and sweet is our Heavenly Mother in the sight of our souls ; precious and lovely are the Gracious Children in the sight of our Heavenly Mother, with mildness and meekness, and all the fair virtues that belong to children in Nature. For of nature the Child despaireth not of the Mother's love, of nature the Child presumeth not of itself, of nature the Child loveth the

---

[1] S. de Cressy has " the loving soul."

Mother and each one of the other [children].   These are the fair virtues, with all other that be like, wherewith our Heavenly Mother is served and pleased.

And I understood none higher stature in this life than Childhood, in feebleness and failing of might and of wit, unto the time that our Gracious Mother hath brought us up to our Father's Bliss.[1]   And then shall it verily be known to us His meaning in those sweet words where He saith : *All shall be well: and thou shalt see, thyself, that all manner of things shall be well.*   And then shall the Bliss of our Mother, in Christ, be new to begin in the Joys of our God : which new beginning shall last without end, new beginning.

Thus I understood that all His blessed children which be come out of Him by Nature shall be brought again into Him by Grace.

THE FIFTEENTH REVELATION

CHAPTER LXIV

"Thou shalt come up above."   " A very fair creature, a little Child—nimble and lively, whiter than lily "

AFORE this time I had great longing and desire of God's gift to be delivered of this world and of this life.   For oftentimes I beheld the woe that is here, and the weal and the bliss that is being there : (and if there had been no pain in this life but the absence of our Lord, methought it was some-time more than I might bear ;) and this made me to mourn, and eagerly to

[1] " Our fader bliss."

long. And also from mine own wretchedness, sloth, and weakness, me liked not to live and to travail, as me fell to do.

And to all this our courteous Lord answered for comfort and patience, and said these words: *Suddenly thou shalt be taken from all thy pain, from all thy sickness, from all thy distress* [1] *and from all thy woe. And thou shalt come up above and thou shalt have me to thy meed, and thou shalt be fulfilled of love and of bliss. And thou shalt never have no manner of pain, no manner of misliking, no wanting of will; but ever joy and bliss without end. What should it then aggrieve thee to suffer awhile, seeing that it is my will and my worship?*

And in this word: *Suddenly thou shalt be taken,*—I saw that God rewardeth man for the patience that he hath in abiding God's will, and for his time, and [for] that man lengtheneth his patience over the time of his living. For not-knowing of his time of passing, that is a great profit: for if a man knew his time, he should not have patience over that time; but, as God willeth, while the soul is in the body it seemeth to itself that it is ever at the point to be taken. For all this life and this languor that we have here is but a point, and when we are taken suddenly out of pain into bliss then pain shall be nought.

And in this time I saw a body lying on the earth, which body shewed heavy and horrible,[2] without shape and form, as it were a swollen quag of stinking mire.[3] And suddenly out of this body sprang a full fair creature, a little Child, fully shapen and formed, nimble [4] and

---

[1] " disese."   [2] " uggley."
[3] a " bolned quave of styngand myre."   [4] " swifie "=agile, quick.

lively, whiter than lily; which swiftly[1] glided up into heaven. And the swollenness of the body betokeneth great wretchedness of our deadly flesh, and the little-ness of the Child betokeneth the cleanness of purity in the soul. And methought: *With this body abideth*[2] *no fairness of this Child, and on this Child dwelleth no foulness of this body.*

It is more[3] blissful that man be taken from pain, than that pain be taken from man;[3] for if pain be taken from us it may come again: therefore it is a sovereign com-fort and blissful beholding in a loving soul that we shall be taken from pain. For in this behest[4] I saw a marvel-lous compassion that our Lord hath in us for our woe, and a courteous promising[5] of clear deliverance. For He willeth that we be comforted in the overpassing;[6] and *that* He shewed in these words: *And thou shalt come up above, and thou shalt have me to thy meed, and thou shalt be fulfilled of joy and bliss.*

It is God's will that we set the point of our thought in this blissful beholding as often as we may,—and as long time keep us therein with His grace; for this is a blessed contemplation to the soul that is led of God, and full greatly to His worship, for the time that it lasteth. And [when] we fall again to our heaviness, and spiritual blindness, and feeling of pains spiritual and bodily, by our frailty, it is God's will that we know that He hath not forgotten us. And so signifieth He in these words: *And thou shalt never more have pain; no manner of sickness, no manner of misliking, no wanting of will; but ever joy and*

---

[1] " sharply." [2] " beleveth."
[3] "full blissful . . . mor than." [4] *i.e.* promise, proclamation.
[5] " behoting." [6] *i.e.* the exceeding fulness of heavenly bliss.

L

bliss without end. What should it then aggrieve thee to suffer awhile, seeing it is my will and my worship?

It is God's will that we take His behests [1] and His comfortings as largely and as mightily as we may take them, and also He willeth that we take our abiding and our troubles [2] as lightly as we may take them, and set them at nought. For the more lightly we take them, and the less price we set on them, for love, the less pain we shall have in the feeling of them, and the more thanks and meed we shall have for them.

CHAPTER LXV

" The Charity of God maketh in us such a unity that, when it is truly seen, no man can part himself from other "

AND thus I understood that what man or woman with firm will [3] chooseth God in this life, for love, he may be sure that he is loved without end: which endless love worketh in him that grace. For He willeth that we be as assured in hope of the bliss of heaven while we are here, as we shall be in sureness while we are there. And ever the more pleasance and joy that we take in this sureness, with reverence and meekness, the better pleaseth Him, as it was shewed. This reverence that I mean is a holy courteous dread of our Lord, to which meekness is united: and that is, that a creature seeth the Lord marvellous great, and itself marvellous little. For these virtues are had endlessly by the loved of God, and

---

[1] See foot-note 4, p. 161.
[2] " diseases "=discomforts, distresses.   [3] " wilfully."

this may now be seen and felt in measure through the gracious presence of our Lord when it is [seen]: which presence in all things is most desired, for it worketh marvellous assuredness in true faith, and sure hope, by greatness of charity, in dread that is sweet and delectable.

It is God's will that I see myself as much bound [1] to Him in love as if He had done for me all that He hath done; and thus should every soul think inwardly of its [2] Lover. That is to say, the Charity of God maketh in us such a unity that, when it is truly seen, no man can part himself from other. And thus ought our soul to think that God hath done for it [3] all that He hath done.

And this sheweth He to make us to love Him and nought dread but Him. For it is His will that we perceive that all the might of our Enemy is taken into our Friend's hand; and therefore the soul that knoweth assuredly this, he [4] shall not dread but Him that he loveth. All other dread he [4] setteth among passions and bodily sickness and imaginations. And therefore though we be in so much pain, woe, and distress that it seemeth to us we can think [of] right nought but [of] that [which] we are in, or [of] that [which] we feel, [yet] as soon as we may, pass we lightly over, and set we it at nought. And why? For that God willeth we know [Him]; and if we know Him and love Him and reverently dread Him, we shall have peace, and be in great rest, and it shall be great pleasance to us, all that He doeth. And this shewed our Lord in these words: *What should it then aggrieve thee to suffer awhile, sith it is my will and my worship?*

---

[1] " bounden "=beholden.   [2] "his."   [3] "him."   [4] *i.e.* the soul.

Now have I told you of Fifteen Revelations, as God vouchsafed to minister them to [my] mind, renewed by lightings and touchings, I hope of the same Spirit that shewed them all.

Of which Fifteen Shewings the First began early in the morn, about the hour of four; and they lasted, shewing by process full fair and steadily, each following other, till it was nine of the day, overpassed.

CHAPTER LXVI

"All was closed, and I saw no more." "For the folly of feeling a little bodily pain I unwisely lost for the time the comfort of all this blessed Shewing of our Lord God"

AND after this the good Lord shewed the Sixteenth [Revelation] on the night following, as I shall tell after: which Sixteenth was conclusion and confirmation to all Fifteen.

But first me behoveth to tell you as anent my feebleness, wretchedness and blindness.—I have said in the beginning: *And in this [moment] all my pain was suddenly taken from me*: of which pain I had no grief nor distress as long as the Fifteen Shewings lasted following. And at the end all was close, and I saw no more. And soon I felt that I should live and languish;[1] and anon my sickness came again: first in my head with a sound and a din, and suddenly all my body was fulfilled with sickness like as it was afore. And I was as barren and as dry as [if] I never had comfort but little. And as a

1 "langiren."

wretched creature I moaned and cried for feeling of my bodily pains and for failing of comfort, spiritual and bodily.

Then came a Religious person to me and asked me how I fared. I said I had raved to-day. And he laughed loud and heartily.[1] And I said : *The Cross that stood afore my face, methought it bled fast.* And with this word the person that I spake to waxed all sober and marvelled. And anon I was sore ashamed and astonished for my recklessness, and I thought : *This man taketh in sober earnest*[2] *the least word that I might say.* Then said I no more thereof. And when I saw that he took it earnestly and with so great reverence, I wept, full greatly ashamed, and would have been shriven ; but at that time I could tell it no priest, for I thought : *How should a priest believe me? I believe not our Lord God.* This [Shewing] I believed verily for the time that I saw Him, and so was then my will and my meaning ever for to do without end ; but as a fool I let it pass from my mind. Ah ! lo, wretch that I am ! this was a great sin, great unkindness, that I for folly of feeling of a little bodily pain, so unwisely lost for the time the comfort of all this blessed Shewing of our Lord God. Here may you see what I am of myself.

But herein would our Courteous Lord not leave me. And I lay still till night, trusting in His mercy, and then I began to sleep. And in the sleep, at the beginning, methought the Fiend set him on my throat, putting forth a visage full near my face, like a young man's and it was long and wondrous lean : I saw never none such. The

---

[1] "inderly"=inwardly ; so de Cressy ; (Collins has "drolly ").
[2] "sadly "=solidly, soberly.

colour was red like the tilestone when it is new-burnt, with black spots therein like black freckles—fouler than the tilestone. His hair was red as rust, clipped in front,[1] with full locks hanging on the temples. He grinned on me with a malicious semblance, shewing white teeth: and so much methought it the more horrible. Body nor hands had he none shapely, but with his paws he held me in the throat, and would have strangled me, but he might not.

This horrible Shewing was made [whilst I was] sleeping, and so was none other. But in all this time I trusted to be saved and kept by the mercy of God. And our Courteous Lord gave me grace to waken; and scarcely had I my life. The persons that were with me looked on me, and wet my temples, and my heart began to comfort. And anon a light smoke came in the door, with a great heat and a foul stench. I said: *Benedicite Domine! it is all on fire that is here!* And I weened it had been a bodily fire that should have burnt us all to death. I asked them that were with me if they felt any stench. They said, Nay: they felt none. I said: *Blessed be God!* For then wist I well it was the Fiend that was come to tempest me. And anon I took to that [which] our Lord had shewed me on the same day, with all the Faith of Holy Church (for I beheld it is both one), and fled thereto as to my comfort. And anon all

---

[1] "evisid aforn with syde lokks hongyng on the thounys" (or thowngs, or thoungs). Bradley's *Dictionary of Middle English—thun*(?)*wange* = temple, *evesed* p. ple of *efesian* = to clip the edges (*cf. eaves*). The Paris MS. however reads: "His hair was rede as rust not scoryd afore, with syde lockes hangyng on the thouwonges." S. de Cressy gives this as: "his hair was red as rust not scoured; afore with side locks hanging down in flakes."

vanished away, and I was brought to great rest and *dea*
peace, without sickness of body or dread of conscience.

THE SIXTEENTH REVELATION

CHAPTER LXVII

"The place that Jesus taketh in our soul He shall never
remove from, without end :—for in us His homliest home and
His endless dwelling." "Our soul can never have rest in things
that are beneath itself—yet may it not abide in the beholding of
its self"

AND then our Lord opened my spiritual eye and
shewed me my soul in midst of my heart. I saw
the Soul so large as it were an endless world, and as it
were a blissful kingdom. And by the conditions that I
saw therein I understood that it is a worshipful City.
In the midst of that City sitteth our Lord Jesus, God
and Man, a fair Person of large stature, highest Bishop,
most majestic[1] King, most worshipful Lord ; and I saw
Him clad majestically.[1] And worshipfully He sitteth in
the Soul, even-right[2] in peace and rest. And the Godhead ruleth and sustaineth[3] heaven and earth and all that
is,—sovereign Might, sovereign Wisdom, and sovereign
Goodness,—[but] the place that Jesus taketh in *our Soul*
He shall never remove it, without end, as to my sight :
for in us is His *homliest* home and His *endless* dwelling.[4]

And in this [sight] He shewed the satisfying that He

---

[1] "solemnest"; "solemnly"=in state.   [2] *i.e.* straight-set.
[3] "gemeth."   [4] "woning."

hath of the making of Man's Soul. For as well as the Father might make a creature, and as well as the Son could make a creature, so well would the Holy Ghost that Man's Soul were made : and so it was done. And therefore the blessed Trinity enjoyeth without end in the making of Man's Soul : for He saw from without beginning what should please Him without end. All thing that He hath made sheweth His Lordship,—as understanding was given at the same time by example of a creature that is to see great treasures and kingdoms belonging to a lord ; and when it had seen all the nobleness beneath, then, marvelling, it was moved to seek above to the high place where the lord dwelleth, knowing, by reason, that his dwelling is in the worthiest place. And thus I understood in verity that our Soul may never have rest in things that are beneath itself. And when it cometh above all creatures into the Self, yet may it not abide in the beholding of its Self, but all the beholding is blissfully set in God that is the Maker dwelling therein. For in Man's Soul is His very dwelling ; and the highest light and the brightest shining of the City is the glorious love of our Lord, as to my sight.

And what may make us more to enjoy in God than to see in Him that He enjoyeth in the highest of all His works ? For I saw in the same Shewing that if the blessed Trinity might have made Man's Soul any better, any fairer, any nobler than it was made, He should not have been full pleased with the making of Man's Soul. And He willeth that our hearts be mightily raised above the deepness of the earth and all vain sorrows, and rejoice [1] in Him.

[1] " enjoyen."

CHAPTER LXVIII

"He said not: *Thou shalt not be tempested, thou shalt not be travailed, thou shalt not be afflicted*; but He said: *Thou shalt not be overcome*"

THIS was a delectable Sight and a restful Shewing, that it is so *without end*. The beholding of this while we are here is full pleasing to God and full great profit to us ; and the soul that thus beholdeth, it maketh it like to Him that is beheld, and oneth it in rest and peace by His grace. And this was a singular joy and bliss to me that I saw Him *sitting* : for the [quiet] secureness of sitting sheweth endless dwelling.

And He gave me to know soothfastly that it was He that shewed me all afore. And when I had beheld this with heedfulness, then shewed our good Lord words [1] full meekly without voice and without opening of lips, right as He had [afore] done, and said full sweetly : *Wit it now well that it was no raving that thou sawest to-day : but take it and believe it, and keep thee therein, and comfort thee therewith, and trust thou thereto : and thou shalt not be overcome.*

These Last Words were said for believing and true sureness that it is our Lord Jesus that shewed me all. And right as in the first word that our good Lord shewed, signifying His blissful Passion,—*Herewith is the devil overcome*,—right so He said in the last word, with full true secureness, meaning us all : *Thou shalt not be over-*

[1] See lxx. "He shewed it all [the Revelation] again within in my soul."

come. And all this teaching in this true comfort, it is general, to all mine even-Christians, as it is aforesaid: and so is God's will.

And this word: *Thou shalt not be overcome*, was said full clearly [1] and full mightily, for assuredness and comfort against all tribulations that may come. He said not: *Thou shalt not be tempested, thou shalt not be travailed, thou shalt not be afflicted;* but He said: *Thou shalt not be overcome.* God willeth that we take heed to these words, and that we be ever strong in sure trust, in weal and woe. For He loveth and enjoyeth us, and so willeth He that we love and enjoy Him and mightily trust in Him; and *all shall be well.*

And soon after, all was close and I saw no more.

CHAPTER LXIX

" I was delivered from the Enemy by the virtue of Christ's Passion "

AFTER this the Fiend came again with his heat and with his stench, and gave me much ado,[2] the stench was so vile and so painful, and also dreadful and travailous. Also I heard a bodily jangling,[3] as if it had been of two persons; and both, to my thinking, jangled at one time as if they had holden a parliament with a great busy-ness; and all was soft muttering, so that I understood nought that they said. And all this was to stir me to despair, as methought,—seeming to me as [though] they mocked at

---

[1] "sharply"=decisively.   [2] " made me full besy."
[3] *i.e.* gabbling.

praying of prayers[1] which are said boisterously with [the] mouth, failing [of] devout attending and wise diligence : the which we owe to God in our prayers.

And our Lord God gave me grace mightily for to trust in Him, and to comfort my soul with bodily speech as I should have done to another person that had been travailed. Methought *that* busy-ness[2] might not be likened to no bodily busy-ness. My bodily eye I set in the same Cross where I had been in comfort afore that time ; my tongue with speech of Christ's Passion and rehearsing the Faith of Holy Church ; and my heart to fasten on God with all the trust and the might. And I thought to myself, saying : *Thou hast now great busy-ness to keep thee in the Faith for that thou shouldst not be taken of the Enemy : wouldst thou now from this time evermore be so busy to keep thee from sin, this were a good and a sovereign occupation!* For I thought in sooth were I safe from sin, I were full safe from all the fiends of hell and enemies of my soul.

And thus he occupied me all that night, and on the morn till it was about prime day. And anon they were all gone, and all passed ; and they left nothing but stench, and that lasted still awhile ; and I scorned him.

And thus was I delivered from him by the virtue of Christ's Passion : for *therewith is the Fiend overcome*, as our Lord Jesus Christ said afore.

---

[1] " bidding of bedes."   [2] see above, " made me full busy."

CHAPTER LXX

"Above the Faith is no goodness kept in this life, as to my sight, and beneath the Faith is no help of soul; but *in* the Faith, *there* willeth the Lord that we keep us"

IN all this blessed Shewing our good Lord gave understanding that the Sight should pass: which blessed Shewing the Faith keepeth, with His own good will and His grace. For He left with me neither sign nor token whereby I might know it, but He left with me His own blessed word in true understanding, bidding me full mightily that I should believe it. And so I do,— Blessed may He be!—I believe that He is our Saviour that shewed it, and that it is the Faith that He shewed: and therefore I believe it, rejoicing. And thereto I am bounden by all His own meaning, with the next words that follow: *Keep thee therein, and comfort thee therewith, and trust thou thereto.*

Thus I am bounden to keep it in my faith. For on the same day that it was shewed, what time that the Sight was passed, as a wretch I forsook it, and openly I said that I had raved. Then our Lord Jesus of His mercy would not let it perish, but He showed it all again *within in my soul*[1] with more fulness, with the blessed light of His precious love: saying these words full mightily and full meekly: *Wit it now well: it was no raving that thou sawest this day.* As if He had said: *For that the Sight was passed from thee, thou losedst it and hadst*

[1] see ch. lxviii.

not skill to keep [1] *it.*   *But wit* [2] *it now* ; that is to say, *now that thou seest it.*   This was said not only for that same time, but also to set thereupon the ground of my faith when He saith anon following : *But take it, believe it, and keep thee therein and comfort thee therewith and trust thou thereto ; and thou shalt not be overcome.*

In these six words that follow (*Take it*—[etc.] His meaning is to fasten it faithfully in our heart : for He willeth that it dwell with us in faith to our life's end, and after in fulness of joy, desiring that we have ever steadfast trust in His blissful behest—knowing His Goodness.

For our faith is contraried in diverse manners by our own blindness, and our spiritual enemy, within and without ; and therefore our precious Lover helpeth us with spiritual sight and true teaching in sundry manners within and without, whereby that we may know Him. And therefore in whatsoever manner He teacheth us, He willeth that we perceive Him wisely, receive Him sweetly, and keep us in Him faithfully. For above the Faith is no goodness kept in this life, as to my sight, and beneath the Faith is no help of soul ; but in the Faith, there willeth the Lord that we keep us. For we have by His goodness and His own working to keep us in the Faith ; and by His sufferance through ghostly enmity we are assayed in the Faith and made mighty. For if our faith had none enmity, it should deserve no meed, according to the understanding that I have in all our Lord's teaching.

---

[1] " couthest not."
[2] *i.e.* learn, perceive, know for certainty by the conviction of reason and consciousness—grasp once for all the truth beheld.

CHAPTER LXXI

" Three manners of looking seen in our Lord's Countenance "

GLAD and joyous and sweet is the Blissful lovely Cheer[1] of our Lord to our souls. For He [be]holdeth[2] us ever, living in love-longing: and He willeth that *our* soul be in glad cheer to Him, to give Him His meed. And thus, I hope, with His grace He hath [drawn], and more shall draw, the Outer Cheer to the Inner Cheer, and make us all one with Him, and each of us with other, in true lasting joy that is Jesus.

I have signifying of Three manners of Cheer of our Lord. The first is Cheer of Passion, as He shewed while He was here in this life, dying. Though this [manner of] Beholding be mournful and troubled, yet it is glad and joyous: for He is God.—The second manner of Cheer is [of] Ruth and Compassion: and this sheweth He, with sureness of Keeping, to all His lovers that betake them[3] to His mercy. The third is the Blissful Cheer, as it shall be without end: and this was [shewed] oftenest and longest-continued.

And thus in the time of our pain and our woe He

---

[1] " Cher," in earlier chapters rendered by *manner of Countenance* or *Regard*.

[2] The word of the MS. might be: " he havith " (possibly " draweth "), or " behadith " or " behavith." There is a verb " bi-hawen " *to behold*—in other forms bihabben, bi-halden—; and " behave " had the meaning of to *manage, govern.* Elsewhere in the MS. to *regard*, if not *to fix the eyes upon*, is expressed (*e.g.* in xxxix.) simply by *to " holden "* without the prefix. S. de Cressy has here " he beheld."

[3] " that have to " ; S. de C., " have need to."

sheweth us Cheer of His Passion and His Cross, helping us to bear it by His own blessed virtue. And in the
time of our sinning He sheweth to us Cheer of Ruth
and Pity, mightily keeping us and defending us against all
our enemies. And these be the common Cheer which He
sheweth to us in this life ; therewith mingling the third :
and that is His Blissful Cheer, like, in part, as it shall
be in Heaven. And that [shewing is] by gracious touching and sweet lighting of the spiritual life, whereby that
we are kept in sure faith, hope, and charity, with contrition and devotion, and also with contemplation and all
manner of true solace and sweet comforts.

CHAPTER LXXII

" As long as we be meddling with any part of sin we shall never
see clearly the Blissful Countenance of our Lord "

BUT now behoveth me to tell in what manner I saw
sin deadly in the creatures which shall not die for
sin, but live in the joy of God without end.

I saw that two contrary things should never be together in one place. The most contrary that are, is the
highest bliss and the deepest pain. The highest bliss
that is, is to have Him in clarity of endless life, Him
verily seeing, Him sweetly feeling, all-perfectly having
in fulness of joy. And thus was the Blissful Cheer of
our Lord shewed in Pity :[1] in which Shewing I saw that
sin is most contrary,—so far forth that as long as we be

[1] That is : in the Shewing of Pity (Rev. ii.) ch. x., in which it was
shewed *darkly*. S. de Cressy has " in *party* "=*part*, but the word seems
to be " *pite* "=*pity*.

meddling with any part of sin, we shall never see clearly
the Blissful Cheer of our Lord. And the more horrible
and grievous that our sins be, the deeper are we for that
time from this blissful sight. And therefore it seemeth
to us oftentimes as we were in peril of death, in a part
of hell, for the sorrow and pain that the sin is to us.
And thus we are dead for the time from the very sight
of our blissful life. But in all this I saw soothfastly that
we be not dead in the sight of God, nor He passeth
never from us. But He shall never have His full bliss
in us till we have our full bliss in Him, verily seeing His
fair Blissful Cheer. For we are ordained thereto in nature,
and get thereto by grace. Thus I saw how sin is deadly
for a short time in the blessed creatures of endless life.

And ever the more clearly that the soul seeth this
Blissful Cheer by grace of loving, the more it longeth to
see it in fulness. For notwithstanding that our Lord God
dwelleth in us and is here with us, and albeit He claspeth
us and encloseth [1] us for tender love that He may never
leave [2] us, and is more near to us than tongue can tell or
heart can think, yet may we never stint of moaning nor
of weeping nor of longing till when we see Him clearly
in His Blissful Countenance. For in that precious blissful sight there may no woe abide, nor any weal fail.[3]

And in this I saw matter of mirth and matter of moaning: matter of mirth: for our Lord, our Maker, is so
near to us, and in us, and we in Him, by sureness of
keeping through His great goodness; matter of moaning:
for our ghostly eye is so blind and we be so borne down
by weight of our mortal flesh and darkness of sin, that

---

[1] halsith; beclosith. [2] levyn; tellen; thynken; stint; see.
[3] "abiden, ne no wele failen."

we may not see our Lord God clearly in His fair Blissful Cheer. No; and because of this dimness [1] scarsely we can believe and trust His great love and our sureness [2] of keeping. And therefore it is that I say we may never stint of moaning nor of weeping. This "weeping" meaneth not all in pouring out of tears by our bodily eye, but also hath more ghostly understanding. For the kindly [2] desire of our soul is so great and so un-measurable, that if there were given us for our solace and for our comfort all the noble things that ever God made in heaven and in earth, and we saw not the fair Blissful Cheer of Himself, yet we should not stint of moaning nor ghostly weeping, that is to say, of painful longing, till when we [should] see verily the fair Blissful Cheer of our Maker. And if we were in all the pain that heart can think and tongue may tell, if we might in that time see His fair Blissful Cheer, all this pain should not aggrieve us.

Thus is that Blissful Sight [the] end of all manner of pain to the loving soul, and the fulfilling of all manner of joy and bliss. And that shewed He in the high, marvellous words where He said : *I it am that is highest; I it am that is lowest; I it am that is all.*

It belongeth to us to have three manner of knowings : the first is that we know our Lord God; the second is that we know our self : what we are by Him, in Nature

---

[1] "myrkehede, unethes we can leven and trowen."

[2] "sekirnes."

Note.—The words "Blissful Cheer" cannot be rendered by the more beautiful and familiar BLESSED COUNTENANCE, and even "*Blissful* Countenance" might fail to bring out the reference to *one Aspect* of the Divine Face, one part of the threefold Truth.

M

and Grace ; the third is that we know meekly what our self is anent our sin and feebleness. And for these three was all the Shewing made, as to mine understanding.

CHAPTER LXXIII

"Two manners of sickness that we have : impatience, or sloth ;—despair, or mistrustful dread"

ALL the blessed teaching of our Lord was shewed by three parts : that is to say, by bodily sight, and by word formed in mine understanding, and by spiritual sight. For the bodily sight, I have said as I saw, as truly as I can ; and for the words, I have said them right as our Lord shewed them to me ; and for the spiritual sight, I have told some deal, but I may never fully tell it : and therefore of this sight I am stirred to say more, as God will give me grace.

God shewed two manners of sickness that we have : the one is impatience, or sloth : for we bear our travail and our pains heavily ; the other is despair, or doubtful dread, which I shall speak of after. *Generally*, He shewed *sin*, wherein that all is comprehended, but in special He shewed only these two. And these two are they that most do travail and tempest us, according to that which our Lord shewed me ; and of them He would have us be amended. I speak of such men and women as for God's love hate sin and dispose themselves to do God's will : then by our spiritual blindness and bodily heaviness we are most inclining to these. And therefore it is God's will that they be known, for then we shall refuse them as we do other sins.

And for help of this, full meekly our Lord shewed the patience that He had in His Hard Passion; and also the joying and the satisfying that He hath of that Passion, for love. And this He shewed in example that we should gladly and wisely bear our pains, for that is great pleasing to Him and endless profit to us. And the cause why we are travailed with them is for lack in knowing [1] of Love. Though the three Persons in the Trinity [2] be all even [3] in Itself, the soul [4] took most understanding in Love; yea, and He willeth that in all things we have our beholding and our enjoying in Love. And of this knowing are we most blind. For some of us believe that God is Almighty and may do all, and that He is All-Wisdom and can do all; but that He is All-Love and will do all, there we stop short. [5] And this not-knowing it is, that hindereth most God's lovers, as to my sight.

For when we begin to hate sin, and amend us by the ordinance of Holy Church, yet there dwelleth a dread that letteth us, because of the beholding of our self and of our sins afore done. And some of us because of our every-daily sins: for we hold not our Covenants, nor keep we our cleanness that our Lord setteth us in, but fall oftentimes into so much wretchedness that shame it is to see it. And the beholding of this maketh us so sorry and so heavy, that scarsely we can find any comfort.

And this dread we take sometime for a meekness, but it is a foul blindness and a weakness. [6] And we cannot

---

[1] " for *unknowing*." [2] seen as Might, Wisdom, Love. [3] *i.e.* equal.
[4] *i.e.* Julian (xiii., xxiv., xlvi.). [5] "astynten."
[6] S. de Cressy: "a wickedness"; but the MS. word is "waykenes."

despise it as we do another sin, that we know [as sin] : for it cometh [subtly] of Enmity, and it is against truth. For it is God's will that of all the properties of the blissful Trinity, we should have most sureness and comfort in Love : for Love maketh Might and Wisdom full meek to us. For right as by the courtesy of God He forgiveth our sin after the time that we repent us, right so willeth He that *we* forgive our sin, as anent our unskilful heaviness and our doubtful dreads.

CHAPTER LXXIV

"There is no dread that fully pleaseth God in us but reverent dread"

FOR I understand [that there be] four manner of dreads. One is the dread of an affright that cometh to a man suddenly by frailty. This dread doeth good, for it helpeth to purge man, as doeth bodily sickness or such other pain as is not sin. For all such pains help man if they be patiently taken. The second is dread of pain, whereby man is stirred and wakened from sleep of sin. He is not able for the time to perceive the soft comfort of the Holy Ghost, till he have understanding of this dread of pain, of bodily death, of spiritual enemies ; and this dread stirreth us to seek comfort and mercy of God, and thus this dread helpeth us,[1] and enableth us to have contrition by the blissful touching of the Holy Ghost. The third is doubtful dread. Doubt-

---

[1] Here the transcriber of the B. Mus. MS. repeats (by mistake, no doubt) "to seek," etc. S. de Cressy : "helpeth us as an entry."

ful dread in as much as it draweth to despair, God will
have it turned in us into love by the knowing of love :
that is to say, that the bitterness of doubt be turned into
the sweetness of natural love by grace. For it may
never please our Lord that His servants doubt in His
Goodness. The fourth is reverent dread : for there is
no dread that fully pleaseth God in us but reverent
dread. And that is full soft, for the more it is had, the
less it is felt for sweetness of love.

Love and Dread are brethren, and they are rooted in
us by the Goodness of our Maker, and they shall never
be taken from us without end. We have of nature to
love and we have of grace to love : and we have of
nature to dread and we have of grace to dread. It
belongeth to the Lordship and to the Fatherhood to be
dreaded, as it belongeth to the Goodness to be loved :
and it belongeth to us that are His servants and His
children to dread Him for Lordship and Fatherhood, as
it belongeth to us to love Him for Goodness.

And though this reverent-dread and love be not parted
asunder, yet they are not both one, but they are two in
property and in working, and neither of them may be
had without other. Therefore I am sure, he that loveth,
he dreadeth, though that he feel it but a little.

All dreads other than reverent dread that are proffered
to us, though they come under the colour of holiness yet
are not so true, and hereby may they be known asunder.—
That dread that maketh us hastily to flee from all that is
not good and fall into our Lord's breast, as the Child into
the Mother's bosom,[1] with all our intent and with all our
mind, knowing our feebleness and our great need,

---

[1] S. de Cressy : " Mothers Arme," but MS. (B.M.) " Moder barme."

knowing His everlasting goodness and His blissful love, only seeking to Him for salvation, cleaving to [Him] with sure trust : that dread that bringeth us into this working, it is natural,[1] gracious, good and true. And all that is contrary to this, either it is wrong, or it is mingled with wrong. Then is this the remedy, to know them both and refuse the wrong.

For the natural property of dread which we have in this life by the gracious working of the Holy Ghost, the same shall be in heaven afore God, gentle, courteous, and full delectable. And thus we shall in love be homely and near to God, and we shall in dread be gentle and courteous to God : and both alike equal.

Desire we of our Lord God to dread Him reverently, to love Him meekly, to trust in Him mightily ; for when we dread Him reverently and love Him meekly our trust is never in vain. For the more that we trust, and the more mightily, the more we please and worship our Lord that we trust in. And if we fail in this reverent dread and meek love (as God forbid we should !), our trust shall soon be misruled for the time. And therefore it needeth us much to pray our Lord of grace that we may have this reverent dread and meek love, of His gift, in heart and in work. For without this, no man may please God.

1 " kinde."

CHAPTER LXXV

" We shall see verily the cause of all things that He hath done; and evermore we shall see the cause of all things that He hath permitted "

I SAW that God can do all that we need. And these three that I shall speak of we need: love, longing, pity. Pity in love keepeth us in the time of our need; and longing in the same love draweth us up into Heaven. For the Thirst of God is to have the general Man unto Him: in which thirst He hath drawn His Holy that be now in bliss; and getting His lively members, ever He draweth and drinketh, and yet He thirsteth and longeth.

I saw three manners of longing in God, and all to one end; of which we have the same in us, and by the same virtue and for the same end.

The first is, that He longeth to teach us to know Him and love Him evermore, as it is convenient and speedful to us. The second is, that He longeth to have us up to His Bliss, as souls are when they are taken out of pain into Heaven. The third is to fulfill us in bliss; and that shall be on the Last Day, fulfilled ever to last. For I saw, as it is known in our Faith, that the pain and the sorrow shall be ended to all that shall be saved. And not only we shall receive the same bliss that souls afore have had in heaven, but also we shall receive a new [bliss], which plenteously shall be flowing out of God into us and shall fulfill us; and these be the goods which

He hath ordained to give us from without beginning. These goods are treasured and hid in Himself; for unto that time [no] Creature is mighty nor worthy to receive them.

In this [fulfilling] we shall see verily the cause of all things that He hath done; and evermore we shall see the cause of all things that He hath suffered.[1] And the bliss and the fulfilling shall be so deep and so high that, for wonder and marvel, all creatures shall have to God so great reverent dread, overpassing that which hath been seen and felt before, that the pillars of heaven shall tremble and quake. But this manner of trembling and dread shall have no pain; but it belongeth to the worthy might of God thus to be beholden by His creatures, in great dread trembling and quaking for meekness of joy, marvelling at the greatness of God the Maker and at the littleness of all that is made. For the beholding of this maketh the creature marvellously meek and mild.

Wherefore God willeth—and also it belongeth to us, both in nature and grace—that we wit and know of this, desiring this sight and this working; for it leadeth us in right way, and keepeth us in true life, and oneth us to God. And as good as God is, so great He is; and as much as it belongeth to His goodness to be loved, so much it belongeth to His greatness to be dreaded. For this reverent dread is the fair courtesy that is in Heaven afore God's face. And as much as He shall then be known and loved overpassing that He is now, in so much He shall be dreaded overpassing that He is now.

---

[1] *i.e.* permitted; "all that is good our Lord doeth, and that which is evil our Lord suffereth," xxxv.

Wherefore it behoveth needs to be that all Heaven and earth shall tremble and quake when the pillars shall tremble and quake.

CHAPTER LXXVI

"The soul that beholdeth the fair nature of our Lord Jesus, it hateth no hell but sin"

I SPEAK but little of reverent dread, for I hope it may be seen in this matter aforesaid. But well I wot our Lord shewed me no souls but those that dread Him. For well I wot the soul that truly taketh the teaching of the Holy Ghost, it hateth more sin for vileness and horribleness than it doth all the pain that is in hell. For the soul that beholdeth the fair nature [1] of our Lord Jesus, it hateth no hell but sin, as to my sight. And therefore it is God's will that we know sin, and pray busily and travail earnestly and seek teaching meekly that we fall not blindly therein ; and if we fall, that we rise readily. For it is the most pain that the soul may have, to turn from God any time by sin.

The soul that willeth to be in rest when [an] other man's sin cometh to mind, he shall flee it as the pain of hell, seeking unto God for remedy, for help against it. For the beholding of other man's sins, it maketh as it were a thick mist afore the eyes of the soul, and we cannot, for the time, see the fairness of God, but if we may behold them with contrition with him, with compassion on him, and with holy desire to God for him. For without this

[1] " kindness."

it harmeth [1] and tempesteth and hindereth the soul that beholdeth them. For this I understood in the Shewing of Compassion.

In this blissful Shewing of our Lord I have understanding of two contrary things: the one is the most wisdom that any creature may do in this life, the other is the most folly. The most wisdom is for a creature to do after the will and counsel of his highest sovereign Friend. This blessed Friend is Jesus, and it is His will and His counsel that we hold us with Him, and fasten us to Him homely—evermore, in what state soever that we be; for whether-so that we be foul or clean, we are all one in His loving. For weal nor for woe He willeth never we flee from Him. But because of the changeability that we are in, in our self, we fall often into sin. Then we have this [doubting dread] by the stirring of our enemy and by our own folly and blindness: for they say thus: *Thou seest well thou art a wretched creature, a sinner, and also unfaithful. For thou keepest not the Command* [2]; *thou dost promise oftentimes our Lord that thou shalt do better, and anon after, thou fallest again into the same, especially into sloth and losing of time.* (For that is the beginning of sin, as to my sight,—and especially to the creatures that have given them to serve our Lord with inward beholding of His blessed Goodness.) And this maketh us adread to appear afore our courteous Lord. Thus is it our enemy that would put us aback [3] with his false dread, [by reason] of our wretchedness, through pain that he threateth us with. For it is his meaning to

---

[1] " noyith."

[2] S. de Cressy—" thy Covenant."

[3] " on bakke."

make us so heavy and so weary in this, that we should let out of mind the fair, Blissful Beholding of our Ever-lasting Friend.

CHAPTER LXXVII

" Accuse not thyself overmuch, deeming that thy tribulation and thy woe is all thy fault."   " All thy living is penance profitable."   " In the remedy He willeth that we rejoice "

OUR good Lord shewed the enmity of the Fiend : in which Shewing I understood that all that is contrary to love and peace is of the Fiend and of his part.   And we have, of our feebleness and our folly, to fall; and we have, of mercy and grace of the Holy Ghost, to rise to more joy.   And if our enemy aught winneth of us by our falling, (for it is his pleasure,[1]) he loseth manifold more in our rising by charity and meekness.   And this glorious rising, it is to him so great sorrow and pain for the hate that he hath to our soul, that he burneth continually in envy.   And all this sorrow that he would make us to have, it shall turn to himself.   And for this it was that our Lord scorned him, and [it was] this [that] made me mightily to laugh.

Then is this the remedy, that we be aware of our wretchedness and flee to our Lord : for ever the more needy that we be, the more speedful it is to us to draw nigh to Him.[2]   And let us say thus in our thinking : *I know*

---

[1] S. de Cressy, "likeness"; Collins, "business." The word may be "Lifenes"=lefness, pleasure; lif=lef=lief=(Morris' *Specimens of Early English*) pleasing, dear.   [2] "neyghen him."

well I have a shrewd pain; but our Lord is All-Mighty and may punish me mightily; and He is All-Wisdom and can punish me discerningly; and He is All-Goodness and loveth me full tenderly. And in this beholding it is necessary for us to abide; for it is a lovely meekness of a sinful soul, wrought by mercy and grace of the Holy Ghost, when we willingly and gladly take the scourge and chastening of our Lord that Himself will give us. And it shall be full tender and full easy, if that we will only hold us satisfied with Him and with all His works.

For the penance that man taketh of himself was not shewed me : that is to say, it was not shewed specified. But specially and highly and with full lovely manner of look was it shewed that we shall meekly bear and suffer the penance that God Himself giveth us, with mind in His blessed Passion. (For when we have mind in His blessed Passion, with pity and love, then we suffer with Him like as His friends did that saw it. And this was shewed in the Thirteenth Shewing, near the beginning, where it speaketh of Pity.) For He saith : *Accuse not [thy]self overdone much, deeming that thy tribulation and thy woe is all for thy fault; for I will not that thou be heavy or sorrowful indiscreetly. For I tell thee, howsoever thou do, thou shalt have woe. And therefore I will that thou wisely know thy penance; and [thou] shalt see in truth that all thy living is penance profitable.*

This place is prison and this life is penance, and in the remedy He willeth that we rejoice. The remedy is that our Lord is with us, keeping and leading into the fulness of joy. For this is an endless joy to us in our Lord's signifying, that He that shall be our bliss when we are there, He is our keeper while we are here. **Our** way and our heaven is true love and sure trust; and of this He gave understanding in all [the Shewings] and especially in the Shewing of the Passion where He made me mightily to choose Him for my heaven.[1]

Flee we to our Lord and we shall be comforted, touch we Him and we shall be made clean, cleave we to Him and we shall be sure,[2] and safe from all manner of peril.

For our courteous Lord willeth that we should be as homely with Him as heart may think or soul may desire. But [let us] beware that we take not so recklessly this homeliness as to leave courtesy. For our Lord Himself is sovereign homeliness, and as homely as He is, so courteous He is: for He is very courteous. And the blessed creatures that shall be in heaven with Him without end, He will have them like to Himself in all things. And to be like our Lord perfectly, it is our very salvation and our full bliss.

And if we wot not how we shall do all this, desire we of our Lord and He shall teach us: for it is His own good-pleasure and His worship; blessed may He be!

CHAPTER LXXVIII

"Though we be highly lifted up into contemplation by the special gift of our Lord, yet it is needful to us to have knowledge and sight of our sin and our feebleness"

OUR Lord of His mercy sheweth us our sin and our feebleness by the sweet gracious light of Himself; for our sin is so vile and so horrible that He of His

---

[1] ch. xix.   [2] "sekir."

courtesy will not shew it to us but by the light of His grace and mercy. Of four things therefore it is His will that we have knowing : the first is, that He is our Ground from whom we have all our life and our being. The second is, that He keepeth us mightily and mercifully in the time that we are in our sin and among all our enemies, that are full fell upon us ; and so much we are in the more peril for [that] we give them occasion thereto, and know not our own need.[1] The third is, how courteously He keepeth us, and *maketh us to know* that we go amiss. The fourth is, how steadfastly He abideth us and changeth no regard :[2] for He willeth that we be turned [again], and oned to Him in love as He is to us.

And thus by this gracious knowing we may see our sin profitably without despair. For truly we need to see it, and by the sight we shall be made ashamed of our self and brought down as anent our pride and pre-sumption ; for it behoveth us verily to see that of our-selves we are right nought but sin and wretchedness. And thus by the sight of the less that our Lord sheweth us, the more is reckoned[3] which we see not. For He of His courtesy measureth the sight to us ; for it is so vile and so horrible that we should not endure to see it as it is. And by this meek knowing after this manner, through contrition and grace we shall be broken from all that is not our Lord. And then shall our blessed Saviour perfectly heal us, and one us to Him.

This breaking and this healing our Lord meaneth for the general Man. For he that is highest and nearest

---

[1] See ch. xxxix. p. 81. [2] " chere "=manner of looking on us ; mien.
[3] S. de Cressy : " wasted," but the indistinct word of the Brit. Mus. MS. is probably " *castid*," for " cast," or " *casten* "=conjectured.

with God, he may see himself sinful—and needeth to—
with me; and I that am the least and lowest that shall
be saved, I may be comforted with him that is highest:
so hath our Lord oned us in charity; [as] where He
shewed me that I should sin.[1]

And for joy that I had in beholding of Him I attended
not readily to that Shewing, and our courteous Lord
stopped there and would not further teach me till that
He gave me grace and will to attend. And hereby was I
learned that though we be highly lifted up into contemplation by the special gift of our Lord, yet it is needful to
us therewith to have knowing and sight of our sin and
our feebleness. For without this knowing we may not
have true meekness, and without this [meekness] we may
not be saved.

And afterward, also, I saw that we may not have this
knowing from our self; nor from none of all our spiritual
enemies : for they will us not so great good. For if it
were by their will, we should not see it until our ending
day. Then be we greatly beholden[2] to God for that
He will Himself, for love, shew it to us in time of mercy
and grace.

CHAPTER LXXIX

"I was taught that I should see mine own sin, and not other
men's sin except it may be for comfort and help of my fellow-
Christians" (lxxvi.)

ALSO I had of this [Revelation] more understanding.
In that He shewed me that I should sin, I took it
nakedly to mine own singular person, for I was none

---

[1] ch. xxxvii.   [2] *i.e.* in gratitude.

otherwise shewed at that time. But by the high, gracious comfort of our Lord that followed after, I saw that His meaning was for the general Man: that is to say, All-Man; which is sinful and shall be unto the last day. Of which Man I am a member, as I hope, by the mercy of God. For the blessed comfort that I saw, it is large enough for us all. And here was I learned that I should see mine own sin, and not other men's sins but if it may be for comfort and help of mine even-Christians.

And also in this same Shewing where I saw that I should sin, there was I learned to be in dread for unsureness of myself. For I wot not how I shall fall, nor I know not the measure nor the greatness of sin; for that would I have wist, with dread, and thereto I had none answer.

Also our courteous Lord in the same time He shewed full surely and mightily the endlessness and the unchangeability of His love; and, afterward, that by His great goodness and His grace inwardly keeping, the love of Him and our soul shall never be disparted in two, without end.[1]

And thus in this dread I have matter of meekness that saveth me from presumption, and in the blessed Shewing of Love I have matter of true comfort and of joy that saveth me from despair. All this homely Shewing of our courteous Lord, it is a lovely lesson and a sweet, gracious teaching of Himself in comforting of our soul. For He willeth that we [should] know by the sweetness and homely loving of Him, that all that we see or feel, within or without, that is contrary to this is of the enemy and not of God. And thus:—If we be stirred

[1] See xxxvii., xl., xlviii., lxi., lxxxii.

to be the more reckless of our living or of the keeping of our hearts because that we have knowing of this plenteous love, then need we greatly to beware. For this stirring, if it come, is untrue ; and greatly we ought to hate it, for it all hath no likeness of God's will. And when that we be fallen, by frailty or blindness, then our courteous Lord toucheth us and stirreth us and calleth us ; and then willeth He that we see our wretchedness and meekly be aware of it.[1] But He willeth not that we abide thus, nor He willeth not that we busy us greatly about our accusing, nor He willeth not that we be wretched over our self ;[2] but He willeth that we hastily turn ourselves unto Him. For He standeth all aloof and abideth us sorrowfully and mournfully till when we come, and hath haste to have us to Him. For we are His joy and His delight, and He is our salve and our life.

When I say He standeth all alone, I leave the speaking of the blessed Company of heaven, and speak of His office and His working here on earth,—upon the condition of the Shewing.

CHAPTER LXXX

" Himself is nearest and meekest, highest and lowest, and doeth all." " Love suffereth never to be without Pity "

BY three things man standeth in this life ; by which three God is worshipped, and we be speeded,[3] kept and saved.

The first is, use of man's Reason natural ; the second

---

[1] "ben it aknowen." S. de Cressy, " be it a knowen."

[2] MS. "wretchful of our selfe." S. de Cressy, "wretchful on our self."

[3] *i.e.* helped onwards.

N

is, common teaching of Holy Church; the third is, inward gracious working of the Holy Ghost. And these three be all of one God: God is the ground of our natural reason; and God, the teaching of Holy Church; and God is the Holy Ghost. And all be sundry gifts to which He willeth that we have great regard, and attend us thereto. For these work in us continually all together; and these be great things. Of which great things He willeth that we have knowing here as it were in an A.B.C., that is to say, that we have a little knowing; whereof we shall have fulness in Heaven. And that is for to speed us.

We know in our Faith that God alone took our nature, and none but He; and furthermore that Christ alone did all the works that belong to our salvation, and none but He; and right so He alone doeth now the last end: that is to say, He dwelleth here with us, and ruleth us and governeth us in this living, and bringeth us to His bliss. And this shall He do as long as any soul is in earth that shall come to heaven,—and so far forth that if there were no such soul but one, He should be withal alone till He had brought him up to His bliss. I believe and understand the ministration of angels, as clerks tell us: but it was not shewed me. For Himself is nearest and meekest, highest and lowest, and doeth all. And not only all that we need, but also He doeth all that is worshipful, to our joy in heaven.

And where I say that He abideth sorrowfully and moaning, it meaneth all the true feeling that *we* have in our self, in contrition and compassion, and all sorrowing and moaning that we are not oned with our Lord. And all such that is speedful, it is Christ in us. And though some of us feel it seldom, it passeth never from Christ till what time He hath brought us out of all our woe. For love suffereth never to be without pity. And what time that we fall into sin and leave the mind of Him and the keeping of our own soul, then keepeth Christ alone all the charge ; and thus standeth He sorrowfully and moaning.

Then belongeth it to us for reverence and kindness to turn us hastily to our Lord and leave Him not alone. He is here alone with us all : that is to say, only for us He is here. And what time I am strange to Him by sin, despair or sloth, then I let my Lord stand alone, in as much as it is in me. And thus it fareth with us all which be sinners. But though it be so that we do thus oftentimes, His Goodness suffereth us never to be alone, but lastingly He is with us, and tenderly He excuseth us, and ever shieldeth us from blame in His sight.

CHAPTER LXXXI

"God seeth all our living a penance : for nature-longing of our love is to Him a lasting penance in us." "His love maketh Him to long "

OUR Good Lord shewed Himself in diverse manners both in heaven and in earth, but I saw Him take no place save in man's soul.

He shewed Himself in earth in the sweet Incarnation and in His blessed Passion. And in other manner He shewed Himself in earth [as in the Revelation] where I say : *I saw God in a Point*.[1] And in another manner He shewed Himself in earth thus as it were in pilgrimage :

[1] ch. xi.

that is to say, He is here with us, leading us, and shall be till when He hath brought us all to His bliss in heaven. He shewed Himself diverse times reigning, as it is aforesaid; but principally in man's soul. He hath taken there His resting-place and His worshipful City: out of which worshipful See He shall never rise nor remove without end.

Marvellous and stately[1] is the place where the Lord dwelleth, and therefore He willeth that we readily answer to[2] His gracious touching, more rejoicing in His whole love than sorrowing in our often fallings. For it is the most worship to Him of anything that we may do, that we live gladly and merrily, for His love, in our penance. For He beholdeth us so tenderly that He seeth all our living [here] a penance: for nature's longing in us is to Him aye-lasting penance in us[3]: which penance He worketh in us and mercifully He helpeth us to bear it. For His love maketh *Him* to long [for us]; His wisdom and His truth with His rightfulness maketh *Him* to suffer us [to be] here: and in this same manner [of longing and abiding] He willeth to see it in us. For this is our natural penance,—and the highest, as to my sight. For this penance goeth[4] never from us till what time that we be fulfilled, when we shall have Him to our meed. And therefore He willeth that we set our hearts in the Overpassing[5]: that is to say, from the pain that we feel into the bliss that we trust.

---

[1] " solemne."   [2] " entenden to "＝turn our attention, respond to.
[3] or, as in S. de Cressy, " For kind longing in us to him is a lasting penance in us."   [4] " cometh."
[5] The exceeding Bliss. " Our light affliction, which is but for a moment, worketh for us a far more exceeding and eternal weight of glory."—2 Cor. iv. 17.

CHAPTER LXXXII

" In falling and in rising we are ever preciously
kept in one Love "

BUT here shewed our courteous Lord the moaning
and the mourning of the soul, signifying thus:
*I know well thou wilt live for my love, joyously and gladly
suffering all the penance that may come to thee; but in as much
as thou livest not without sin thou wouldest suffer, for my love,
all the woe, all the tribulation and distress that might come to
thee. And it is sooth.*[1] *But be not greatly aggrieved with
sin that falleth to thee against thy will.*

And here I understood that [which was shewed] that
the Lord beholdeth the servant with pity and not with
blame.[2] For this passing life asketh[3] not to live all
without blame and sin. He loveth us endlessly, and
we sin customably, and He sheweth us full mildly, and
then we sorrow and mourn discreetly, turning us unto
the beholding of His mercy, cleaving to His love and
goodness, seeing that He is our medicine, perceiving
that we do nought but sin. And thus by the meekness
we get by the sight of our sin, faithfully knowing His
everlasting love, Him thanking and praising, we please
Him:—*I love thee, and thou lovest me, and our love shall not
be disparted in two: for thy profit I suffer* [*these things to
come*]. And all this was shewed in spiritual understanding, saying these blessed words: *I keep thee full surely.*

[1] *i.e.* truth. See xxvii., " It is sooth that sin is cause of all this
pain."   [2] ch. li.

[3] *i.e.* "demandeth not that we live."

And by the great desire that I saw in our blessed Lord that we shall live in this manner,—that is to say, in longing and enjoying, as all this lesson of love sheweth,—thereby I understood that that which is contrarious to us is not of Him but of enmity; and He willeth that we know it by the sweet gracious light of His kind love. If any such lover be in earth which is contiuually kept from falling, I know it not: for it was not shewed me. But this was shewed: that in falling and in rising we are ever preciously kept in one Love. For in the Beholding of God we fall not, and in the beholding of self we stand not; and both these [manners of beholding] be sooth[1] as to my sight. But the Beholding of our Lord God is the highest soothness.[1] Then are we greatly bound to God[2] [for] that He willeth in this living to shew us this high soothness. And I understood that while we be in this life it is full speedful to us that we see both these at once. For the higher Beholding keepeth us in spiritual solace and true enjoying in God; [and] that other that is the lower Beholding keepeth us in dread and maketh us ashamed of ourself. But our good Lord willeth ever that we hold us much more in the Beholding of the higher, and [yet] leave not the knowing of the lower, unto the time that we be brought up above, where we shall have our Lord Jesus unto our meed and be fulfilled of joy and bliss without end.

[1] *i.e.* truth, trueness. "Both these ben soth, as to my syte. But the beholdyng of our Lord God is the heyest sothnes." See chaps. xlv., lii., etc., the two "Deemings": the Beholding by God of the higher Self and the Beholding by man of the lower self.

[2] in gratitude, obligation.

CHAPTER LXXXIII

"Life, Love, and Light"

I HAD, in part, touching, sight, and feeling in three properties of God, in which the strength and effect of all the Revelation standeth: and they were seen in every Shewing, and most properly in the Twelfth, where it saith oftentimes: [*It is I.*] The properties are these: Life, Love, and Light.[1] In life is marvellous homeliness, and in love is gentle courtesy, and in light is endless Nature-hood. These properties were in one Goodness: unto which Goodness my Reason would be oned, and cleave to it with all its might.

I beheld with reverent dread, and highly marvelling in the sight and in the feeling of the sweet accord, that our Reason is in God; understanding that it is the highest gift that we have received; and it is grounded in nature.

Our faith is a light by nature coming of our endless Day, that is our Father, God. In which light our Mother, Christ, and our good Lord, the Holy Ghost, leadeth us in this passing life. This light is measured

---

[1] *Cf.* chs. lxxxv. and lxxxvi. These words might be (as Life, Light, and Love) for the Trinity of *Might* ("the Father willeth"), *Wisdom* ("the Son worketh"), *Love* ("the Holy Ghost confirmeth"): *one Goodness*: or as it is sometimes denoted, the Trinity of *Might, Wisdom, Goodness*: *one Love*. But here the thought seems to be centred in *Light* as the manifestation of Being (of *Kyndhede* = relationships, correspondences of nature): of the Triune Divine Light which in Man is corresponding Reason, Faith, Charity: Charity keeping man, while here, in Faith and Hope; Charity leading him from and through and into the Eternal Divine Love.

discreetly, needfully standing to us in the night. The light is cause of our life; the night is cause of our pain and of all our woe: in which we earn meed and thanks of God. For we, with mercy and grace, steadfastly know and believe our light, going therein wisely and mightily.

And at the end of woe, suddenly our eyes shall be opened, and in clearness of light our sight shall be full: which light is God, our Maker and Holy Ghost, in Christ Jesus our Saviour.

Thus I saw and understood that our faith is our light in our night : which light is God, our endless Day.

CHAPTER LXXXIV

"Charity"

THE light is Charity, and the measuring of this light is done to us profitably by the wisdom of God. For neither is the light so large that we may see our blissful Day, nor is it shut from us; but it is such a light in which we may live meedfully, with travail deserving [1] the endless worship of God. And this was seen in the Sixth Shewing where He said : *I thank thee of thy service and of thy travail.* Thus Charity keepeth us in Faith and Hope, and Hope leadeth us in Charity. And in the end all shall be Charity.

I had three manners of understanding of this light, Charity. The first is Charity unmade; the second is

---

[1] *i.e.* earning the endless praise.

Charity made; the third is Charity given. Charity
unmade is God; Charity made is our soul in God;
Charity given is virtue. And that is a precious gift of
working in which we love God, for Himself; and ourselves, in God; and that which God loveth, for God.

CHAPTER LXXXV

" Lord, blessed mayest Thou be, for it is thus : it is well "

AND in this sight I marvelled highly. For notwithstanding our simple living and our blindness here,
yet endlessly our courteous Lord beholdeth us in this
working, rejoicing; and of all things, we may please
Him best wisely and truly to believe, and to enjoy
with Him and in Him. For as verily as we shall
be in the bliss of God without end, Him praising
and thanking, so verily we have been in the
foresight of God, loved and known in His endless
purpose from without beginning. In which unbegun
love He made us ; and in the same love He keepeth us
and never suffereth us to be hurt [in manner] by which
our bliss might be lost. And therefore when the Doom
is given and we be all brought up above, then shall we
clearly see in God the secret things which be now hid
to us. Then shall none of us be stirred to say in any
wise : *Lord, if it had been thus, then it had been full well;*
but we shall say all with one voice : *Lord, blessed mayst
thou be, for it is thus : it is well ; and now see we verily that
all-thing is done as it was then ordained before that anything
was made.*

CHAPTER LXXXVI

" Love was our Lord's Meaning "

THIS book is begun by God's gift and His grace, but it is not yet performed, as to my sight.

For Charity pray we all; [together] with *God's* working, thanking, trusting, enjoying. For thus will our good Lord be prayed to, as by the understanding that I took of all His own meaning and of the sweet words where He saith full merrily: *I am the Ground of thy beseeching.* For truly I saw and understood in our Lord's meaning that He shewed it for that He willeth to have it known more than it is: in which knowing He will give us grace to love to Him and cleave to Him. For He beholdeth His heavenly treasure with so great love on earth that He willeth to give us more light and solace in heavenly joy, in drawing to Him of our hearts, for sorrow and darkness [1] which we are in.

And from that time that it was shewed I desired oftentimes to learn [2] what was our Lord's meaning. And fifteen years after, and more, I was answered in ghostly understanding, saying thus: *Wouldst thou learn [2] thy Lord's meaning in this thing? Learn it well: Love was His meaning. Who shewed it thee? Love. What shewed He thee? Love. Wherefore shewed it He? For Love. Hold thee therein and thou shalt learn and know more in the same. But thou shalt never know nor learn therein other thing without end.* Thus was I learned [3] that Love was our Lord's meaning.

---

[1] " merkness "=dimness.   [2] " witten "=to see clearly.   [3] " lerid."

And I saw full surely that ere God made us He loved us; which love was never slacked, nor ever shall be. And in this love He hath done all His works; and in this love He hath made all things profitable to us; and in this love our life is everlasting. In our making we had beginning; but the love wherein He made us was in Him from without beginning: in which love we have our beginning. And all this shall we see in God, without end.

POSTSCRIPT BY A SCRIBE

[The Sloane MS. is entitled " Revelations to one who could not read a Letter, Anno Dom. 1373," and each chapter is headed by a few lines denoting its contents. These titles are in language similar to that of the text, and are probably the work of an early scribe. No doubt it is the same scribe who after the last sentence of the book adds the aspiration :] *Which Jesus mot grant us*

Amen.

[And to him also may be assigned this conclusion :—]

Thus endeth the Revelation of Love of the blissid Trinite shewid by our Savior Christ Jesu for our endles comfort and solace and also to enjoyen in him in this passand journey of this life.

Amen Jesu Amen

I pray Almyty God that this booke com not but to the hands of them that will be his faithfull lovers, and to those that will submitt them to the faith of holy Church, and obey the holesom understondying and teching of the men that be of vertuous life, sadde Age and sound lering : ffor this Revelation is hey Divinitye and hey wisdom, wherfore it may not dwelle with him that is thrall to synne and to the Devill.

And beware thou take not on thing after thy affection and liking, and leve another : for that is the condition of an heretique. But take every thing with other. And, trewly understonden, All is according to holy Scripture and groundid in the same. And *that* Jesus, our very love, light and truth, shall shew to all clen soulis that with mekeness aske profe reverently this wisdom of hym.

And thou to whom this boke shall come, thank heyley and hertily our Saviour Christ Jesu that he made these shewings and revelations, for the, and to the, of his endles love, mercy and goodnes for thine and our save guide, to conduct to everlastying bliss : *the which Jesus mot grant us.* AMEN.

GLOSSARY

Adight = prepared, ordained.

Adventure = chance, hazard.

After = according to.

All thing = with the verb singular—kept here chiefly to express *all*, the *whole* of things related to each other, though often, as in the original, meaning simply *every*, *each*. In Early and Middle English *thing* had no *s* in the plural.

And had sometimes the force of *but*, and once or twice in the MS. it is used in its sense of *if*, or of *and though*, or *and when*.

Asseth, *asyeth*, *asyeth-making* = satisfaction; fulfilment (theologically used).

Asketh = requireth, demandeth.

Avisement = consideration; observation with self-consulting.

Beclosed = enclosed.

Behest = promise: a thing proclaimed; afterwards, command.

Behold in = behold. *Beholding* = manner of regarding things.

Belongeth to, *behoveth* = is incumbent, befitteth.

Blissful = used sometimes as *blessed*.

Bodily = perceived by any of the bodily senses, effected by material agency.

Braste = burst.

Busyness = the state of being busy; *great busyness* = much ado.

But if = unless, save.

Cause = reason, end, object.

Cheer = expression of countenance shewing sorrow or gladness; mien.

Close = shut away; hid, or partially hid.

Come from = go from.

Common : the Blessed Common = the Christian Community.

Contrarious = perverse. Various other forms are used from to *contrary*, to oppose.

Could and *can* refer to knowledge and practical skill, ability.

Courteous = gently considerate and fair ; reverentially ceremonious ; Gracious.

Deadly = mortal.

Dearworthy = precious ; beloved and honoured.

Depart = dispart, part.

Deserve = earn.

Disease = distress, trouble, want of ease.

Doom, deeming = judgment. *Doomsman* = priestly confessor.

Enjoy in = enjoy ; rejoice in.

Entend = attend.

Enter = to lead in.

Even = equal ; *even-like ; even-right* = straight, straight-facing.

Even-Christian (*even-cristen,* sing. or pl.) = fellow-Christian. *Hamlet* V. i., "And the more the pity that great folk have countenance in this world to drown or hang themselves more than their even Christian."

Faithfully = trustfully.

For that = because.

Fulfilled of = filled full with. *Fulfilling* = fulfilment, Perfect Bliss.

Garland = crown.

Generally = relating to things or people in general, not "in special."

Grante mercy = (" grand merci ") great thanks.

Have to = betake one's self to.

Hastily = quickly, soon.

Homely = intimate, simple, as of one at home.

Honest = fair, seemly.

If = that (chap. xxxii., "Thou shalt see—if all—shall be well Acts xxvi. 8).

Impropriated (*impropried*) *to* = appropriated to.

Indifferent (to thy sight, chap. li.) = indistinct.

Intellect = understanding, that which is to be understood, inference. xiii.

Intent = attention.

Kind = nature, race, birth, species ; natural, etc. ; *kindly* = as by birth and kinship, natural, filial, gentle, genial, human and humane.

Known = made known.

Languor = to languish.

Learn = teach.

Let, "*letten*" = hinder (letted).

Like (*it liketh him*, *meliketh*) = to suit, be similar to the desire, to be pleasing (Amos iv. 5). *Liking* = pleasure, pleasance.

Likeness ("without any likeness") = comparison.

May, *might*, often for *can* and *could* of modern usage.

Mean = to think, say, signify, intend ; to have in one's mind.

Mean, *means* = medium, intermediary thing, or person, or communication.

Mind = feeling, memory, sympathetic perception or realisation.

Mischief = hurt, injury, harm.

Mights = powers, faculties.

Morrow = morning.

Moaning = sorrowing.

Naked = simple, single, plain, by itself.

Needs = of need ; it *behoveth needs* = is incumbent through necessity.

Oweth = ought, is bound by duty or debt.

Over = upper.

One (oned, oneing) = to make one, unite.

Overpassing = exceeding ; the *overpassing* = the Restoration, the heavenly Fulfilment of the Company of souls made *more* than conquerors ; the Supernal Blessedness.

Pass = to die.

Passing = surpassingly.

Regard, in regard of = in respect of, comparison with. *Regard* = look, sight.

Ready = prepared ; *readily* = quickly.

Sad = sober ("sad votaress," Milton, *Comus*), originally "firm" ("rype and sad corage," Chaucer : *The Clerkes Tale*, 164).

Say = tell.

Skilfully = discerningly, with practical knowledge and ability.

Slade = a steep, hollow place ; a ravine.

So far forth = to such a measure.

Solemn = festal, as of a yearly feast, stately, ceremonial.

Sooth = very reality, that which *is ; soothly, soothfastly.*

Speed = prospering, furtherance, profit.

Stint (" stinten ") = to cease.

Stirring (" stering ") = moving, prompting, motion.

Substantial and *sensual*, relating respectively (in the writer's psychology) to the *Substance* or higher self, and the soul inhabiting the body on earth, called by her the *Sensualite*, and in chap. lvii. *the sensual soul ; cf.* Genesis i. 27, with ii. 7.

Tarry = to vex, delay.

Touch (a) = an instant. *Touching* = influence.

Trow = believe.

Unknowing = ignorance ; *unmade* = not made.

Ween = suppose, expect, think.

Will ; He will = He willeth that. *Wilfully* = with firm will, resolutely.

Wit = to know by perception, to experience, find, learn. Knowledge knows : *Wisdom wits.*

Worship = honour, praise, glory.

Wretch = a poor, a mean creature of no account.

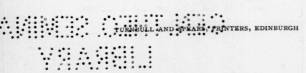TURNBULL AND SPEARS, PRINTERS, EDINBURGH

A CATALOGUE OF BOOKS PUBLISHED BY METHUEN AND COMPANY: LONDON 36 ESSEX STREET W.C.

CONTENTS

FEBRUARY 1906

A CATALOGUE OF

MESSRS. METHUEN'S
PUBLICATIONS

Colonial Editions are published of all Messrs. METHUEN'S Novels issued at a price above 2s. 6d., and similar editions are published of some works of General Literature. These are marked in the Catalogue. Colonial editions are only for circulation in the British Colonies and India.

An asterisk denotes that a book is in the Press.
I.P.L. represents Illustrated Pocket Library.
S.Q.S. represents Social Questions Series.

PART I.—GENERAL LITERATURE

Abbot (Jacob). See Little Blue Books.

Abbott (J. H. M.). Author of 'Tommy Cornstalk.' AN OUTLANDER IN ENGLAND: BEING SOME IMPRESSIONS OF AN AUSTRALIAN ABROAD. *Second Edition. Cr. 8vo. 6s.*
A Colonial Edition is also published.

Acatos (M. J.). See Junior School Books.

Adams (Frank). JACK SPRATT. With 24 Coloured Pictures. *Super Royal 16mo. 2s.*

Adeney (W. F.), M.A. See Bennett and Adeney.

Æschylus. See Classical Translations.

Æsop. See I.P.L.

Ainsworth (W. Harrison). See I.P.L.

Alderson (J. P.). MR. ASQUITH. With Portraits and Illustrations. *Demy 8vo. 7s. 6d. net.*
A Colonial Edition is also published.

Aldis (Janet). MADAME GEOFFRIN, HER SALON, AND HER TIMES. With many Portraits and Illustrations. *Second Edition. Demy 8vo. 10s. 6d. net.*
A Colonial Edition is also published.

Alexander (William), D.D., Archbishop of Armagh. THOUGHTS AND COUNSELS OF MANY YEARS. *Demy 16mo. 2s. 6d.*

Aiken (Henry). THE NATIONAL SPORTS OF GREAT BRITAIN. With descriptions in English and French. With 51 Coloured Plates. *Royal Folio. Five Guineas net.* The Plates can be had separately in a Portfolio. *£3, 3s. net.*
See also I.P.L.

Allen (Jessie). See Little Books on Art.

Allen (J. Romilly), F.S.A. See Antiquary's Books.

Almack (E.). See Little Books on Art.

Amherst (Lady). A SKETCH OF EGYPTIAN HISTORY FROM THE EARLIEST TIMES TO THE PRESENT DAY. With many Illustrations. *Demy 8vo. 10s. 6d. net.*

Anderson (F. M.). THE STORY OF THE BRITISH EMPIRE FOR CHILDREN. With many Illustrations. *Cr. 8vo. 2s.*

Anderson (J. G.), B.A., Examiner to London University, NOUVELLE GRAMMAIRE FRANÇAISE. *Cr. 8vo. 2s.*
EXERCICES DE GRAMMAIRE FRANÇAISE. *Cr. 8vo. 1s. 6d.*

Andrewes (Bishop). PRECES PRIVATAE. Edited, with Notes, by F. E. BRIGHTMAN, M.A., of Pusey House, Oxford. *Cr. 8vo. 6s.*

Anglo=Australian. AFTER-GLOW MEMORIES. *Cr. 8vo. 6s.*
A Colonial Edition is also published.

Aristophanes. THE FROGS. Translated into English by E. W. HUNTINGFORD, M.A. *Cr. 8vo. 2s. 6d.*

Aristotle. THE NICOMACHEAN ETHICS. Edited, with an Introduction and Notes, by JOHN BURNET, M.A., Professor of Greek at St. Andrews. *Cheaper issue. Demy 8vo. 10s. 6d. net.*

Ashton (R.). See Little Blue Books.

Atkins (H. G.). See Oxford Biographies.

Atkinson (C. M.). JEREMY BENTHAM. *Demy 8vo. 5s. net.*

Atkinson (T. D.). A SHORT HISTORY OF ENGLISH ARCHITECTURE. With over 200 Illustrations. *Fcap. 8vo. 3s. 6d. net.*

*A GLOSSARY OF TERMS USED IN ENGLISH ARCHITECTURE. Illustrated. *Fcap. 8vo. 3s. 6d. net.*

Auden (T.), M.A., F.S.A. See Ancient Cities.

Aurelius (Marcus). See Standard Library and W. H. D. Rouse.

Austen (Jane). See Little Library and Standard Library.

Aves (Ernest). See Books on Business.

Bacon (Francis). See Little Library and Standard Library.

Baden-Powell (R. S. S.), Major-General. THE DOWNFALL OF PREMPEH. A Diary of Life in Ashanti, 1895. Illustrated. *Third Edition. Large Cr. 8vo. 6s.*
A Colonial Edition is also published.

THE MATABELE CAMPAIGN, 1896. With nearly 100 Illustrations. *Fourth Edition. Large Cr. 8vo. 6s.*
A Colonial Edition is also published.

*Bagot (Richard). THE LAKE OF COMO. *Cr. 8vo. 3s. 6d. net.*

Bailey (J. C.), M.A. See Cowper.

Baker (W. G.), M.A. See Junior Examination Series.

Baker (Julian L.), F.I.C., F.C.S. See Books on Business.

Balfour (Graham). THE LIFE OF ROBERT LOUIS STEVENSON. *Second Edition. Two Volumes. Demy 8vo. 25s. net.*
A Colonial Edition is also published.

Bally (S. E.). See Commercial Series.

Banks (Elizabeth L.). THE AUTO-BIOGRAPHY OF A 'NEWSPAPER GIRL.' *Second Edition. Cr. 8vo. 6s.*
A Colonial Edition is also published.

Barham (R. H.). See Little Library.

Baring (The Hon. Maurice). WITH THE RUSSIANS IN MANCHURIA. *Third Edition. Demy 8vo. 7s. 6d. net.*
A Colonial Edition is also published.

Baring-Gould (S.). THE LIFE OF NAPOLEON BONAPARTE. With over 450 Illustrations in the Text, and 12 Photogravure Plates. *Gilt top. Large quarto. 36s.*

THE TRAGEDY OF THE CÆSARS. With numerous Illustrations from Busts, Gems, Cameos, etc. *Fifth Edition. Royal 8vo. 10s. 6d. net.*

A BOOK OF FAIRY TALES. With numerous Illustrations by A. J. GASKIN. *Second Edition. Cr. 8vo. Buckram. 6s.*

OLD ENGLISH FAIRY TALES. With numerous Illustrations by F. D. BEDFORD. *Second Edition. Cr. 8vo. Buckram. 6s.*
A Colonial Edition is also published.

THE VICAR OF MORWENSTOW. Revised Edition. With a Portrait. *Cr. 8vo. 3s. 6d.*

DARTMOOR: A Descriptive and Historical Sketch. With Plans and numerous Illustrations. *Cr. 8vo. 6s.*

THE BOOK OF THE WEST. Illustrated. *Two volumes. Vol. I. Devon. Second Edition. Vol. II. Cornwall. Second Edition. Cr. 8vo. 6s. each.*

A BOOK OF NORTH WALES. Illustrated. *Cr. 8vo. 6s.*

A BOOK OF SOUTH WALES. Illustrated. *Cr. 8vo. 6s.*

A BOOK OF BRITTANY. Illustrated. *Cr. 8vo. 6s.*

A BOOK OF THE RIVIERA. Illustrated. *Cr. 8vo. 6s.*
A Colonial Edition is also published.

*THE RHINE. Illustrated. *Cr. 8vo. 6s.*

A BOOK OF GHOSTS. With 8 Illustrations by D. MURRAY SMITH. *Second Edition. Cr. 8vo. 6s.*
A Colonial Edition is also published.

OLD COUNTRY LIFE. With 67 Illustrations. *Fifth Edition. Large Cr. 8vo. 6s.*

A GARLAND OF COUNTRY SONG: English Folk Songs with their Traditional Melodies. Collected and arranged by S. BARING-GOULD and H. F. SHEPPARD. *Demy 4to. 6s.*

SONGS OF THE WEST: Folk Songs of Devon and Cornwall. Collected from the Mouths of the People. By S. BARING-GOULD, M.A., and H. FLEETWOOD SHEPPARD, M.A. New and Revised Edition, under the musical editorship of CECIL J. SHARP, Principal of the Hampstead Conservatoire. *Large Imperial 8vo. 5s. net.*
See also Little Guides and Half-Crown Library.

Barker (Aldred F.). See Textbooks of Technology.

Barnes (W. E.), D.D. See Churchman's Bible.

Barnett (Mrs. P. A.). See Little Library.

Baron (R. R. N.), M.A. FRENCH PROSE COMPOSITION. *Second Edition. Cr. 8vo. 2s. 6d. Key, 3s. net.* See also Junior School Books.

Barron (H. M.), M.A., Wadham College, Oxford. TEXTS FOR SERMONS. With a Preface by Canon SCOTT HOLLAND. *Cr. 8vo. 3s. 6d.*

Bartholomew (J. G.), F.R.S.E. See C. G. Robertson.

Bastable (C. F.), M.A. See S.Q.S.

Batson (Mrs. Stephen). A BOOK OF THE COUNTRY AND THE GARDEN. Illustrated by F. CARRUTHERS GOULD and A. C. GOULD. *Demy 8vo. 10s. 6d.*

A CONCISE HANDBOOK OF GARDEN FLOWERS. *Fcap. 8vo. 3s. 6d.*

Batten (Loring W.), Ph.D., S.T.D. THE HEBREW PROPHET. *Cr. 8vo. 3s. 6d. net.*

Beaman (A. Hulme). PONS ASINORUM; OR, A GUIDE TO BRIDGE. *Second Edition. Fcap. 8vo. 2s.*

Beard (W. S.). See Junior Examination Series and Beginner's Books.

Beckford (Peter). THOUGHTS ON HUNTING. Edited by J. OTHO PAGET, and Illustrated by G. H. JALLAND. *Second Edition. Demy 8vo. 6s.*

Beckford (William). See Little Library.

Beeching (H. C.), M.A., Canon of Westminster. See Library of Devotion.

Begbie (Harold). MASTER WORKERS. Illustrated. *Demy 8vo. 7s. 6d. net.*

Behmen (Jacob). DIALOGUES ON THE SUPERSENSUAL LIFE. Edited by BERNARD HOLLAND. *Fcap. 8vo. 3s. 6d.*

Belloc (Hillaire). PARIS. With Maps and Illustrations. *Cr. 8vo. 6s.*

***MARIE ANTOINETTE.** With many Portraits and Illustrations. *Demy 8vo. 12s. 6d. net.*
    A Colonial Edition is also published.

Bellot (H. H. L.), M.A. THE INNER AND MIDDLE TEMPLE. With numerous Illustrations. *Crown 8vo. 6s. net.*
    See also L. A. A. Jones.

Bennett (W. H.), M.A. A PRIMER OF THE BIBLE. *Second Edition. Cr. 8vo. 2s. 6d.*

Bennett (W. H.) and **Adeney (W. F.).** A BIBLICAL INTRODUCTION. *Third Edition. Cr. 8vo. 7s. 6d.*

Benson (Archbishop) GOD'S BOARD: Communion Addresses. *Fcap. 8vo. 3s. 6d. net.*

Benson (A. C.), M.A. See Oxford Biographies.

Benson (R. M.). THE WAY OF HOLINESS: a Devotional Commentary on the 119th Psalm. *Cr. 8vo. 5s.*

Bernard (E. R.), M.A., Canon of Salisbury. THE ENGLISH SUNDAY. *Fcap. 8vo. 1s. 6d.*

Bertouch (Baroness de). THE LIFE OF FATHER IGNATIUS. Illustrated. *Demy 8vo. 10s. 6d. net.*
    A Colonial Edition is also published.

Betham-Edwards (M.). HOME LIFE IN FRANCE. Illustrated. *Fourth Edition. Demy 8vo. 7s. 6d. net.*
    A Colonial Edition is also published.

Bethune-Baker (J. F.), M.A. See Handbooks of Theology.

Bidez (M.). See Byzantine Texts.

Biggs (C. R. D.), D.D. See Churchman's Bible.

Bindley (T. Herbert), B.D. THE OECUMENICAL DOCUMENTS OF THE FAITH. With Introductions and Notes. *Cr. 8vo. 6s.*

Binns (H. B.). THE LIFE OF WALT WHITMAN. Illustrated. *Demy 8vo. 10s. 6d. net.*
    A Colonial Edition is also published.

Binyon (Laurence). THE DEATH OF ADAM, AND OTHER POEMS. *Cr. 8vo. 3s. 6d. net.*

***WILLIAM BLAKE.** In 2 volumes. *Quarto. £1, 1s. each.*
    Vol. I.—THE BOOK OF JOB.

Birnstingl (Ethel). See Little Books on Art.

Blackmantle (Bernard). See I.P.L.

Blair (Robert). See I.P.L.

Blake (William). See I.P.L. and Little Library.

Blaxland (B.), M.A. See Library of Devotion.

Bloom (T. Harvey), M.A. SHAKESPEARE'S GARDEN. Illustrated. *Fcap. 8vo. 3s. 6d.; leather, 4s. 6d. net.*
    See also Antiquary's Books.

Blouet (Henri). See Beginner's Books.

Boardman (T. H.), M.A. See Textbooks of Science.

Bodley (J. E. C.), Author of 'France.' THE CORONATION OF EDWARD VII. *Demy 8vo. 21s. net.* By Command of the King.

Body (George), D.D. THE SOUL'S PILGRIMAGE: Devotional Readings from his writings. Selected by J. H. BURN, B.D., F.R.S.E. *Pott 8vo. 2s. 6d.*

Bona (Cardinal). See Library of Devotion.

Boon (F. C.). See Commercial Series.

Borrow (George). See Little Library.

Bos (J. Ritzema). AGRICULTURAL ZOOLOGY. Translated by J. R. AINSWORTH DAVIS, M.A. With 155 Illustrations. *Cr. 8vo. Third Edition. 3s. 6d.*

Botting (C. G.), B.A. EASY GREEK EXERCISES. *Cr. 8vo. 2s.* See also Junior Examination Series.

Boulton (E. S.), M.A. GEOMETRY ON MODERN LINES. *Cr. 8vo. 2s.*

Boulton (William B.). THOMAS GAINSBOROUGH. With 40 Illustrations. *Second Ed. Demy 8vo. 7s. 6d. net.*
SIR JOSHUA REYNOLDS, P.R.A. With 49 Illustrations. *Demy 8vo. 7s. 6d. net.*

Bowden (E. M.). THE IMITATION OF BUDDHA: Being Quotations from Buddhist Literature for each Day in the Year. *Fifth Edition. Cr. 16mo. 2s. 6d.*

Boyle (W.). CHRISTMAS AT THE ZOO. With Verses by W. BOYLE and 24 Coloured Pictures by H. B. NEILSON. *Super Royal 16mo. 2s.*

Brabant (F. G.), M.A. See Little Guides.

Bradley (J. W.). See Little Books on Art.

***Brailsford (H. N.).** MACEDONIA. Illustrated. *Demy 8vo. 12s. 6d. net.*

Brodrick (Mary) and **Morton (Anderson).** A CONCISE HANDBOOK OF EGYPTIAN ARCHÆOLOGY. Illustrated. *Cr. 8vo. 3s. 6d.*

Brooke (A. S.), M.A. SLINGSBY AND SLINGSBY CASTLE. Illustrated. *Cr. 8vo. 7s. 6d.*

Brooks (E. W.). See Byzantine Texts.

Brown (P. H.), LL.D., Fraser Professor of Ancient (Scottish) History at the University of Edinburgh. SCOTLAND IN THE TIME OF QUEEN MARY. *Demy 8vo. 7s. 6d. net.*

Browne (Sir Thomas). See Standard Library.

Brownell (C. L.). THE HEART OF JAPAN. Illustrated. *Third Edition. Cr. 8vo. 6s.; also Demy 8vo. 6d.*
    A Colonial Edition is also published.

Browning (Robert). See Little Library.

Buckland (Francis T.). CURIOSITIES OF NATURAL HISTORY. Illustrated by H. B. NEILSON. *Cr. 8vo. 3s. 6d.*

Buckton (A. M.) THE BURDEN OF ENGELA : a Ballad-Epic. *Second Edition. Cr. 8vo. 3s. 6d. net.*
EAGER HEART : A Mystery Play. *Fourth Edition. Cr. 8vo. 1s. net.*

Budge (E. A. Wallis). THE GODS OF THE EGYPTIANS. With over 100 Coloured Plates and many Illustrations. *Two Volumes. Royal 8vo. £3, 3s. net.*

Bull (Paul), Army Chaplain. GOD AND OUR SOLDIERS. *Second Edition. Cr. 8vo. 6s.*
A Colonial Edition is also published.

Bulley (Miss). See S.Q.S.

Bunyan (John). THE PILGRIM'S PROGRESS. Edited, with an Introduction, by C. H. FIRTH, M.A. With 39 Illustrations by R. ANNING BELL. *Cr. 8vo. 6s.*
See also Library of Devotion and Standard Library.

Burch (G. J.), M.A., F.R.S. A MANUAL OF ELECTRICAL SCIENCE. Illustrated. *Cr. 8vo. 3s.*

Burgess (Gelett). GOOPS AND HOW TO BE THEM. Illustrated. *Small 4to. 6s.*

Burke (Edmund). See Standard Library.

Burn (A. E.), D.D., Prebendary of Lichfield. See Handbooks of Theology.

Burn (J. H.), B.D. See Library of Devotion.

Burnand (Sir F. C.) RECORDS AND REMINISCENCES. With a Portrait by H. v. HERKOMER. *Cr. 8vo. Fourth and Cheaper Edition. 6s.*
A Colonial Edition is also published.

Burns (Robert), THE POEMS OF. Edited by ANDREW LANG and W. A. CRAIGIE. With Portrait. *Third Edition. Demy 8vo, gilt top. 6s.*

Burnside (W. F.), M.A. OLD TESTAMENT HISTORY FOR USE IN SCHOOLS. *Cr. 8vo. 3s. 6d.*

Burton (Alfred). See I.P.L.

Butler (Joseph). See Standard Library.

Caldecott (Alfred), D.D. See Handbooks of Theology.

Calderwood (D. S.), Headmaster of the Normal School, Edinburgh. TEST CARDS IN EUCLID AND ALGEBRA. In three packets of 40, with Answers. *1s.* each. Or in three Books, price *2d.*, *2d.*, and *3d.*

Cambridge (Ada) [Mrs. Cross]. THIRTY YEARS IN AUSTRALIA. *Demy 8vo. 7s. 6d.*
A Colonial Edition is also published.

Canning (George). See Little Library.

Capey (E. F. H.). See Oxford Biographies.

Careless (John). See I.P.L.

Carlyle (Thomas). THE FRENCH REVOLUTION. Edited by C. R. L. FLETCHER, Fellow of Magdalen College, Oxford. *Three Volumes. Cr. 8vo. 18s.*

THE LIFE AND LETTERS OF OLIVER CROMWELL. With an Introduction by C. H. FIRTH, M.A., and Notes and Appendices by Mrs. S. C. LOMAS. *Three Volumes. Demy 8vo. 18s. net.*

Carlyle (R. M. and A. J.), M.A. See Leaders of Religion.

****Carpenter (Margaret).** THE CHILD IN ART. Illustrated. *Cr. 8vo. 6s.*

Chamberlin (Wilbur B.). ORDERED TO CHINA. *Cr. 8vo. 6s.*
A Colonial Edition is also published.

Channer (C. C.) and Roberts (M. E.). LACEMAKING IN THE MIDLANDS, PAST AND PRESENT. With 16 full-page Illustrations. *Cr. 8vo. 2s. 6d.*

Chapman (S. J.). See Books on Business.

Chatterton (Thomas). See Standard Library.

Chesterfield (Lord), THE LETTERS OF, TO HIS SON. Edited, with an Introduction by C. STRACHEY, and Notes by A. CALTHROP. *Two Volumes. Cr. 8vo. 12s.*

****Chesterton (G. K.).** DICKENS. With Portraits and Illustrations. *Demy 8vo. 7s. 6d. net.*
A Colonial Edition is also published.

Christian (F. W.). THE CAROLINE ISLANDS. With many Illustrations and Maps. *Demy 8vo. 12s. 6d. net.*

Cicero. See Classical Translations.

Clarke (F. A.), M.A. See Leaders of Religion.

Cleather (A. L.) and Crump (B.). RICHARD WAGNER'S MUSIC DRAMAS : Interpretations, embodying Wagner's own explanations. *In Four Volumes. Fcap 8vo. 2s. 6d. each.*
VOL. I.—THE RING OF THE NIBELUNG.
VOL. II.—PARSIFAL, LOHENGRIN, and THE HOLY GRAIL.
VOL. III.—TRISTAN AND ISOLDE.

Clinch (G.). See Little Guides.

Clough (W. T.). See Junior School Books.

Coast (W. G.), B.A. EXAMINATION PAPERS IN VERGIL. *Cr. 8vo. 2s.*

Cobb (T.). See Little Blue Books.

Cobb (W. F.), M.A. THE BOOK OF PSALMS : with a Commentary. *Demy 8vo. 10s. 6d. net.*

Coleridge (S. T.), SELECTIONS FROM. Edited by ARTHUR SYMONS. *Fcap. 8vo. 2s. 6d. net.*

Collingwood (W. G.). See Half-Crown Library.

Collins (W. E.), M.A. See Churchman's Library.

Colonna. HYPNEROTOMACHIA POLIPHILI UBI HUMANA OMNIA NON NISI SOMNIUM ESSE DOCET ATQUE OBITER PLURIMA SCITU SANE QUAM DIGNA COMMEMORAT. An edition limited to 350 copies on handmade paper. *Folio. Three Guineas net.*

Combe (William). See I.P.L.

Cook (A. M.), M.A. See E. C. Marchant.

Cooke-Taylor (R. W.). See S.Q.S.

Corelli (Marie). THE PASSING OF THE GREAT QUEEN : *Fcap. 4to. 1s.*

A CHRISTMAS GREETING. *Cr. 4to. 1s.*

Corkran (Alice). See Little Books on Art.

Cotes (Rosemary). DANTE'S GARDEN. With a Frontispiece. *Second Edition. Fcap. 8vo. 2s. 6d.; leather, 3s. 6d. net.*

BIBLE FLOWERS. With a Frontispiece and Plan. *Fcap. 8vo. 2s. 6d. net.*

Cowley (Abraham). See Little Library.

Cowper (William), THE POEMS OF. Edited with an Introduction and Notes by J. C. BAILEY, M.A. Illustrated, including two unpublished designs by WILLIAM BLAKE. *Demy 8vo. 10s. 6d. net.*

Cox (J. Charles), LL.D., F.S.A. See Little Guides, The Antiquary's Books, and Ancient Cities.

Cox (Harold), B.A. See S.Q.S.

Crabbe (George). See Little Library.

Craigie (W. A.). A PRIMER OF BURNS. *Cr. 8vo. 2s. 6d.*

Craik (Mrs.). See Little Library.

Crashaw (Richard). See Little Library.

Crawford (F. G.). See Mary C. Danson.

*Cross (J. A.). A LITTLE BOOK OF RELIGION. *Fcap. 8vo. 2s. 6d. net.*

Crouch (W.). BRYAN KING. With a Portrait. *Cr. 8vo. 3s. 6d. net.*

Cruikshank (G.). THE LOVING BALLAD OF LORD BATEMAN. With 11 Plates. *Cr. 16mo. 1s. 6d. net.*

Crump (B.). See A. L. Cleather.

Cunliffe (Sir F. H. E.), Fellow of All Souls' College, Oxford. THE HISTORY OF THE BOER WAR. With many Illustrations, Plans, and Portraits. *In 2 vols. Quarto. 15s. each.*

A Colonial Edition is also published.

Cunynghame (H.), C.B., See Connoisseur's Library.

Cutts (E. L.), D.D. See Leaders of Religion.

Daniell (G. W.), M.A. See Leaders of Religion.

Danson (Mary C.) and Crawford (F. G.). FATHERS IN THE FAITH. *Fcap. 8vo. 1s. 6d.*

Dante. LA COMMEDIA DI DANTE. The Italian Text edited by PAGET TOYNBEE, M.A., D.Litt. *Cr. 8vo. 6s.*

THE PURGATORIO OF DANTE. Translated into Spenserian Prose by C. GORDON WRIGHT. With the Italian text. *Fcap. 8vo. 2s. 6d. net.*

See also Paget Toynbee, Little Library and Standard Library.

Darley (George). See Little Library.

D'Arcy (R. F.), M.A. A NEW TRIGONOMETRY FOR BEGINNERS. *Cr. 8vo. 2s. 6d.*

Davenport (Cyril). See Connoisseur's Library and Little Books on Art.

*Davey (Richard). THE PAGEANT OF LONDON With 40 Illustrations in Colour by JOHN FULLEYLOVE, R. I. *In Two Volumes. Demy 8vo. 7s. 6d. net.* Each volume may be purchased separately.

VOL. I.—TO A.D. 1500.
VOL. II.—A.D. 1500 TO 1900.

Davis (H. W. C.), M.A., Fellow and Tutor of Balliol College, Author of 'Charlemagne.' ENGLAND UNDER THE NORMANS AND ANGEVINS : 1066-1272. With Maps and Illustrations. *Demy 8vo. 10s. 6d.. net.*

Dawson (A. J.). MOROCCO. Illustrated *Demy 8vo. 10s. 6d. net.*

Deane (A. C.). See Little Library.

Delbos (Leon). THE METRIC SYSTEM. *Cr. 8vo. 2s.*

Demosthenes. THE OLYNTHIACS AND PHILIPPICS. Translated by OTHO HOLLAND. *Cr. 8vo. 2s. 6d.*

Demosthenes. AGAINST CONON AND CALLICLES. Edited by F. DARWIN SWIFT, M.A. *Fcap. 8vo. 2s.*

Dickens (Charles). See Little Library and I.P.L.

Dickinson (Emily). POEMS. *Cr. 8vo. 4s. 6d. net.*

Dickinson (G. L.), M.A., Fellow of King's College, Cambridge. THE GREEK VIEW OF LIFE. *Fourth Edition. Cr. 8vo. 2s. 6d.*

Dickson (H. N.). F.R.Met. Soc. METEOROLOGY. Illustrated. *Cr. 8vo. 2s. 6d.*

Dilke (Lady). See S.Q.S.

Dillon (Edward). See Connoisseur's Library and Little Books on Art.

Ditchfield (P. H.), M.A., F.S.A. THE STORY OF OUR ENGLISH TOWNS. With an Introduction by AUGUSTUS JESSOPP, D.D. *Second Edition. Cr. 8vo. 6s.*

OLD ENGLISH CUSTOMS: Extant at the Present Time. *Cr. 8vo. 6s.* See also Half-crown Library.

Dixon (W. M.), M.A. A PRIMER OF TENNYSON. *Second Edition. Cr. 8vo. 2s. 6d.*

ENGLISH POETRY FROM BLAKE TO BROWNING. *Second Edition. Cr. 8vo. 2s. 6d.*

Dole (N. H.). FAMOUS COMPOSERS. With Portraits. *Two Volumes. Demy 8vo. 12s. net.*

Doney (May). SONGS OF THE REAL. *Cr. 8vo. 3s. 6d. net.*

A volume of poems.

Douglas (James). THE MAN IN THE PULPIT. *Cr. 8vo. 2s. 6d. net.*

Dowden (J.), D.D., Lord Bishop of Edinburgh. See Churchman's Library.

Drage (G.). See Books on Business.

Driver (S. R.), D.D., D.C.L., Canon of Christ Church, Regius Professor of Hebrew in the University of Oxford. SERMONS ON SUBJECTS CONNECTED WITH THE OLD TESTAMENT. *Cr. 8vo.* 6s. See also Westminster Commentaries.

Dry (Wakeling). See Little Guides.

Dryhurst (A. R.). See Little Books on Art.

Duguid (Charles). See Books on Business.

Dunn (J. T.), D.Sc., and **Mundella** (V. A.). GENERAL ELEMENTARY SCIENCE. With 114 Illustrations. *Second Edition. Cr. 8vo.* 3s. 6d.

Dunstan (A. E.), B.Sc. See Junior School Books and Textbooks of Science.

Durham (The Earl of). A REPORT ON CANADA. With an Introductory Note. *Demy 8vo.* 4s. 6d. net.

Dutt (W. A.). A POPULAR GUIDE TO NORFOLK. *Medium 8vo.* 6d. net.
THE NORFOLK BROADS. With coloured Illustrations by FRANK SOUTH-GATE. *Cr. 8vo.* 6s. See also Little Guides.

Earle (John), Bishop of Salisbury. MICRO-COSMOGRAPHIE, OR A PIECE OF THE WORLD DISCOVERED. *Post 16mo.* 2s net.

Edmonds (Major J. E.), R.E.; D.A.Q.-M.G. See W. Birkbeck Wood.

Edwards (Clement). See S.Q.S.

Edwards (W. Douglas). See Commercial Series.

Egan (Pierce). See I.P.L.

*__Egerton__ H. E., M.A. A HISTORY OF BRITISH COLONIAL POLICY. New and Cheaper Issue. *Demy 8vo.* 7s. 6d. net.
A Colonial Edition is also published.

Ellaby (C. G.). See The Little Guides.

Ellerton (F. G.). See S. J. Stone.

Ellwood (Thomas), THE HISTORY OF THE LIFE OF. Edited by C. G. CRUMP, M.A. *Cr. 8vo.* 6s.

Epictetus. See W. H. D. Rouse.

Erasmus. A Book called in Latin EN-CHIRIDION MILITIS CHRISTIANI, and in English the Manual of the Christian Knight.
From the edition printed by Wynken de Worde, 1533. *Fcap. 8vo* 3s. 6d. net.

Fairbrother (W. H.), M.A. THE PHILO-SOPHY OF T. H. GREEN. *Second Edition. Cr. 8vo.* 3s. 6d.

Farrer (Reginald). THE GARDEN OF ASIA. *Second Edition. Cr. 8vo.* 6s.
A Colonial Edition is also published.

*__Fea__ (Allan). BEAUTIES OF THE SEVENTEENEH CENTURY. With 100 Illustrations. *Demy 8vo.* 12s. 6d. net.

FELISSA; OR, THE LIFE AND OPINIONS OF A KITTEN OF SENTI-MENT. With 12 Coloured Plates. *Post 16mo.* 2s. 6d. net.

Ferrier (Susan). See Little Library.

Fidler (T. Claxton), M.Inst. C.E. See Books on Business.

Fielding (Henry). See Standard Library.

Finn (S. W.), M.A. See Junior Examination Series.

Firth (C. H.), M.A. CROMWELL'S ARMY: A History of the English Soldier during the Civil Wars, the Commonwealth, and the Protectorate. *Cr. 8vo.* 6s.

Fisher (G. W.), M.A. ANNALS OF SHREWSBURY SCHOOL. Illustrated. *Demy 8vo.* 10s. 6d.

FitzGerald (Edward). THE RUBAIYAT OF OMAR KHAYYÁM. Printed from the Fifth and last Edition. With a Com-mentary by Mrs. STEPHEN BATSON, and a Biography of Omar by E. D. ROSS. *Cr. 8vo.* 6s. See also Miniature Library.

*__FitzGerald__ (H. P.). A CONCISE HAND-BOOK OF CLIMBERS, TWINERS, AND WALL SHRUBS. Illustrated. *Fcap. 8vo.* 3s. 6d. net.

Flecker (W. H.), M.A., D.C.L., Headmaster of the Dean Close School, Cheltenham. THE STUDENT'S PRAYER BOOK. THE TEXT OF MORNING AND EVENING PRAYER AND LITANY. With an Introduc-tion and Notes. *Cr. 8vo.* 2s. 6d.

Flux (A. W.), M.A., William Dow Professor of Political Economy in M'Gill University, Montreal. ECONOMIC PRINCIPLES. *Demy 8vo.* 7s. 6d. net.

Fortescue (Mrs. G.). See Little Books on Art.

Fraser (David). A MODERN CAM-PAIGN; OR, WAR AND WIRELESS TELEGRAPHY IN THE FAR EAST. Illustrated. *Cr. 8vo.* 6s.
A Colonial Edition is also published.

Fraser (J. F.). ROUND THE WORLD ON A WHEEL. With 100 Illustrations. *Fourth Edition Cr. 8vo.* 6s.
A Colonial Edition is also published.

French (W.), M.A. See Textbooks of Science.

Freudenreich (Ed. von). DAIRY BAC-TERIOLOGY. A Short Manual for the Use of Students. Translated by J. R. AINSWORTH DAVIS, M.A. *Second Edition. Revised. Cr. 8vo.* 2s. 6d.

Fulford (H. W.), M.A. See Churchman's Bible.

C. G., and F. C. G. JOHN BULL'S AD-VENTURES IN THE FISCAL WON-DERLAND. By CHARLES GEAKE. With 46 Illustrations by F. CARRUTHERS GOULD. *Second Edition. Cr. 8vo.* 1s. net.

*__Gallaher__ (D.) and Stead (D. W.). THE COMPLETE RUGBY FOOTBALLER. With an Account of the Tour of the New Zealanders in England. With Illustra-tions. *Demy 8vo.* 10s. 6d. net.

Gallichan (W. M.). See Little Guides.

Gambado (Geoffrey, Esq.). See I.P.L.

Gaskell (Mrs.). See Little Library and Standard Library.

Gasquet, the Right Rev. Abbot, O.S.B. See Antiquary's Books.

George (H. B.), M.A., Fellow of New College, Oxford. BATTLES OF ENGLISH HISTORY. With numerous Plans. *Fourth Edition.* Revised, with a new Chapter including the South African War. *Cr. 8vo.* 3s. 6d.

A HISTORICAL GEOGRAPHY OF THE BRITISH EMPIRE. *Second Edition. Cr. 8vo.* 3s. 6d.

Gibbins (H. de B.), Litt.D., M.A. INDUSTRY IN ENGLAND: HISTORICAL OUTLINES. With 5 Maps. *Fourth Edition. Demy 8vo.* 10s. 6d.

A COMPANION GERMAN GRAMMAR. *Cr. 8vo.* 1s. 6d.

THE INDUSTRIAL HISTORY OF ENGLAND. *Tenth Edition.* Revised. With Maps and Plans. *Cr. 8vo.* 3s.

ENGLISH SOCIAL REFORMERS. *Second Edition. Cr. 8vo.* 2s. 6d.

See also Commercial Series and S.Q.S.

Gibbon (Edward). THE DECLINE AND FALL OF THE ROMAN EMPIRE. A New Edition, edited with Notes, Appendices, and Maps, by J. B. BURY, M.A., Litt.D., Regius Professor of Greek at Cambridge. *In Seven Volumes. Demy 8vo. Gilt top,* 8s. 6d. *each. Also, Cr. 8vo.* 6s. *each.*

MEMOIRS OF MY LIFE AND WRITINGS. Edited by G. BIRKBECK HILL, LL.D. *Demy 8vo, Gilt top.* 8s. 6d. *Also Cr. 8vo.* 6s.

See also Standard Library.

Gibson (E. C. S.), D.D., Lord Bishop of Gloucester. See Westminster Commentaries, Handbooks of Theology, and Oxford Biographies.

Gilbert (A. R.). See Little Books on Art.

Gloag (M.). See K. Wyatt.

Godfrey (Elizabeth). A BOOK OF REMEMBRANCE. Edited by. *Fcap. 8vo.* 2s. 6d. *net.*

Godley (A. D.), M.A., Fellow of Magdalen College, Oxford. LYRA FRIVOLA. *Third Edition. Fcap. 8vo.* 2s. 6d.

VERSES TO ORDER. *Second Edition. Fcap. 8vo.* 2s. 6d.

SECOND STRINGS. *Fcap. 8vo.* 2s. 6d.

Goldsmith (Oliver). THE VICAR OF WAKEFIELD. *Fcap. 32mo.* With 10 Plates in Photogravure by Tony Johannot. *Leather,* 2s. 6d. *net.* See also I.P.L. and Standard Library.

Goodrich-Freer (A.). IN A SYRIAN SADDLE. *Demy 8vo.* 7s. 6d. *net.*

A Colonial Edition is also published.

Goudge (H. L.), M.A., Principal of Wells Theological College. See Westminster Commentaries.

Graham (P. Anderson). See S.Q.S.

Granger (F. S.), M.A., Litt.D. PSYCHOLOGY. *Second Edition. Cr. 8vo.* 2s.6d.

THE SOUL OF A CHRISTIAN. *Cr. 8vo.* 6s.

Gray (E. M'Queen). GERMAN PASSAGES FOR UNSEEN TRANSLATION. *Cr. 8vo.* 2s. 6d.

Gray (P. L.), B.Sc. THE PRINCIPLES OF MAGNETISM AND ELECTRICITY: an Elementary Text-Book. With 181 Diagrams. *Cr. 8vo.* 3s. 6d.

Green (G. Buckland), M.A., late Fellow of St. John's College, Oxon. NOTES ON GREEK AND LATIN SYNTAX. *Cr. 8vo.* 3s. 6d.

Green (E. T.), M.A. See Churchman's Library.

Greenidge (A. H. J.), M.A. A HISTORY OF ROME: During the Later Republic and the Early Principate. *In Six Volumes. Demy 8vo.* Vol. I. (133-104 B.C.). 10s. 6d. *net.*

Greenwell (Dora). See Miniature Library.

Gregory (R. A.). THE VAULT OF HEAVEN. A Popular Introduction to Astronomy. Illustrated. *Cr. 8vo.* 2s. 6d.

Gregory (Miss E. C.). See Library of Devotion.

Greville Minor. A MODERN JOURNAL. Edited by J. A. SPENDER. *Cr. 8vo.* 3s. 6d. *net.*

Grubb (H. C.). See Textbooks of Technology.

Guiney (Louisa I.). HURRELL FROUDE: Memoranda and Comments. Illustrated. *Demy 8vo.* 10s. 6d. *net.*

Gwynn (M. L.). A BIRTHDAY BOOK. New and cheaper issue. *Royal 8vo.* 5s. *net.*

Hackett (John), B.D. A HISTORY OF THE ORTHODOX CHURCH OF CYPRUS. With Maps and Illustrations. *Demy 8vo.* 15s. *net.*

Haddon (A. C.), Sc.D., F.R.S. HEAD-HUNTERS BLACK, WHITE, AND BROWN. With many Illustrations and a Map. *Demy 8vo.* 15s.

Hadfield (R. A.). See S.Q.S.

Hall (R. N.) and Neal (W. G.). THE ANCIENT RUINS OF RHODESIA. Illustrated *Second Edition, revised. Demy 8vo.* 10s. 6d. *net.*

A Colonial Edition is also published.

Hall (R. N.). GREAT ZIMBABWE. With numerous Plans and Illustrations. *Second Edition. Royal 8vo.* 21s. *net.*

Hamilton (F. J.), D.D. See Byzantine Texts.

Hammond (J. L.). CHARLES JAMES FOX. *Demy 8vo.* 10s. 6d.

Hannay (D.). A SHORT HISTORY OF THE ROYAL NAVY, Illustrated. *Two Volumes. Demy 8vo.* 7s. 6d. *each.* Vol. I. 1200-1688.

Hannay (James O.), M.A. THE SPIRIT AND ORIGIN OF CHRISTIAN MONASTICISM. *Cr. 8vo.* 6s.

THE WISDOM OF THE DESERT. *Fcap. 8vo.* 3s. 6d. *net.*

Hare (A. T.), M.A. THE CONSTRUCTION OF LARGE INDUCTION COILS With numerous Diagrams. *Demy 8vo.* 6s.

Harrison (Clifford). READING AND READERS. *Fcap. 8vo. 2s. 6d.*

Hawthorne (Nathaniel). See Little Library. HEALTH, WEALTH AND WISDOM. *Cr. 8vo. 1s. net.*

Heath (Frank R.). See Little Guides.

Heath (Dudley). See Connoisseur's Library.

Hello (Ernest). STUDIES IN SAINT-SHIP. Translated from the French by V. M. CRAWFORD. *Fcap 8vo. 3s. 6d.*

Henderson (B. W.), Fellow of Exeter College, Oxford. THE LIFE AND PRINCIPATE OF THE EMPEROR NERO. Illustrated. *New and cheaper issue. Demy 8vo. 7s. 6d. net.* AT INTERVALS. *Fcap 8vo. 2s. 6d. net.*

Henderson (T. F.). See Little Library and Oxford Biographies.

Henley (W. E.). See Half-Crown Library.

Henson (H. H.), B.D., Canon of Westminster. APOSTOLIC CHRISTIANITY: As Illustrated by the Epistles of St. Paul to the Corinthians. *Cr. 8vo. 6s.* LIGHT AND LEAVEN: HISTORICAL AND SOCIAL SERMONS. *Cr. 8vo. 6s.* DISCIPLINE AND LAW. *Fcap. 8vo. 2s. 6d.*

Herbert (George). See Library of Devotion.

Herbert of Cherbury (Lord). See Miniature Library.

Hewins (W. A. S.), B.A. ENGLISH TRADE AND FINANCE IN THE SEVENTEENTH CENTURY. *Cr. 8vo. 2s. 6d.*

Hewitt (Ethel M.) A GOLDEN DIAL. A Day Book of Prose and Verse. *Fcap. 8vo. 2s. 6d. net.*

Heywood (W.). PALIO AND PONTE: A Book of Tuscan Games. Illustrated. *Royal 8vo. 21s. net.*

Hilbert (T.). See Little Blue Books.

Hill (Clare). See Textbooks of Technology.

Hill (Henry), B.A., Headmaster of the Boy's High School, Worcester, Cape Colony. A SOUTH AFRICAN ARITHMETIC. *Cr. 8vo. 3s. 6d.*

Hillegas (Howard C.). WITH THE BOER FORCES. With 24 Illustrations. *Second Edition. Cr. 8vo. 6s.* A Colonial Edition is also published.

Hirst (F. W.) See Books on Business.

Hobhouse (Emily). THE BRUNT OF THE WAR. With Map and Illustrations. *Cr. 8vo. 6s.* A Colonial Edition is also published.

Hobhouse (L. T.), Fellow of C.C.C., Oxford. THE THEORY OF KNOWLEDGE. *Demy 8vo. 10s. 6d. net.*

Hobson (J. A.), M.A. INTERNATIONAL TRADE: A Study of Economic Principles. *Cr. 8vo. 2s. 6d. net.* PROBLEMS OF POVERTY. *Fifth Edition. Cr. 8vo. 2s. 6d.*

Hodgkin (T.), D.C.L. See Leaders of Religion.

Hodgson (Mrs. W.) HOW TO IDENTIFY OLD CHINESE PORCELAIN. *Second Edition. Post 8vo. 6s.*

Hogg (Thomas Jefferson). SHELLEY AT OXFORD. With an Introduction by R. A. STREATFEILD. *Fcap. 8vo. 2s. net.*

Holden-Stone (G. de). See Books on Business.

Holdich (Sir T. H.), K.C.I.E. THE INDIAN BORDERLAND: being a Personal Record of Twenty Years. Illustrated. *Demy 8vo. 10s. 6d. net.* A Colonial Edition is also published.

Holdsworth (W. S.), M.A. A HISTORY OF ENGLISH LAW. *In Two Volumes. Vol. I. Demy 8vo. 10s. 6d. net.*

Holland (Canon Scott). See Library of Devotion.

Holt (Emily). THE SECRET OF POPULARITY: How to Achieve Social Success. *Cr. 8vo. 3s. 6d. net.* A Colonial Edition is also published.

Holyoake (G. J.). THE CO-OPERATIVE MOVEMENT TO-DAY. *Fourth Edition. Cr. 8vo. 2s. 6d.*

Hone (Nathaniel J.). See Antiquary's Books.

Hoppner. See Little Galleries.

Horace. See Classical Translations.

Horsburgh (E. L. S.), M.A. WATERLOO: A Narrative and Criticism. With Plans. *Second Edition. Cr. 8vo. 5s.* See also Oxford Biographies.

Horth (A. C.). See Textbooks of Technology.

Horton (R. F.), D.D. See Leaders of Religion.

Hosie (Alexander). MANCHURIA. With Illustrations and a Map. *Second Edition. Demy 8vo. 7s. 6d. net.* A Colonial Edition is also published.

How (F. D.). SIX GREAT SCHOOLMASTERS. With Portraits and Illustrations. *Second Edition. Demy 8vo. 7s. 6d.*

Howell (G.). See S. Q. S.

Hudson (Robert). MEMORIALS OF A WARWICKSHIRE PARISH. Illustrated. *Demy 8vo. 15s. net.*

Hughes (C. E.). THE PRAISE OF SHAKESPEARE. An English Anthology. With a Preface by SIDNEY LEE. *Demy 8vo. 3s. 6d. net.*

Hughes (Thomas). TOM BROWN'S SCHOOLDAYS. With an Introduction and Notes by VERNON RENDALL. *Leather. Royal 32mo. 2s. 6d. net.*

Hutchinson (Horace G.) THE NEW FOREST. Illustrated in colour with 50 Pictures by WALTER TYNDALE and 4 by Miss LUCY KEMP WELCH. *Large Demy 8vo. 21s. net.*

Hutton (A. W.), M.A. See Leaders of Religion and Library of Devotion.

Hutton (Edward). THE CITIES OF UMBRIA. With many Illustrations, of which 20 are in Colour, by A. PISA. *Second Edition. Cr. 8vo. 6s.* A Colonial Edition is also published.

ENGLISH LOVE POEMS. Edited with an Introduction. *Fcap. 8vo.* 3s. 6d. *net.*

Hutton (R. H.). See Leaders of Religion.

Hutton (W. H.), M.A. THE LIFE OF SIR THOMAS MORE. With Portraits. *Second Edition. Cr. 8vo.* 5s. See also Leaders of Religion.

Hyett (F. A.). A SHORT HISTORY OF FLORENCE. *Demy 8vo.* 7s. 6d. *net.*

Ibsen (Henrik). BRAND. A Drama. Translated by WILLIAM WILSON. *Third Edition. Cr. 8vo.* 3s. 6d.

Inge (W. R.), M.A., Fellow and Tutor of Hertford College, Oxford. CHRISTIAN MYSTICISM. The Bampton Lectures for 1899. *Demy 8vo.* 12s. 6d. *net.* See also Library of Devotion.

Innes (A. D.), M.A. A HISTORY OF THE BRITISH IN INDIA. With Maps and Plans. *Cr. 8vo.* 6s.
ENGLAND UNDER THE TUDORS. With Maps. *Demy 8vo.* 10s. 6d. *net.*

Jackson (C. E.), B.A. See Textbooks of Science.

Jackson (S.), M.A. See Commercial Series.

Jackson (F. Hamilton). See Little Guides.

Jacob (F.), M.A. See Junior Examination Series.

Jeans (J. Stephen). See S. Q. S. and Business Books.

Jeffreys (D. Gwyn). DOLLY'S THEATRICALS. Described and Illustrated with 24 Coloured Pictures. *Super Royal 16mo.* 2s. 6d.

Jenks (E.), M.A., Reader of Law in the University of Oxford. ENGLISH LOCAL GOVERNMENT. *Cr. 8vo.* 2s. 6d.

Jenner (Mrs. H.). See Little Books on Art.

Jessopp (Augustus), D.D. See Leaders of Religion.

*****Jevons (F. B.),** M.A., Litt.D., Principal of Hatfield Hall, Durham. RELIGION IN EVOLUTION. *Cr. 8vo.* 3s. 6d. *net.*
See also Churchman's Library and Handbooks of Theology.

Johnson (Mrs. Barham). WILLIAM BODHAM DONNE AND HIS FRIENDS. Illustrated. *Demy 8vo.* 10s. 6d. *net.*

Johnston (Sir H. H.), K.C.B. BRITISH CENTRAL AFRICA. With nearly 200 Illustrations and Six Maps. *Third Edition. Cr. 4to.* 18s. *net.*
A Colonial Edition is also published.

Jones (R. Crompton), M.A. POEMS OF THE INNER LIFE. Selected by. *Eleventh Edition. Fcap. 8vo.* 2s. 6d. *net.*

Jones (H.). See Commercial Series.

Jones (L. A. Atherley), K.C., M.P., and **Bellot (Hugh H. L.).** THE MINERS' GUIDE TO THE COAL MINES REGULATION ACTS. *Cr. 8vo.* 2s. 6d. *net.*
*****COMMERCE IN WAR. *Demy 8vo.* 21s. *net.*

Jonson (Ben). See Standard Library.

Julian (Lady) of Norwich. REVELATIONS OF DIVINE LOVE. Edited by GRACE WARRACK. *Cr. 8vo.* 3s. 6d.

Juvenal. See Classical Translations.

'Kappa.' LET YOUTH BUT KNOW: A Plea for Reason in Education. *Cr. 8vo.* 3s. 6d. *net.*

Kaufmann (M.). See S. Q. S.

Keating (J. F.), D.D. THE AGAPE AND THE EUCHARIST. *Cr. 8vo.* 3s. 6d.

Keats (John). THE POEMS OF. Edited with Introduction and Notes by E. de Selincourt, M.A. *Demy 8vo.* 7s. 6d. *net.* See also Little Library, Standard Library, and E. de Selincourt.

Keble (John). THE CHRISTIAN YEAR. With an Introduction and Notes by W. LOCK, D.D., Warden of Keble College. Illustrated by R. ANNING BELL. *Third Edition. Fcap. 8vo.* 3s. 6d. ; *padded morocco,* 5s. See also Library of Devotion.

Kempis (Thomas à). THE IMITATION OF CHRIST. With an Introduction by DEAN FARRAR. Illustrated by C. M. GERE. *Third Edition. Fcap. 8vo.* 3s. 6d.; *padded morocco.* 5s. See also Library of Devotion and Standard Library.
Also Translated by C. BIGG, D.D. *Cr. 8vo.* 3s. 6d

Kennedy (Bart.). THE GREEN SPHINX. *Cr. 8vo.* 3s. 6d. *net.*
A Colonial Edition is also published.

Kennedy (James Houghton), D.D., Assistant Lecturer in Divinity in the University of Dublin. ST. PAUL'S SECOND AND THIRD EPISTLES TO THE CORINTHIANS. With Introduction, Dissertations and Notes. *Cr. 8vo.* 6s.

Kestell (J. D.). THROUGH SHOT AND FLAME : Being the Adventures and Experiences of J. D. KESTELL, Chaplain to General Christian de Wet. *Cr. 8vo.* 6s.
A Colonial Edition is also published.

Kimmins (C. W.), M.A. THE CHEMISTRY OF LIFE AND HEALTH. Illustrated. *Cr. 8vo.* 2s. 6d.

Kinglake (A. W.). See Little Library.

Kipling (Rudyard). BARRACK-ROOM BALLADS. 73rd Thousand. *Twenty-first Edition. Cr. 8vo.* 6s.
A Colonial Edition is also published.
THE SEVEN SEAS. 62nd Thousand. *Tenth Edition. Cr. 8vo.* 6s.
A Colonial Edition is also published.
THE FIVE NATIONS. 41st Thousand. *Second Edition. Cr. 8vo.* 6s.
A Colonial Edition is also published.
DEPARTMENTAL DITTIES. *Sixteenth Edition. Cr. 8vo.* 6s.
A Colonial Edition is also published.

*****Knight (Albert E.).** THE COMPLETE CRICKETER. Illustrated. *Demy 8vo.* 7s. 6d. *net.*
A Colonial Edition is also published.

Knowling (R. J.), M.A., Professor of New Testament Exegesis at King's College, London. See Westminster Commentaries.

Lamb (Charles and Mary), THE WORKS OF. Edited by E. V. LUCAS. Illustrated. *In Seven Volumes. Demy 8vo. 7s. 6d. each.*
THE LIFE OF. See E. V. Lucas.
See also Little Library.

Lambert (F. A. H.). See Little Guides.

Lambros (Professor). See Byzantine Texts.

Lane-Poole (Stanley). A HISTORY OF EGYPT IN THE MIDDLE AGES. Fully Illustrated. *Cr. 8vo. 6s.*

Langbridge (F.), M.A. BALLADS OF THE BRAVE: Poems of Chivalry, Enterprise, Courage, and Constancy. *Second Edition. Cr. 8vo. 2s. 6d.*

Law (William). See Library of Devotion and Standard Library.

Leach (Henry). THE DUKE OF DEVONSHIRE. A Biography. With 12 Illustrations. *Demy 8vo. 12s. 6d. net.*
A Colonial Edition is also published.

*Le Braz (Anatole). THE LAND OF PARDONS. Translated by FRANCES M. GOSTLING. Illustrated in colour. *Crown 8vo. 6s.*

Lee (Captain L. Melville). A HISTORY OF POLICE IN ENGLAND. *Cr. 8vo. 3s. 6d. net.*

Leigh (Percival). THE COMIC ENGLISH GRAMMAR. Embellished with upwards of 50 characteristic Illustrations by JOHN LEECH. *Post 16mo. 2s. 6d. net.*

Lewes (V. B.), M.A. AIR AND WATER. Illustrated. *Cr. 8vo. 2s. 6d.*

*Lewis (Mrs. Gwynn). A CONCISE HANDBOOK OF GARDEN SHRUBS. Illustrated. *Fcap. 8vo. 3s. 6d. net.*

Lisle (Fortunéede). See Little Books on Art.

Littlehales (H.). See Antiquary's Books.

Lock (Walter), D.D., Warden of Keble College. ST. PAUL, THE MASTERBUILDER. *Second Edition. Cr. 8vo. 3s. 6d.*
THE BIBLE AND CHRISTIAN LIFE. *Cr. 8vo. 6s.*
See also Leaders of Religion and Library of Devotion.

Locker (F.). See Little Library.

Longfellow (H. W.). See Little Library.

Lorimer (George Horace). LETTERS FROM A SELF-MADE MERCHANT TO HIS SON. *Fourteenth Edition. Cr. 8vo. 6s.*
A Colonial Edition is also published.
OLD GORGON GRAHAM. *Second Edition. Cr. 8vo. 6s.*
A Colonial Edition is also published.

Lover (Samuel). See I. P. L.

E. V. L. and C. L. G. ENGLAND DAY BY DAY: Or, The Englishman's Handbook to Efficiency. Illustrated by GEORGE MORROW. *Fourth Edition. Fcap. 4to. 1s. net.*

Lucas (E. V.). THE LIFE OF CHARLES LAMB. With numerous Portraits and Illustrations. *Third Edition. Two Vols. Demy 8vo. 21s. net.*
A Colonial Edition is also published.
A WANDERER IN HOLLAND. With many Illustrations, of which 20 are in Colour by HERBERT MARSHALL. *Fifth Edition. Cr. 8vo. 6s.*
A Colonial Edition is also published.
THE OPEN ROAD: a Little Book for Wayfarers. *Ninth Edition. Fcap. 8vo. 5s.; India Paper, 7s. 6d.*
THE FRIENDLY TOWN: a Little Book for the Urbane. *Second Edition. Fcap. 8vo. 5s.; India Paper, 7s. 6d.*

Lucian. See Classical Translations.

Lyde (L. W.), M.A. See Commercial Series.

Lydon (Noel S.). See Junior School Books.

Lyttelton (Hon. Mrs. A.). WOMEN AND THEIR WORK. *Cr. 8vo. 2s. 6d.*

M. M. HOW TO DRESS AND WHAT TO WEAR. *Cr. 8vo. 1s. net.*

Macaulay (Lord). CRITICAL AND HISTORICAL ESSAYS. Edited by F. C. MONTAGUE, M.A. *Three Volumes. Cr. 8vo. 18s.*
The only edition of this book completely annotated.

M'Allen (J. E. B.), M.A. See Commercial Series.

MacCulloch (J. A.). See Churchman's Library.

MacCunn (Florence A.). MARY STUART. With over 60 Illustrations, including a Frontispiece in Photogravure. *Demy 8vo. 10s. 6d. net.*
A Colonial Edition is also published. See also Leaders of Religion.

McDermott (E. R.). See Books on Business.

M'Dowall (A. S.). See Oxford Biographies.

Mackay (A. M.). See Churchman's Library.

Magnus (Laurie), M.A. A PRIMER OF WORDSWORTH. *Cr. 8vo. 2s. 6d.*

Mahaffy (J. P.), Litt.D. A HISTORY OF THE EGYPT OF THE PTOLEMIES. Fully Illustrated. *Cr. 8vo. 6s.*

Maitland (F. W.), LL.D., Downing Professor of the Laws of England in the University of Cambridge. CANON LAW IN ENGLAND. *Royal 8vo. 7s. 6d.*

Malden (H. E.), M.A. ENGLISH RECORDS. A Companion to the History of England. *Cr. 8vo. 3s. 6d.*
THE ENGLISH CITIZEN: HIS RIGHTS AND DUTIES. *Third Edition. Cr. 8vo. 1s. 6d.*
A SCHOOL HISTORY OF SURREY. Illustrated. *Cr. 8vo. 1s. 6d.*

Marchant (E. C.), M.A., Fellow of Peterhouse, Cambridge. A GREEK ANTHOLOGY. *Second Edition. Cr. 8vo. 3s. 6d.*

Marchant (C. E.), M.A., and **Cook (A. M.)**, M.A. PASSAGES FOR UNSEEN TRANSLATION. *Third Edition. Cr. 8vo. 3s. 6d.*

Marlowe (Christopher). See Standard Library.

Marr (J. E.), F.R.S., Fellow of St John's College, Cambridge. THE SCIENTIFIC STUDY OF SCENERY. *Second Edition.* Illustrated. *Cr. 8vo.* 6s.

AGRICULTURAL GEOLOGY. Illustrated. *Cr. 8vo.* 6s.

Marvell (Andrew). See Little Library.

Masefield (John). SEA LIFE IN NELSON'S TIME. Illustrated. *Cr. 8vo.* 3s. 6d. net.

*ON THE SPANISH MAIN. With Portraits and Illustrations. *Demy 8vo.* 10s. 6d. net.

A Colonial Edition is also published.

Maskell (A.). See Connoisseur's Library.

Mason (A. J.), D.D. See Leaders of Religion.

Massee (George). THE EVOLUTION OF PLANT LIFE: Lower Forms. Illustrated. *Cr. 8vo.* 2s. 6d.

Massinger (P.). See Standard Library.

Masterman (C. F. G.), M.A. TENNYSON AS A RELIGIOUS TEACHER. *Cr. 8vo.* 6s.

*Matheson (Hon. E. F.). COUNSELS OF LIFE. *Fcap. 8vo.* 3s. 6d. net.

May (Phil). THE PHIL MAY ALBUM. *Second Edition.* 4to. 1s. net.

Mellows (Emma S.). A SHORT STORY OF ENGLISH LITERATURE. *Cr. 8vo.* 3s. 6d.

Methuen (A. M. S.). THE TRAGEDY OF SOUTH AFRICA. *Cr. 8vo.* 2s. net. Also Cr. 8vo. 3d. net.

A revised and enlarged edition of the author's 'Peace or War in South Africa.'

ENGLAND'S RUIN : DISCUSSED IN SIXTEEN LETTERS TO THE RIGHT HON. JOSEPH CHAMBERLAIN, M.P. *Seventh Edition. Cr. 8vo.* 3d. net.

Michell (E. B.). THE ART AND PRACTICE OF HAWKING. With 3 Photogravures by G. E. LODGE, and other Illustrations. *Demy 8vo.* 10s. 6d.

Millais (J. G.). THE LIFE AND LETTERS OF SIR JOHN EVERETT MILLAIS, President of the Royal Academy. With many Illustrations, of which 2 are in Photogravure. *New Edition. Demy 8vo.* 7s. 6d. net.

A Colonial Edition is also published.

*Millin (G. F.). PICTORIAL GARDENING. Illustrated. *Cr. 8vo.* 3s. 6d. net.

Millis (C. T.), M.I.M.E. See Textbooks of Technology.

Milne (J. G.), M.A. A HISTORY OF ROMAN EGYPT. Fully Illustrated. *Cr. 8vo.* 6s.

Milton (John), THE POEMS OF, BOTH ENGLISH AND LATIN, Compos'd at several times. Printed by his true Copies.

The Songs were set in Musick by Mr. HENRY LAWES, Gentleman of the Kings Chappel, and one of His Majesties Private Musick.

Printed and publish'd according to Order. Printed by RUTH RAWORTH for HUMPHREY MOSELEY, and are to be sold at the signe of the Princes Armes in Pauls Churchyard, 1645.

See also Little Library Standard Library, and R. F. Towndrow.

Minchin (H. C.), M.A. See R. Peel.

Mitchell (P. Chalmers), M.A. OUTLINES OF BIOLOGY. Illustrated. *Second Edition. Cr. 8vo.* 6s.

Mitton (G. E.). JANE AUSTEN AND HER TIMES. With many Portraits and Illustrations. *Second Edition. Demy 8vo.* 10s. 6d. net.

A Colonial Edition is also published.

'**Moil (A.).**' See Books on Business.

Moir (D. M.). See Little Library.

Money (L. G. Chiozza). RICHES AND POVERTY *Second Edition Demy 8vo.* 5s. net.

Montaigne. See C. F. Pond.

Moore (H. E.). See S. Q. S.

Moran (Clarence G.). See Books on Business.

More (Sir Thomas). See Standard Library.

Morfill (W. R.), Oriel College, Oxford. A HISTORY OF RUSSIA FROM PETER THE GREAT TO ALEXANDER II. With Maps and Plans. *Cr. 8vo.* 3s. 6d.

Morich (R. J.), late of Clifton College. See School Examination Series.

*Morris (J.). THE MAKERS OF JAPAN. With many portraits and Illustrations. *Demy 8vo.* 12s. 6d. net.

A Colonial Edition is also published.

Morris (J. E.). See Little Guides.

Morton (Miss Anderson). See Miss Brodrick.

THE MOTOR YEAR-BOOK FOR 1906. With many Illustrations and Diagrams. *Demy 8vo.* 7s. 6d. net.

Moule (H. C. G.), D.D., Lord Bishop of Durham. See Leaders of Religion.

Muir (M. M. Pattison), M.A. THE CHEMISTRY OF FIRE. Illustrated. *Cr. 8vo.* 2s. 6d.

Mundella (V. A.), M.A. See J. T. Dunn.

Munro (R.), LL.D. See Antiquary's Books.

Naval Officer (A). See I. P. L.

Neal (W. G.). See R. N. Hall.

Newman (J. H.) and others. See Library of Devotion.

Nichols (J. B. B.). See Little Library.

Nicklin (T.), M.A. EXAMINATION PAPERS IN THUCYDIDES. *Cr. 8vo.* 2s.

Nimrod. See I. P. L.

*Norgate (G. Le G.). SIR WALTER SCOTT. Illustrated. *Demy 8vo.* 7s. 6d. net.

Norregaard (B. W.). THE GREAT SIEGE: The Investment and Fall of Port Arthur. Illustrated. *Demy 8vo.* 10s. 6d. net.

Northcote (James), R.A. THE CONVERSATIONS OF JAMES NORTHCOTE, R.A., AND JAMES WARD. Edited by ERNEST FLETCHER. With many Portraits. *Demy 8vo.* 10s. 6d.

Norway (A. H.). NAPLES. With 25 Coloured Illustrations by MAURICE GREIFFENHAGEN. A New Edition. *Cr. 8vo.* 6s.

Novalis. THE DISCIPLES AT SAÏS AND OTHER FRAGMENTS. Edited by Miss UNA BIRCH. *Fcap. 8vo.* 3s. 6d.

*****Oldfield (W. J.),** Canon of Lincoln. PRIMER OF RELIGION. *Fcap 8vo.* 2s. 6d.

Oliphant (Mrs.). See Leaders of Religion.

Oman (C. W. C.), M.A., Fellow of All Souls', Oxford. A HISTORY OF THE ART OF WAR. Vol. II.: The Middle Ages, from the Fourth to the Fourteenth Century. Illustrated. *Demy 8vo.* 10s. 6d. net.

Ottley (R. L.), D.D. See Handbooks of Theology and Leaders of Religion.

Overton (J. H.). See Leaders of Religion.

Owen (Douglas). See Books on Business.

Oxford (M. N.), of Guy's Hospital. A HANDBOOK OF NURSING. *Third Edition. Cr. 8vo.* 3s. 6d.

Pakes (W. C. C.). THE SCIENCE OF HYGIENE. Illustrated. *Demy 8vo.* 15s.

Palmer (Frederick). WITH KUROKI IN MANCHURIA. Illustrated. *Third Edition. Demy 8vo.* 7s. 6d. net.
A Colonial Edition is also published.

Parker (Gilbert). A LOVER'S DIARY. *Fcap. 8vo.* 5s.

*****Parkes (A. K.).** SMALL LESSONS ON GREAT TRUTHS. *Fcap. 8vo.* 1s. 6d.

Parkinson (John). PARADISI IN SOLE PARADISUS TERRESTRIS, OR A GARDEN OF ALL SORTS OF PLEASANT FLOWERS. *Folio.* £4, 4s. net.

Parmenter (John). HELIO-TROPES, OR NEW POSIES FOR SUNDIALS, 1625. Edited by PERCIVAL LANDON. *Quarto.* 3s. 6d. net.

Parmentier (Prof. Leon). See Byzantine Texts.

Pascal. See Library of Devotion.

Paston (George). SOCIAL CARICATURES IN THE EIGHTEENTH CENTURY. *Imperial Quarto.* £2, 12s. 6d. net. See also Little Books on Art and I.P.L.

Paterson (W. R.) (Benjamin Swift). LIFE'S QUESTIONINGS. *Cr. 8vo.* 3s. 6d. net.

Patterson (A. H.). NOTES OF AN EAST COAST NATURALIST. Illustrated in Colour by F. SOUTHGATE. *Second Edition. Cr. 8vo.* 6s.

NATURE IN EASTERN NORFOLK. A series of observations on the Birds, Fishes, Mammals, Reptiles, and stalk-eyed Crustaceans found in that neighbourhood, with a list of the species. With 12 Illustrations in colour, by FRANK SOUTHGATE. *Second Edition. Cr. 8vo.* 6s.

Peacock (N.). See Little Books on Art.

Pearce (E. H.), M.A. ANNALS OF CHRIST'S HOSPITAL. Illustrated. *Demy 8vo.* 7s. 6d.

Peel (Robert), and **Minchin (H. C.),** M.A. OXFORD. With 100 Illustrations in Colour. *Cr. 8vo.* 6s.

Peel (Sidney), late Fellow of Trinity College, Oxford, and Secretary to the Royal Commission on the Licensing Laws. PRACTICAL LICENSING REFORM. *Second Edition. Cr. 8vo.* 1s. 6d.

Peters (J. P.), D.D. See Churchman's Library.

Petrie (W. M. Flinders), D.C.L., LL.D., Professor of Egyptology at University College. A HISTORY OF EGYPT, FROM THE EARLIEST TIMES TO THE PRESENT DAY. Fully Illustrated. *In six volumes. Cr. 8vo.* 6s. each.

VOL. I. PREHISTORIC TIMES TO XVIth DYNASTY. *Fifth Edition.*

VOL. II. THE XVIITH AND XVIIITH DYNASTIES. *Fourth Edition.*

VOL. III. XIXTH TO XXXTH DYNASTIES.

VOL. IV. THE EGYPT OF THE PTOLEMIES. J. P. MAHAFFY, Litt.D.

VOL. V. ROMAN EGYPT. J. G. MILNE, M.A.

VOL. VI. EGYPT IN THE MIDDLE AGES. STANLEY LANE-POOLE, M.A.

RELIGION AND CONSCIENCE IN ANCIENT EGYPT. Illustrated. *Cr 8vo.* 2s. 6d.

SYRIA AND EGYPT, FROM THE TELL EL AMARNA TABLETS. *Cr. 8vo.* 2s. 6d.

EGYPTIAN TALES. Illustrated by TRISTRAM ELLIS. *In Two Volumes. Cr. 8vo.* 3s. 6d. each.

EGYPTIAN DECORATIVE ART. With 120 Illustrations. *Cr. 8vo.* 3s. 6d.

Phillips (W. A.). See Oxford Biographies.

Phillpotts (Eden). MY DEVON YEAR. With 38 Illustrations by J. LEY PETHYBRIDGE. *Second and Cheaper Edition. Large Cr. 8vo.* 6s.

UP ALONG AND DOWN ALONG. Illustrated by CLAUDE SHEPPERSON. *Cr. 4to.* 5s. net.
A volume of poems.

Pienaar (Philip). WITH STEYN AND DE WET. *Second Edition. Cr. 8vo.* 3s. 6d.
A Colonial Edition is also published.

Plarr (Victor G.) and **Walton (F. W.).** A SCHOOL HISTORY OF MIDDLESEX. Illustrated. *Cr. 8vo.* 1s. 6d.

Plato. See Standard Library.

Plautus. THE CAPTIVI. Edited, with an Introduction, Textual Notes, and a Commentary, by W. M. LINDSAY, Fellow of Jesus College, Oxford. *Demy 8vo.* 10s. 6d. *net.*

Plowden-Wardlaw (J. T.), B.A., King's College, Cambridge. See School Examination Series.

Pocock (Roger). A FRONTIERSMAN. *Third Edition. Cr. 8vo.* 6s.
A Colonial Edition is also published.

Podmore (Frank). MODERN SPIRITUALISM. *Two Volumes. Demy 8vo.* 21s. *net.*
A History and a Criticism.

Poer (J. Patrick Le). A MODERN LEGIONARY. *Cr. 8vo.* 6s.
A Colonial Edition is also published.

Pollard (Alice). See Little Books on Art.

Pollard (A. W.). OLD PICTURE BOOKS. Illustrated. *Demy 8vo.* 7s. 6d. *net.*

Pollard (Eliza F.). See Little Books on Art.

Pollock (David), M.I.N.A. See Books on Business.

Pond (C. F.). A DAY BOOK OF MONTAIGNE. Edited by. *Fcap. 8vo.* 3s. 6d. *net.*

Potter (M. C.), M.A., F.L.S. A TEXTBOOK OF AGRICULTURAL BOTANY. Illustrated. *Second Edition. Cr. 8vo.* 4s. 6d.

Power (J. O'Connor). THE MAKING OF AN ORATOR. *Cr. 8vo.* 6s.

Pradeau (G.). A KEY TO THE TIME ALLUSIONS IN THE DIVINE COMEDY. With a Dial. *Small quarto.* 3s. 6d.

Prance (G.). See Half-Crown Library.

Prescott (O. L.). ABOUT MUSIC, AND WHAT IT IS MADE OF. *Cr. 8vo.* 3s. 6d. *net.*

Price (L. L.), M.A., Fellow of Oriel College, Oxon. A HISTORY OF ENGLISH POLITICAL ECONOMY. *Fourth Edition. Cr. 8vo.* 2s. 6d.

Primrose (Deborah). A MODERN BŒOTIA. *Cr. 8vo.* 6s.

Pugin and Rowlandson. THE MICROCOSM OF LONDON, OR LONDON IN MINIATURE. With 104 Illustrations in colour. *In Three Volumes. Small 4to.* £3, 3s. *net.*

'Q' (A. T. Quiller Couch). See Half-Crown Library.

Quevedo Villegas. See Miniature Library.

G.R. and E.S. THE WOODHOUSE CORRESPONDENCE. *Cr. 8vo.* 6s.
A Colonial Edition is also published.

Rackham (R. B.), M.A. See Westminster Commentaries.

Randolph (B. W.), D.D. See Library of Devotion.

Rannie (D. W.), M.A. A STUDENT'S HISTORY OF SCOTLAND. *Cr. 8vo.* 3s. 6d.

Rashdall (Hastings), M.A., Fellow and Tutor of New College, Oxford. DOCTRINE AND DEVELOPMENT. *Cr. 8vo.* 6s.

Rawstorne (Lawrence, Esq.). See I.P.L.

*Raymond (Walter). A SCHOOL HISTORY OF SOMERSETSHIRE. Illustrated. *Cr. 8vo.* 1s. 6d.

A Real Paddy. See I.P.L.

Reason (W.), M.A. See S.Q.S.

Redfern (W. B.), Author of 'Ancient Wood and Iron Work in Cambridge,' etc. ROYAL AND HISTORIC GLOVES AND ANCIENT SHOES. Profusely Illustrated in colour and half-tone. *Quarto,* £2, 2s. *net.*

Reynolds. See Little Galleries.

*Rhodes (W. E.). A SCHOOL HISTORY OF LANCASHIRE. Illustrated. *Cr. 8vo.* 1s. 6d.

Roberts (M. E.). See C. C. Channer.

Robertson (A.), D.D., Lord Bishop of Exeter. REGNUM DEI. The Bampton Lectures of 1901. *Demy 8vo.* 12s. 6d. *net.*

Robertson (C. Grant). M.A., Fellow of All Souls' College, Oxford, Examiner in the Honours School of Modern History, Oxford, 1901-1904. SELECT STATUTES, CASES, AND CONSTITUTIONAL DOCUMENTS, 1660-1832. *Demy 8vo.* 10s. 6d. *net.*

Robertson (C. Grant) and Bartholomew (J. G.), F.R.S.E., F.R.G.S. A HISTORICAL AND MODERN ATLAS OF THE BRITISH EMPIRE. *Quarto.* 4s. 6d. *net.*

Robertson (Sir G. S.), K.C.S.I. See Half-Crown Library.

Robinson (A. W.), M.A. See Churchman's Bible.

Robinson (Cecilia). THE MINISTRY OF DEACONESSES. With an Introduction by the late Archbishop of Canterbury. *Cr. 8vo.* 3s. 6d.

Robinson (F. S.). See Connoisseur's Library.

Rochefoucauld (La). See Little Library.

Rodwell (G.), B.A. NEW TESTAMENT GREEK. A Course for Beginners. With a Preface by WALTER LOCK, D.D., Warden of Keble College. *Fcap. 8vo.* 3s. 6d.

Roe (Fred). ANCIENT COFFERS AND CUPBOARDS: Their History and Description. Illustrated. *Quarto.* £3, 3s. *net.*
OLD OAK FURNITURE. With many Illustrations by the Author, including a frontispiece in colour. *Demy 8vo.* 10s. 6d. *net.*

Rogers (A. G. L.), M.A. See Books on Business.

Roscoe (E. S.). ROBERT HARLEY, EARL OF OXFORD. Illustrated. *Demy 8vo.* 7s. 6d.
This is the only life of Harley in existence.
See also Little Guides.

Rose (Edward). THE ROSE READER. Illustrated. *Cr. 8vo. 2s. 6d.* Also in 4 Parts. Parts I. and II. 6d. each; Part III. 8d.; Part IV. 10d.

*Rouse (W. H. D.). WORDS OF THE ANCIENT WISE: Thoughts from Epictetus and Marcus Aurelius. Edited by. *Fcap. 8vo. 3s. 6d. net.*

Rowntree (Joshua). THE IMPERIAL DRUG TRADE. *Second Edition. Cr. 8vo. 5s. net.*

Rubie (A. E.), D.D. See Junior School Books.

Russell (W. Clark). THE LIFE OF ADMIRAL LORD COLLINGWOOD. With Illustrations by F. BRANGWYN. *Fourth Edition. Cr. 8vo. 6s.*
A Colonial Edition is also published.

St. Anslem. See Library of Devotion.

St. Augustine. See Library of Devotion.

St. Cyres (Viscount). See Oxford Biographies.

St. Francis of Assisi. See Standard Library.

'Saki' (H. Munro). REGINALD. *Second Edition. Fcap. 8vo. 2s. 6d. net.*

Sales (St. Francis de). See Library of Devotion.

Salmon (A. L.). A POPULAR GUIDE TO DEVON. *Medium 8vo. 6d. net.* See also Little Guides.

Sargeant (J.), M.A. ANNALS OF WESTMINSTER SCHOOL. Illustrated. *Demy 8vo. 7s. 6d.*

Sathas (C.). See Byzantine Texts.

Schmitt (John). See Byzantine Texts.

Scott (A. M.). WINSTON SPENCER CHURCHILL. With Portraits and Illustrations. *Cr. 8vo. 3s. 6d.*
A Colonial Edition is also published.

Seeley (H. G.), F.R.S. DRAGONS OF THE AIR. Illustrated. *Cr. 8vo. 6s.*

*Selincourt (E. de). A DAY BOOK OF KEATS. Edited by. *Fcap. 8vo. 3s. 6d. net.*

Sells (V. P.), M.A. THE MECHANICS OF DAILY LIFE. Illustrated. *Cr. 8vo. 2s. 6d.*

Selous (Edmund). TOMMY SMITH'S ANIMALS. Illustrated by G. W. ORD. *Fourth Edition. Fcap. 8vo. 2s. 6d.*

Settle (J. H.). ANECDOTES OF SOLDIERS, in Peace and War. *Cr. 8vo. 3s. 6d. net.*
A Colonial Edition is also published.

Shakespeare (William).
THE FOUR FOLIOS, 1623; 1632; 1664; 1685. Each *Four Guineas net*, or a complete set, *Twelve Guineas net.*
The Arden Shakespeare.
Demy 8vo. 2s. 6d. net each volume. General Editor, W. J. CRAIG. An Edition of Shakespeare in single Plays. Edited with a full Introduction, Textual Notes, and a Commentary at the foot of the page.

HAMLET. Edited by EDWARD DOWDEN, Litt.D.
ROMEO AND JULIET. Edited by EDWARD DOWDEN, Litt.D.
KING LEAR. Edited by W. J. CRAIG.
JULIUS CAESAR. Edited by M. MACMILLAN, M.A.
THE TEMPEST. Edited by MORETON LUCE.
OTHELLO. Edited by H. C. HART.
TITUS ANDRONICUS. Edited by H. B. BAILDON.
CYMBELINE. Edited by EDWARD DOWDEN.
THE MERRY WIVES OF WINDSOR. Edited by H. C. HART.
A MIDSUMMER NIGHT'S DREAM. Edited by H. CUNINGHAM.
KING HENRY V. Edited by H. A. EVANS.
ALL'S WELL THAT ENDS WELL. Edited by W. O. BRIGSTOCKE.
THE TAMING OF THE SHREW. Edited by R. WARWICK BOND.
TIMON OF ATHENS. Edited by K. DEIGHTON.
MEASURE FOR MEASURE. Edited by H. C. HART.
*TWELFTH NIGHT. Edited by MORETON LUCE.
THE MERCHANT OF VENICE. Edited by C. KNOX POOLER.
*TROILUS AND CRESSIDA. Edited by K. DEIGHTON.

The Little Quarto Shakespeare. Edited by W. J. CRAIG. With Introductions and Notes. *Pott 16mo. In 40 Volumes. Leather, price 1s. net each volume.* Mahogany Revolving Book Case. *10s. net.*
See also Standard Library.

Sharp (A.). VICTORIAN POETS. *Cr. 8vo. 2s. 6d.*

Sharp (Cecil). See S. Baring-Gould.

Sharp (Mrs. E. A.). See Little Books on Art.

Shedlock (J. S.) THE PIANOFORTE SONATA. *Cr. 8vo. 5s.*

Shelley (Percy B.). ADONAIS; an Elegy on the death of John Keats, Author of 'Endymion,' etc. Pisa. From the types of Didot, 1821. *2s. net.*

Sheppard (H. F.), M.A. See S. Baring-Gould.

Sherwell (Arthur), M.A. See S.Q.S.

Shipley (Mary E.). AN ENGLISH CHURCH HISTORY FOR CHILDREN. With a Preface by the Bishop of Gibraltar. With Maps and Illustrations. Part I. *Cr. 8vo. 2s. 6d. net.*

Sichel (Walter). DISRAELI: A Study in Personality and Ideas. With 3 Portraits. *Demy 8vo. 12s. 6d. net.*
A Colonial Edition is also published.
See also Oxford Biographies.

Sime (J.). See Little Books on Art.

Simonson (G. A.). FRANCESCO GUARDI. With 41 Plates. *Imperial 4to. £2, 2s. net.*

Sketchley (R. E. D.). See Little Books on Art.

Skipton (H. P. K.). See Little Books on Art.

Sladen (Douglas). SICILY: The New Winter Resort. With over 200 Illustrations. *Second Edition. Cr. 8vo. 5s. net.*

Small (Evan), M.A. THE EARTH. An Introduction to Physiography. Illustrated. *Cr. 8vo. 2s. 6d.*

Smallwood (M. G.). See Little Books on Art.

Smedley (F. E.). See I.P.L.

Smith (Adam). THE WEALTH OF NATIONS. Edited with an Introduction and numerous Notes by EDWIN CANNAN, M.A. *Two volumes. Demy 8vo. 21s. net.*
See also English Library.

Smith (Horace and James). See Little Library.

Smith (H. Bompas), M.A. A NEW JUNIOR ARITHMETIC. *Crown 8vo. 2s. 6d.*

Smith (R. Mudie). THOUGHTS FOR THE DAY. Edited by. *Fcap. 8vo. 3s. 6d. net.*

Smith (Nowell C.). See W. Wordsworth.

Smith (John Thomas). A BOOK FOR A RAINY DAY: Or Recollections of the Events of the Years 1766-1833. Edited by WILFRED WHITTEN. Illustrated. *Demy 8vo. 12s. 6d. net.*

Snell (F. J.). A BOOK OF EXMOOR. Illustrated. *Cr. 8vo. 6s.*

Snowden (C. E.). A HANDY DIGEST OF BRITISH HISTORY. *Demy 8vo. 4s. 6d.*

Sophocles. See Classical Translations.

Sornet (L. A.). See Junior School Books.

South (Wilton E.), M.A. See Junior School Books.

Southey (R.). ENGLISH SEAMEN. Edited by DAVID HANNAY.
Vol. I. (Howard, Clifford, Hawkins, Drake, Cavendish). *Second Edition. Cr. 8vo. 6s.*
Vol. II. (Richard Hawkins, Grenville, Essex, and Raleigh). *Cr. 8vo. 6s.*
See also Standard Library.

Spence (C. H.), M.A. See School Examination Series.

Spooner (W. A.), M.A. See Leaders of Religion.

*Staley (Edgcumbe). THE GUILDS OF FLORENCE. Illustrated. *Royal 8vo. 21s. net.*

Stanbridge (J. W.), B.D. See Library of Devotion.

'Stancliffe.' GOLF DO'S AND DONT'S. *Second Edition. Fcap. 8vo. 1s.*

Stead (D. W.). See D. Gallaher.

Stedman (A. M. M.), M.A.
INITIA LATINA: Easy Lessons on Elementary Accidence. *Eighth Edition. Fcap. 8vo. 1s.*

FIRST LATIN LESSONS. *Ninth Edition. Cr. 8vo. 2s.*

FIRST LATIN READER. With Notes adapted to the Shorter Latin Primer and Vocabulary. *Sixth Edition revised. 18mo. 1s. 6d.*

EASY SELECTIONS FROM CÆSAR. The Helvetian War. *Second Edition 18mo. 1s.*

EASY SELECTIONS FROM LIVY. The Kings of Rome. *18mo. Second Edition. 1s. 6d.*

EASY LATIN PASSAGES FOR UNSEEN TRANSLATION. *Tenth Edition Fcap. 8vo. 1s. 6d.*

EXEMPLA LATINA. First Exercises in Latin Accidence. With Vocabulary. *Third Edition. Cr. 8vo. 1s.*

EASY LATIN EXERCISES ON THE SYNTAX OF THE SHORTER AND REVISED LATIN PRIMER. With Vocabulary. *Tenth and Cheaper Edition, re-written. Cr. 8vo. 1s. 6d. Original Edition. 2s. 6d.* KEY, 3s. net.

THE LATIN COMPOUND SENTENCE: Rules and Exercises. *Second Edition. Cr. 8vo. 1s. 6d.* With Vocabulary. 2s.

NOTANDA QUAEDAM: Miscellaneous Latin Exercises on Common Rules and Idioms. *Fourth Edition. Fcap. 8vo. 1s. 6d.* With Vocabulary. 2s. Key, 2s. net.

LATIN VOCABULARIES FOR REPETITION: Arranged according to Subjects. *Thirteenth Edition. Fcap. 8vo. 1s. 6d.*

A VOCABULARY OF LATIN IDIOMS. *18mo. Second Edition. 1s.*

STEPS TO GREEK. *Second Edition, revised. 18mo. 1s.*

A SHORTER GREEK PRIMER. *Cr. 8vo. 1s. 6d.*

EASY GREEK PASSAGES FOR UNSEEN TRANSLATION. *Third Edition, revised. Fcap. 8vo. 1s. 6d.*

GREEK VOCABULARIES FOR REPETITION. Arranged according to Subjects. *Fourth Edition. Fcap. 8vo. 1s. 6d.*

GREEK TESTAMENT SELECTIONS. For the use of Schools. With Introduction, Notes, and Vocabulary. *Fourth Edition. Fcap. 8vo. 2s. 6d.*

STEPS TO FRENCH. *Seventh Edition. 18mo. 8d.*

FIRST FRENCH LESSONS. *Seventh Edition, revised. Cr. 8vo. 1s.*

EASY FRENCH PASSAGES FOR UNSEEN TRANSLATION. *Fifth Edition, revised. Fcap. 8vo. 1s. 6d.*

EASY FRENCH EXERCISES ON ELE-
MENTARY SYNTAX. With Vocabu-
lary. *Fourth Edition. Cr. 8vo. 2s. 6d.*
KEY. 3s. net.

FRENCH VOCABULARIES FOR RE-
PETITION: Arranged according to Sub-
jects. *Twelfth Edition. Fcap. 8vo. 1s.*
See also School Examination Series.

Steel (R. Elliott), M.A., F.C.S. THE
WORLD OF SCIENCE. With 147
Illustrations. *Second Edition. Cr. 8vo. 2s. 6d.*
See also School Examination Series.

Stephenson (C.), of the Technical College,
Bradford, and Suddards (F.) of the
Yorkshire College, Leeds. ORNAMEN-
TAL DESIGN FOR WOVEN FABRICS.
Illustrated. *Demy 8vo. Third Edition.*
7s. 6d.

Stephenson (J.), M.A. THE CHIEF
TRUTHS OF THE CHRISTIAN
FAITH. *Crown 8vo. 3s. 6d.*

Sterne (Laurence). See Little Library.

Sterry (W.). M.A. ANNALS OF ETON
COLLEGE. Illustrated. *Demy 8vo. 7s. 6d.*

Steuart (Katherine). BY ALLAN
WATER. *Second Edition. Cr. 8vo. 6s.*

Stevenson (R. L.) THE LETTERS OF
ROBERT LOUIS STEVENSON TO
HIS FAMILY AND FRIENDS.
Selected and Edited by SIDNEY COLVIN.
Sixth Edition. Cr. 8vo. 12s.
LIBRARY EDITION. *Demy 8vo. 2 vols. 25s.*
net.
A Colonial Edition is also published.

VAILIMA LETTERS. With an Etched
Portrait by WILLIAM STRANG. *Fifth
Edition. Cr. 8vo. Buckram. 6s.*
A Colonial Edition is also published.

THE LIFE OF R. L. STEVENSON. See
G. Balfour.

Stevenson (M. I.). FROM SARANAC
TO THE MARQUESAS. Being Letters
written by Mrs. M. I. STEVENSON during
1887-8. *Cr. 8vo. 6s. net.*
A Colonial Edition is also published.

LETTERS FROM SAMOA. Edited and
arranged by M. C. BALFOUR. With many
Illustrations. *Cr. 8vo. 6s. net.*

Stoddart (Anna M.). See Oxford Biographies.

Stokes (F. G.), B.A. HOURS WITH
RABELAIS. From the translation of SIR
T. URQUHART and P. A. MOTTEUX. With
a Portrait in Photogravure. *Cr. 8vo. 3s. 6d.
net.*

Stone (S. J.). POEMS AND HYMNS.
With a Memoir by F. G. ELLERTON,
M.A. With Portrait. *Cr. 8vo. 6s.*

*Storr (Vernon F.), M.A., Lecturer in
the Philosophy of Religion in Cambridge
University; Examining Chaplain to the
Archbishop of Canterbury; formerly Fellow
of University College, Oxford. DEVELOP-
MENT AND DIVINE PURPOSE. *Cr.
8vo. 5s. net.*

Straker (F.). See Books on Business.

Streane (A. W.), D.D. See Churchman's
Bible.

Stroud (H.), D.Sc., M.A. See Textbooks of
Science.

Strutt (Joseph). THE SPORTS AND
PASTIMES OF THE PEOPLE OF
ENGLAND. Illustrated by many engrav-
ings. Revised by J. CHARLES COX, LL.D.,
F.S.A. *Quarto. 21s. net.*

Stuart (Capt. Donald). THE STRUGGLE
FOR PERSIA. With a Map. *Cr. 8vo. 6s.*

*Sturch (F.), Staff Instructor to the Surrey
County Council. SOLUTIONS TO THE
CITY AND GUILDS QUESTIONS
IN MANUAL INSTRUCTION DRAW-
ING. *Imp. 4to. 5s. net.*

Suckling (Sir John). FRAGMENTA
AUREA: a Collection of all the Incom-
parable Peeces, written by. And published
by a friend to perpetuate his memory.
Printed by his own copies.
Printed for HUMPHREY MOSELEY, and
are to be sold at his shop, at the sign of the
Princes Arms in St. Paul's Churchyard,
1646.

Suddards (F.). See C. Stephenson.

Surtees (R. S.). See I.P.L.

Swift (Jonathan). THE JOURNAL TO
STELLA. Edited by G. A. AITKEN. *Cr.
8vo. 6s.*

Symes (J. E.), M.A. THE FRENCH
REVOLUTION. *Second Edition. Cr. 8vo.
2s. 6d.*

Sympson (E. M.), M.A., M.D. See Ancient
Cities.

Syrett (Netta). See Little Blue Books.

Tacitus. AGRICOLA. With Introduction
Notes, Map, etc. By R. F. DAVIS, M.A.,
Fcap. 8vo. 2s.

GERMANIA. By the same Editor. *Fcap.
8vo. 2s.* See also Classical Translations.

Tallack (W.). HOWARD LETTERS
AND MEMORIES. *Demy 8vo. 10s. 6d.
net.*

Tauler (J.). See Library of Devotion.

Taunton (E. L.). A HISTORY OF THE
JESUITS IN ENGLAND. Illustrated.
Demy 8vo. 21s. net.

Taylor (A. E.). THE ELEMENTS OF
METAPHYSICS. *Demy 8vo. 10s. 6d. net.*

Taylor (F. G.), M.A. See Commercial Series.

Taylor (I. A.). See Oxford Biographies.

Taylor (T. M.), M.A., Fellow of Gonville
and Caius College, Cambridge. A CON-
STITUTIONAL AND POLITICAL
HISTORY OF ROME. *Cr. 8vo. 7s. 6d.*

Tennyson (Alfred, Lord). THE EARLY
POEMS OF. Edited, with Notes and
an Introduction, by J. CHURTON COLLINS,
M.A. *Cr. 8vo. 6s.*

IN MEMORIAM, MAUD, AND THE
PRINCESS. Edited by J. CHURTON
COLLINS, M.A. *Cr. 8vo. 6s.* See also
Little Library.

Terry (C. S.).   See Oxford Biographies.

Terton (Alice). LIGHTS AND SHADOWS IN A HOSPITAL. *Cr. 8vo.* 3s. 6d.

Thackeray (W. M.).   See Little Library.

Theobald (F. V.), M.A. INSECT LIFE. Illustrated. *Second Ed. Revised. Cr. 8vo.* 2s. 6d.

Thompson (A. W.).   See Little Guides.

Tileston (Mary W.). DAILY STRENGTH FOR DAILY NEEDS. *Twelfth Edition. Medium 16mo.* 2s. 6d. net. Also an edition in superior binding, 6s.

Tompkins (H. W.), F.R.H.S.   See Little Guides.

Towndrow (R. F.). A DAY BOOK OF MILTON. Edited by. *Fcap. 8vo.* 3s. 6d. net.

Townley (Lady Susan). MY CHINESE NOTE-BOOK   With 16 Illustrations and 2 Maps. *Third Edition. Demy 8vo.* 10s. 6d. net.
    A Colonial Edition is also published.

*****Toynbee (Paget),** M.A., D.Litt. DANTE IN ENGLISH LITERATURE. *Demy 8vo.* 12s. 6d. net.
    See also Oxford Biographies.

Trench (Herbert). DEIRDRE WED and Other Poems. *Cr. 8vo.* 5s.

Trevelyan (G. M.), Fellow of Trinity College, Cambridge. ENGLAND UNDER THE STUARTS. With Maps and Plans. *Second Edition. Demy 8vo.* 10s. 6d. net.

Troutbeck (G. E.).   See Little Guides.

Tyler (E. A.), B.A., F.C.S.   See Junior School Books.

Tyrell-Gill (Frances).   See Little Books on Art.

Vardon (Harry). THE COMPLETE GOLFER. Illustrated. *Sixth Edition. Demy 8vo.* 10s. 6d. net.
    A Colonial Edition is also published.

Vaughan (Henry).   See Little Library.

Voegelin (A.), M.A.   See Junior Examination Series.

Waddell (Col. L. A.), LL.D., C.B. LHASA AND ITS MYSTERIES. With a Record of the Expedition of 1903-1904. With 2000 Illustrations and Maps. *Demy 8vo.* 21s. net.
    *Also Third and Cheaper Edition. With 155 Illustrations and Maps. *Demy 8vo.* 10s. 6d. net.

Wade (G. W.), D.D. OLD TESTAMENT HISTORY. With Maps. *Third Edition. Cr. 8vo.* 6s.

Wagner (Richard).   See A. L. Cleather.

Wall (J. C.). DEVILS. Illustrated by the Author and from photographs. *Demy 8vo.* 4s. 6d. net.   See also Antiquary's Books.

Walters (H. B.).   See Little Books on Art.

Walton (F. W.).   See Victor G. Plarr.

Walton (Izaac) and **Cotton (Charles).** See I.P.L., English Library, and Little Library.

Warmelo (D. S. Van). ON COMMANDO. With Portrait. *Cr. 8vo.* 3s. 6d.
    A Colonial Edition is also published.

Warren-Vernon (Hon. William), M.A. READINGS ON THE INFERNO OF DANTE, chiefly Based on the Commentary of BENVENUTO DA IMOLA. With an Introduction by the Rev. Dr. MOORE. In Two Volumes. *Second Edition. Cr. 8vo.* 15s. net.

Waterhouse (Mrs. Alfred). WITH THE SIMPLE-HEARTED : Little Homilies to Women in Country Places. *Second Edition. Small Pott 8vo.* 2s. net.   See also Little Library.

Weatherhead (T. C.), M.A. EXAMINATION PAPERS IN HORACE. *Cr. 8vo.* 2s.   See also Junior Examination Series.

Webb (W. T.).   See Little Blue Books.

Webber (F. C.).   See Textbooks of Technology.

Wells (Sidney H.).   See Textbooks of Science.

Wells (J.), M.A., Fellow and Tutor of Wadham College. OXFORD AND OXFORD LIFE. *Third Edition. Cr. 8vo.* 3s. 6d.
A SHORT HISTORY OF ROME. *Sixth Edition.* With 3 Maps. *Cr. 8vo.* 3s. 6d.
    See also Little Guides.

'Westminster Gazette' Office Boy (Francis Brown). THE DOINGS OF ARTHUR. *Cr. 4to.* 2s. 6d. net.

Wetmore (Helen C.). THE LAST OF THE GREAT SCOUTS ('Buffalo Bill'). Illustrated. *Second Edition. Demy 8vo.* 6s.
    A Colonial Edition is also published.

Whibley (C).   See Half-crown Library.

Whibley (L.), M.A., Fellow of Pembroke College, Cambridge. GREEK OLIGARCHIES : THEIR ORGANISATION AND CHARACTER. *Cr. 8vo.* 6s.

Whitaker (G. H.), M.A.   See Churchman's Bible.

White (Gilbert). THE NATURAL HISTORY OF SELBORNE. Edited by L. C. MIALL, F.R.S., assisted by W. WARDE FOWLER, M.A. *Cr. 8vo.* 6s.   See also Standard Library.

Whitfield (E. E.).   See Commercial Series.

Whitehead (A. W.). GASPARD DE COLIGNY. Illustrated. *Demy 8vo.* 12s. 6d. net.

Whiteley (R. Lloyd), F.I.C., Principal of the Municipal Science School, West Bromwich. AN ELEMENTARY TEXT-BOOK OF INORGANIC CHEMISTRY. *Cr. 8vo.* 2s. 6d.

Whitley (Miss).   See S.Q.S.

Whitten (W.).   See John Thomas Smith.

Whyte (A. G.), B.Sc.   See Books on Business.

Wilberforce (Wilfrid).   See Little Books on Art.

Wilde (Oscar). DE PROFUNDIS. *Sixth Edition. Cr. 8vo.* 5s. net.
    A Colonial Edition is also published.

Wilkins (W. H.), B.A. See S.Q.S.

Wilkinson (J. Frome). See S.Q.S.

*__Williams (A.).__ PETROL PETER: or Mirth for Motorists. Illustrated in Colour by A. W. MILLS. *Demy 4to. 3s. 6d. net.*

Williamson (M. G.). See Ancient Cities.

Williamson (W.). THE BRITISH GARDENER. Illustrated. *Demy 8vo. 10s. 6d.*

Williamson (W.), B.A. See Junior Examination Series, Junior School Books, and Beginner's Books.

Willson (Beckles). LORD STRATHCONA: the Story of his Life. Illustrated. *Demy 8vo. 7s. 6d.*
A Colonial Edition is also published.

Wilmot-Buxton (E. M.). MAKERS OF EUROPE. *Cr. 8vo. Fourth Ed. 3s. 6d.*
A Text-book of European History for Middle Forms.

THE ANCIENT WORLD. With Maps and Illustrations. *Cr. 8vo. 3s. 6d.*
See also Beginner's Books.

Wilson (Bishop.). See Library of Devotion.

Wilson (A. J.). See Books on Business.

Wilson (H. A.). See Books on Business.

Wilton (Richard), M.A. LYRA PASTORALIS : Songs of Nature, Church, and Home. *Pott 8vo. 2s. 6d.*

Winbolt (S. E.), M.A. EXERCISES IN LATIN ACCIDENCE. *Cr. 8vo. 1s. 6d.*

LATIN HEXAMETER VERSE : An Aid to Composition. *Cr. 8vo. 3s. 6d.* KEY, *5s. net.*

Windle (B. C. A.), D.Sc., F.R.S. See Antiquary's Books, Little Guides and Ancient Cities.

Winterbotham (Canon), M.A., B.Sc., LL.B. See Churchman's Library.

Wood (J. A. E.). See Textbooks of Technology.

Wood (J. Hickory). DAN LENO. Illustrated. *Third Edition. Cr. 8vo. 6s.*
A Colonial Edition is also published.

Wood (W. Birkbeck), M.A., late Scholar of Worcester College, Oxford, and **Edmonds (Major J. E.)**, R.E., D.A.Q.-M.G. A HISTORY OF THE CIVIL WAR IN THE UNITED STATES. With an Introduction by H. SPENSER WILKINSON. With 24 Maps and Plans. *Demy 8vo. 12s. 6d. net.*

Wordsworth (Christopher). See Antiquary's Books.

*__Wordsworth (W.).__ THE POEMS OF. With Introduction and Notes by NOWELL C. SMITH, Fellow of New College, Oxford. *In Four Volumes. Demy 8vo. 5s. net each.* See also Little Library.

Wordsworth (W.) and Coleridge (S. T.). See Little Library.

Wright (Arthur), M.A., Fellow of Queen's College, Cambridge See Churchman's Library.

Wright (C. Gordon). See Dante.

Wright (J. C.). TO-DAY. *Fcap. 16mo. 1s. net.*

Wright (Sophie). GERMAN VOCABULARIES FOR REPETITION. *Fcap. 8vo. 1s. 6d.*

Wrong (George M.), Professor of History in the University of Toronto. THE EARL OF ELGIN. Illustrated. *Demy 8vo. 7s. 6d. net.*
A Colonial Edition is also published.

Wyatt (Kate) and Gloag (M.). A BOOK OF ENGLISH GARDENS. With 24 Illustrations in Colour. *Cr. 8vo. 10s. 6s. net.*

Wylde (A. B.). MODERN ABYSSINIA. With a Map and a Portrait. *Demy 8vo. 15s. net.*
A Colonial Edition is also published

Wyndham (George). THE POEMS OF WILLIAM SHAKESPEARE. With an Introduction and Notes. *Demy 8vo. Buckram, gilt top. 10s. 6d.*

Wyon (R.). See Half-crown Library.

Yeats (W. B.). AN ANTHOLOGY OF IRISH VERSE. *Revised and Enlarged Edition. Cr. 8vo. 3s. 6d.*

Young (Filson). THE COMPLETE MOTORIST. With 138 Illustrations. *Fifth Edition. Demy 8vo. 12s. 6d. net.*
A Colonial Edition is also published.

Young (T. M.). THE AMERICAN COTTON INDUSTRY: A Study of Work and Workers. *Cr. 8vo. Cloth, 2s. 6d. ; paper boards, 1s. 6d.*

Zimmern (Antonia). WHAT DO WE KNOW CONCERNING ELECTRICITY? *Fcap. 8vo. 1s. 6d. net.*

Ancient Cities

General Editor, B. C. A. WINDLE, D.Sc., F.R.S.

Cr. 8vo. 4s. 6d. net.

CHESTER. By B. C. A. Windle, D.Sc. F.R.S. Illustrated by E. H. New.

SHREWSBURY. By T. Auden, M.A., F.S.A. Illustrated.

CANTERBURY. By J. C. Cox, LL.D., F.S.A. Illustrated.

*EDINBURGH. By M. G. Williamson. Illustrated by Herbert Railton.

*LINCOLN. By E. Mansel Sympson, M.A., M.D. Illustrated by E. H. New.

Antiquary's Books, The

General Editor, J. CHARLES COX, LL.D., F.S.A.

A series of volumes dealing with various branches of English Antiquities: comprehensive and popular, as well as accurate and scholarly.

Demy 8vo.   7s. 6d. net.

ENGLISH MONASTIC LIFE. By the Right Rev. Abbot Gasquet, O.S B. Illustrated. *Third Edition.*

REMAINS OF THE PREHISTORIC AGE IN ENGLAND. By B. C. A. Windle, D.Sc., F.R.S. With numerous Illustrations and Plans.

OLD SERVICE BOOKS OF THE ENGLISH CHURCH. By Christopher Wordsworth, M.A., and Henry Littlehales. With Coloured and other Illustrations.

CELTIC ART. By J. Romilly Allen, F.S.A. With numerous Illustrations and Plans.

ARCHÆOLOGY AND FALSE ANTIQUITIES. By R. Munro, LL.D. Illustrated.

SHRINES OF BRITISH SAINTS. By J. C. Wall. With numerous Illustrations and Plans.

THE ROYAL FORESTS OF ENGLAND. By J. C. Cox, LL.D., F.S.A. Illustrated.

*THE MANOR AND MANORIAL RECORDS. By Nathaniel J. Hone. Illustrated.

*SEALS. By J. Harvey Bloom. Illustrated.

Beginner's Books, The

Edited by W. WILLIAMSON, B.A.

EASY FRENCH RHYMES. By Henri Blouet. Illustrated. *Fcap. 8vo.* 1s.

EASY STORIES FROM ENGLISH HISTORY. By E. M. Wilmot-Buxton, Author of ' Makers of Europe.' *Cr. 8vo.* 1s.

EASY EXERCISES IN ARITHMETIC. Arranged by W. S. Beard. *Fcap. 8vo.* Without Answers, 1s. With Answers, 1s. 3d.

EASY DICTATION AND SPELLING. By W. Williamson, B.A. *Fourth Edition. Fcap. 8vo.* 1s.

Business, Books on

Cr. 8vo.   2s. 6d. net.

A series of volumes dealing with all the most important aspects of commercial and financial activity. The volumes are intended to treat separately all the considerable industries and forms of business, and to explain accurately and clearly what they do and how they do it. Some are Illustrated. The first volumes are—

PORTS AND DOCKS. By Douglas Owen.

RAILWAYS. By E. R. McDermott.

THE STOCK EXCHANGE. By Chas. Duguid. *Second Edition.*

THE BUSINESS OF INSURANCE. By A. J. Wilson.

THE ELECTRICAL INDUSTRY: LIGHTING, TRACTION, AND POWER. By A. G. Whyte, B.Sc.

THE SHIPBUILDING INDUSTRY: Its History, Science, Practice, and Finance. By David Pollock, M.I.N.A.

THE MONEY MARKET. By F. Straker.

THE BUSINESS SIDE OF AGRICULTURE. By A. G. L. Rogers, M.A.

LAW IN BUSINESS. By H. A. Wilson.

THE BREWING INDUSTRY. By Julian L. Baker, F.I.C., F.C.S.

THE AUTOMOBILE INDUSTRY. By G. de H. Stone.

MINING AND MINING INVESTMENTS. By ' A. Moil.'

THE BUSINESS OF ADVERTISING. By Clarence G. Moran, Barrister-at-Law. Illustrated.

TRADE UNIONS. By G. Drage.

CIVIL ENGINEERING. By T. Claxton Fidler, M.Inst. C.E. Illustrated.

THE IRON TRADE. By J. Stephen Jeans. Illustrated.

MONOPOLIES, TRUSTS, AND KARTELLS. By F. W. Hirst.

THE COTTON INDUSTRY AND TRADE. By Prof. S. J. Chapman, Dean of the Faculty of Commerce in the University of Manchester. Illustrated.

*THE COAL INDUSTRY. By Ernest Aves. Illustrated.

Byzantine Texts

Edited by J. B. BURY, M.A., Litt.D.

A series of texts of Byzantine Historians, edited by English and foreign scholars.

ZACHARIAH OF MITYLENE. Translated by F. J. Hamilton, D.D., and E. W. Brooks. *Demy 8vo.* 12s. 6d. net.

EVAGRIUS. Edited by Léon Parmentier and M. Bidez. *Demy 8vo.* 10s. 6d. net.

THE HISTORY OF PSELLUS. Edited by C. Sathas. *Demy 8vo.* 15s. net.

ECTHESIS CHRONICA. Edited by Professor Lambros. *Demy 8vo.* 7s. 6d. net.

THE CHRONICLE OF MOREA. Edited by John Schmitt. *Demy 8vo.* 15s. net.

Churchman's Bible, The

General Editor, J. H. BURN, B.D., F.R.S.E.

A series of Expositions on the Books of the Bible, which will be of service to the general reader in the practical and devotional study of the Sacred Text.

Each Book is provided with a full and clear Introductory Section, in which is stated what is known or conjectured respecting the date and occasion of the composition of the Book, and any other particulars that may help to elucidate its meaning as a whole. The Exposition is divided into sections of a convenient length, corresponding as far as possible with the divisions of the Church Lectionary. The Translation of the Authorised Version is printed in full, such corrections as are deemed necessary being placed in footnotes.

THE EPISTLE OF ST. PAUL THE APOSTLE TO THE GALATIANS. Edited by A. W. Robinson, M.A. *Second Edition. Fcap. 8vo.* 1s. 6d. net.

ECCLESIASTES. Edited by A. W. Streane, D.D. *Fcap. 8vo.* 1s. 6d. net.

THE EPISTLE OF ST. PAUL THE APOSTLE TO THE PHILIPPIANS. Edited by C. R. D. Biggs, D.D. *Second Edition. Fcap 8vo.* 1s. 6d. net.

THE EPISTLE OF ST. JAMES. Edited by H. W. Fulford, M.A. *Fcap. 8vo.* 1s. 6d. net.

ISAIAH. Edited by W. E. Barnes, D.D. *Two Volumes. Fcap. 8vo.* 2s. net each. With Map.

THE EPISTLE OF ST. PAUL THE APOSTLE TO THE EPHESIANS. Edited by G. H. Whitaker, M.A. *Fcap. 8vo.* 1s. 6d. net.

Churchman's Library, The

General Editor, J. H. BURN, B.D., F.R.S.E.

THE BEGINNINGS OF ENGLISH CHRISTIANITY. By W. E. Collins, M.A. With Map. *Cr. 8vo.* 3s. 6d.

SOME NEW TESTAMENT PROBLEMS. By Arthur Wright, M.A. *Cr. 8vo.* 6s.

THE KINGDOM OF HEAVEN HERE AND HEREAFTER. By Canon Winterbotham, M.A., B.Sc., LL.B. *Cr. 8vo.* 3s. 6d.

THE WORKMANSHIP OF THE PRAYER BOOK: Its Literary and Liturgical Aspects. By J. Dowden, D.D. *Second Edition. Cr. 8vo.* 3s. 6d.

EVOLUTION. By F. B. Jevons, M.A., Litt.D *Cr. 8vo.* 3s. 6d.

THE OLD TESTAMENT AND THE NEW SCHOLARSHIP. By J. W. Peters, D.D. *Cr. 8vo.* 6s.

THE CHURCHMAN'S INTRODUCTION TO THE OLD TESTAMENT. By A. M. Mackay, B.A. *Cr. 8vo.* 3s. 6d.

THE CHURCH OF CHRIST. By E. T. Green, M.A. *Cr. 8vo.* 6s.

COMPARATIVE THEOLOGY. By J. A. MacCulloch. *Cr. 8vo.* 6s.

Classical Translations

Edited by H. F. FOX, M.A., Fellow and Tutor of Brasenose College, Oxford.

Crown 8vo.

A series of Translations from the Greek and Latin Classics, distinguished by literary excellence as well as by scholarly accuracy.

ÆSCHYLUS — Agamemnon, Choephoroe, Eumenides. Translated by Lewis Campbell, LL.D. 5s.

CICERO — De Oratore I. Translated by E. N. P. Moor, M.A. 3s. 6d.

CICERO — Select Orations (Pro Milone, Pro Mureno, Philippic II., in Catilinam). Translated by H. E. D. Blakiston, M.A. 5s.

CICERO — De Natura Deorum. Translated by F. Brooks, M.A. 3s. 6d.

[Continued.

CLASSICAL TRANSLATIONS—*continued.*

CICERO—De Officiis. Translated by G. B. Gardiner, M.A. 2s. 6d.

HORACE—The Odes and Epodes. Translated by A. D. Godley, M.A. 2s.

LUCIAN—Six Dialogues (Nigrinus, Icaro-Menippus, The Cock, The Ship, The Parasite, The Lover of Falsehood) Translated by S. T. Irwin, M.A. 3s. 6d.

SOPHOCLES—Electra and Ajax. Translated by E. D. A. Morshead, M.A. 2s. 6d.

TACITUS—Agricola and Germania. Translated by R. B. Townshend. 2s. 6d.

THE SATIRES OF JUVENAL. Translated by S. G. Owen. 2s. 6d.

Commercial Series

Edited by H. DE B. GIBBINS, Litt.D., M.A.

Crown 8vo.

A series intended to assist students and young men preparing for a commercial career, by supplying useful handbooks of a clear and practical character, dealing with those subjects which are absolutely essential in the business life.

COMMERCIAL EDUCATION IN THEORY AND PRACTICE. By E. E. Whitfield, M.A. 5s.
An introduction to Methuen's Commercial Series treating the question of Commercial Education fully from both the point of view of the teacher and of the parent.

BRITISH COMMERCE AND COLONIES FROM ELIZABETH TO VICTORIA. By H. de B. Gibbins, Litt.D., M.A. *Third Edition.* 2s.

COMMERCIAL EXAMINATION PAPERS. By H. de B. Gibbins, Litt.D., M.A. 1s. 6d.

THE ECONOMICS OF COMMERCE. By H. de B. Gibbins, Litt.D., M.A. *Second Edition.* 1s. 6d.

A GERMAN COMMERCIAL READER. By S. E. Bally. With Vocabulary. 2s.

A COMMERCIAL GEOGRAPHY OF THE BRITISH EMPIRE. By L. W. Lyde, M.A. *Fourth Edition.* 2s.

A COMMERCIAL GEOGRAPHY OF FOREIGN NATIONS. By F. C. Boon, B.A. 2s.

A PRIMER OF BUSINESS. By S. Jackson, M.A. *Third Edition.* 1s. 6d.

COMMERCIAL ARITHMETIC. By F. G. Taylor, M.A. *Fourth Edition.* 1s. 6d.

FRENCH COMMERCIAL CORRESPONDENCE. By S. E. Bally. With Vocabulary. *Third Edition.* 2s.

GERMAN COMMERCIAL CORRESPONDENCE. By S. E. Bally. With Vocabulary. *Second Edition.* 2s. 6d.

A FRENCH COMMERCIAL READER. By S. E. Bally. With Vocabulary. *Second Edition.* 2s.

PRECIS WRITING AND OFFICE CORRESPONDENCE. By E. E. Whitfield, M.A. *Second Edition.* 2s.

A GUIDE TO PROFESSIONS AND BUSINESS. By H. Jones. 1s. 6d.

THE PRINCIPLES OF BOOK-KEEPING BY DOUBLE ENTRY. By J. E. B. M'Allen, M.A. 2s.

COMMERCIAL LAW. By W. Douglas Edwards. *Second Edition.* 2s.

Connoisseur's Library, The

Wide Royal 8vo. 25s. net.

A sumptuous series of 20 books on art, written by experts for collectors, superbly illustrated in photogravure, collotype, and colour. The technical side of the art is duly treated. The first volumes are—

MEZZOTINTS. By Cyril Davenport. With 40 Plates in Photogravure.

PORCELAIN. By Edward Dillon. With 19 Plates in Colour, 20 in Collotype, and 5 in Photogravure.

MINIATURES. By Dudley Heath. With 9 Plates in Colour, 15 in Collotype, and 15 in Photogravure.

IVORIES. By A. Maskell. With 80 Plates in Collotype and Photogravure.

ENGLISH FURNITURE. By F. S. Robinson. With 160 Plates in Collotype and one in Photogravure. *Second Edition.*

*EUROPEAN ENAMELS. By H. Cunynghame, C.B. With many Plates in Collotype and a Frontispiece in Photogravure.

Devotion, The Library of

With Introductions and (where necessary) Notes.

Small Pott 8vo, cloth, 2s. ; leather, 2s. 6d. net.

These masterpieces of devotional literature are furnished with such Introductions and Notes as may be necessary to explain the standpoint of the author and the obvious difficulties of the text, without unnecessary intrusion between the author and the devout mind.

THE CONFESSIONS OF ST. AUGUSTINE. Edited by C. Bigg, D.D. *Fifth Edition.*

THE CHRISTIAN YEAR. Edited by Walter Lock, D.D. *Third Edition.*

THE IMITATION OF CHRIST. Edited by C. Bigg, D.D. *Fourth Edition.*

A BOOK OF DEVOTIONS. Edited by J. W. Stanbridge. B.D. *Second Edition.*

LYRA INNOCENTIUM. Edited by Walter Lock, D.D.

A SERIOUS CALL TO A DEVOUT AND HOLY LIFE. Edited by C. Bigg, D.D. *Second Edition.*

THE TEMPLE. Edited by E. C. S. Gibson, D.D. *Second Edition.*

A GUIDE TO ETERNITY. Edited by J. W. Stanbridge, B.D.

THE PSALMS OF DAVID. Edited by B. W. Randolph, D.D.

LYRA APOSTOLICA. By Cardinal Newman and others. Edited by Canon Scott Holland and Canon H. C. Beeching, M.A.

THE INNER WAY. By J. Tauler. Edited by A. W. Hutton, M.A.

THE THOUGHTS OF PASCAL. Edited by C. S. Jerram, M.A.

ON THE LOVE OF GOD. By St. Francis de Sales. Edited by W. J. Knox-Little, M.A.

A MANUAL OF CONSOLATION FROM THE SAINTS AND FATHERS. Edited by J. H. Burn, B.D.

THE SONG OF SONGS. Edited by B. Blaxland, M.A.

THE DEVOTIONS OF ST. ANSELM. Edited by C. C. J. Webb, M.A.

GRACE ABOUNDING. By John Bunyan. Edited by S. C. Freer, M.A.

BISHOP WILSON'S SACRA PRIVATA. Edited by A. E. Burn, B.D.

LYRA SACRA : A Book of Sacred Verse. Edited by H. C. Beeching, M.A., Canon of Westminster.

A DAY BOOK FROM THE SAINTS AND FATHERS. Edited by J. H. Burn, B.D.

HEAVENLY WISDOM. A Selection from the English Mystics. Edited by E. C. Gregory.

LIGHT, LIFE, AND LOVE. A Selection from the German Mystics. Edited by W. R. Inge, M.A.

*AN INTRODUCTION TO THE DEVOUT LIFE. By St. Francis de Sales. Translated and Edited by T. Barns, M.A.

Standard Library, The

In Sixpenny Volumes.

THE STANDARD LIBRARY is a new series of volumes containing the great classics of the world, and particularly the finest works of English literature. All the great masters will be represented, either in complete works or in selections. It is the ambition of the publishers to place the best books of the Anglo-Saxon race within the reach of every reader, so that the series may represent something of the diversity and splendour of our English tongue. The characteristics of THE STANDARD LIBRARY are four :—1. SOUNDNESS OF TEXT. 2. CHEAPNESS. 3. CLEARNESS OF TYPE. 4. SIMPLICITY. The books are well printed on good paper at a price which on the whole is without parallel in the history of publishing. Each volume contains from 100 to 250 pages, and is issued in paper covers, Crown 8vo, at Sixpence net, or in cloth gilt at One Shilling net. In a few cases long books are issued as Double Volumes or as Treble Volumes.

The following books are ready with the exception of those marked with a †, which denotes that the book is nearly ready :—

THE MEDITATIONS OF MARCUS AURELIUS. The translation is by R. Graves.

THE NOVELS OF JANE AUSTEN. In 5 volumes. VOL. I.—Sense and Sensibility.

ESSAYS AND COUNSELS and THE NEW ATLANTIS. By Francis Bacon, Lord Verulam.

†RELIGIO MEDICI and URN BURIAL. By Sir Thomas Browne. The text has been collated by A. R. Waller.

THE PILGRIM'S PROGRESS. By John Bunyan.

REFLECTIONS ON THE FRENCH REVOLUTION. By Edmund Burke.

†THE ANALOGY OF RELIGION, NATURAL AND REVEALED. By Joseph Butler, D.D.

[Continued.

THE STANDARD LIBRARY—*continued*.

THE POEMS OF THOMAS CHATTERTON. In 2 volumes.
  †Vol. I.—Miscellaneous Poems.
  †Vol. II.—The Rowley Poems.
†VITA NUOVA. By Dante. Translated into English by D G. Rossetti.
TOM JONES. By Henry Fielding. Treble Vol.
†CRANFORD. By Mrs. Gaskell.
THE HISTORY OF THE DECLINE AND FALL OF THE ROMAN EMPIRE. By Edward Gibbon. In 7 volumes.
  Vol. V. is nearly ready.
  The Text and Notes have been revised by J. B. Bury, Litt. D., but the Appendices of the more expensive edition are not given.
†THE VICAR OF WAKEFIELD. By Oliver Goldsmith.
THE POEMS AND PLAYS OF OLIVER GOLDSMITH.
THE WORKS OF BEN JONSON.
  †Vol. I.—The Case is Altered. Every Man in His Humour. Every Man out of His Humour.
  The text has been collated by H. C. Hart.
THE POEMS OF JOHN KEATS. Double volume.
  The Text has been collated by E. de Selincourt.
ON THE IMITATION OF CHRIST. By Thomas à Kempis.
  The translation is by C. Bigg, DD., Canon of Christ Church.
†A SERIOUS CALL TO A DEVOUT AND HOLY LIFE. By William Law.
THE PLAYS OF CHRISTOPHER MARLOWE.
  †Vol. I.—Tamburlane the Great.
THE PLAYS OF PHILIP MASSINGER.
  †Vol. I.—The Duke of Milan.

THE POEMS OF JOHN MILTON. In 2 volumes.
  †Vol. I.—Paradise Lost.
THE PROSE WORKS OF JOHN MILTON.
  †Vol. I.—Eikonoklastes and The Tenure of Kings and Magistrates.
SELECT WORKS OF SIR THOMAS MORE.
  †Vol. I.—Utopia and Poems.
†THE REPUBLIC OF PLATO. Translated by Sydenham and Taylor. Double Volume. The translation has been revised by W. H. D. Rouse.
†THE LITTLE FLOWERS OF ST. FRANCIS. Translated by W. Heywood.
THE WORKS OF WILLIAM SHAKESPEARE. In 10 volumes.
  VOL. I.—The Tempest; The Two Gentlemen of Verona; The Merry Wives of Windsor; Measure for Measure; The Comedy of Errors.
  VOL. II.—Much Ado About Nothing; Love's Labour's Lost; A Midsummer Night's Dream; The Merchant of Venice; As You Like It.
  VOL. III.—The Taming of the Shrew; All's Well that Ends Well; Twelfth Night; The Winter's Tale.
  Vol. IV.—The Life and Death of King John; The Tragedy of King Richard the Second; The First Part of King Henry IV.; The Second Part of King Henry IV.
  †Vol. V.—The Life of King Henry V.; The First Part of King Henry VI.; The Second Part of King Henry VI.
THE LIFE OF NELSON. By Robert Southey.
†THE NATURAL HISTORY AND ANTIQUITIES OF SELBORNE. By Gilbert White.

Half-Crown Library

Crown 8vo.   *2s. 6d. net.*

THE LIFE OF JOHN RUSKIN. By W. G. Collingwood, M.A. With Portraits. *Sixth Edition.*
ENGLISH LYRICS. By W. E. Henley. *Second Edition.*
THE GOLDEN POMP. A Procession of English Lyrics. Arranged by A. T. Quiller Couch. *Second Edition.*
CHITRAL: The Story of a Minor Siege. By Sir G. S. Robertson, K.C.S.I. *Third Edition.* Illustrated.

STRANGE SURVIVALS AND SUPERSTITIONS. By S. Baring-Gould. *Third Edition.*
YORKSHIRE ODDITIES AND STRANGE EVENTS. By S. Baring-Gould. *Fourth Edition.*
ENGLISH VILLAGES. By P. H. Ditchfield, M.A., F.S.A. Illustrated.
A BOOK OF ENGLISH PROSE. By W. E. Henley and C. Whibley.
THE LAND OF THE BLACK MOUNTAIN. Being a Description of Montenegro. By R. Wyon and G. Prance. With 40 Illustrations.

Illustrated Pocket Library of Plain and Coloured Books, The

Fcap 8vo.   *3s. 6d. net each volume.*

A series, in small form, of some of the famous illustrated books of fiction and general literature. These are faithfully reprinted from the first or best editions without introduction or notes. The Illustrations are chiefly in colour.

COLOURED BOOKS

OLD COLOURED BOOKS. By George Paston. With 16 Coloured Plates. *Fcap. 8vo. 2s. net.*
THE LIFE AND DEATH OF JOHN MYTTON, ESQ.

By Nimrod. With 18 Coloured Plates by Henry Alken and T. J. Rawlins. *Third Edition.*

[*Continued.*

THE LIFE OF A SPORTSMAN. By Nimrod. With 35 Coloured Plates by Henry Alken.

HANDLEY CROSS. By R. S. Surtees. With 17 Coloured Plates and 100 Woodcuts in the Text by John Leech.

MR. SPONGE'S SPORTING TOUR. By R. S. Surtees. With 13 Coloured Plates and 90 Woodcuts in the Text by John Leech.

JORROCKS' JAUNTS AND JOLLITIES. By R. S. Surtees. With 15 Coloured Plates by H. Alken.

This volume is reprinted from the extremely rare and costly edition of 1843, which contains Alken's very fine illustrations instead of the usual ones by Phiz.

ASK MAMMA. By R. S. Surtees. With 13 Coloured Plates and 70 Woodcuts in the Text by John Leech.

THE ANALYSIS OF THE HUNTING FIELD. By R. S. Surtees. With 7 Coloured Plates by Henry Alken, and 43 Illustrations on Wood.

THE TOUR OF DR. SYNTAX IN SEARCH OF THE PICTURESQUE. By William Combe. With 30 Coloured Plates by T. Rowlandson.

THE TOUR OF DOCTOR SYNTAX IN SEARCH OF CONSOLATION. By William Combe. With 24 Coloured Plates by T. Rowlandson.

THE THIRD TOUR OF DOCTOR SYNTAX IN SEARCH OF A WIFE. By William Combe. With 24 Coloured Plates by T. Rowlandson.

THE HISTORY OF JOHNNY QUAE GENUS: the Little Foundling of the late Dr. Syntax. By the Author of 'The Three Tours.' With 24 Coloured Plates by Rowlandson.

THE ENGLISH DANCE OF DEATH, from the Designs of T. Rowlandson, with Metrical Illustrations by the Author of 'Doctor Syntax.' *Two Volumes.*

This book contains 76 Coloured Plates.

THE DANCE OF LIFE: A Poem. By the Author of 'Doctor Syntax.' Illustrated with 26 Coloured Engravings by T. Rowlandson.

LIFE IN LONDON: or, the Day and Night Scenes of Jerry Hawthorn, Esq., and his Elegant Friend, Corinthian Tom. By Pierce Egan. With 36 Coloured Plates by I. R. and G. Cruikshank. With numerous Designs on Wood.

REAL LIFE IN LONDON: or, the Rambles and Adventures of Bob Tallyho, Esq., and his Cousin, The Hon. Tom Dashall. By an Amateur (Pierce Egan). With 31 Coloured Plates by Alken and Rowlandson, etc. *Two Volumes.*

THE LIFE OF AN ACTOR. By Pierce Egan. With 27 Coloured Plates by Theodore Lane, and several Designs on Wood.

THE VICAR OF WAKEFIELD. By Oliver Goldsmith. With 24 Coloured Plates by T. Rowlandson.

THE MILITARY ADVENTURES OF JOHNNY NEWCOME. By an Officer. With 15 Coloured Plates by T. Rowlandson.

THE NATIONAL SPORTS OF GREAT BRITAIN. With Descriptions and 51 Coloured Plates by Henry Alken.

This book is completely different from the large folio edition of 'National Sports' by the same artist, and none of the plates are similar.

THE ADVENTURES OF A POST CAPTAIN. By A Naval Officer. With 24 Coloured Plates by Mr. Williams.

GAMONIA: or, the Art of Preserving Game; and an Improved Method of making Plantations and Covers, explained and illustrated by Lawrence Rawstorne, Esq. With 15 Coloured Plates by T. Rawlins.

AN ACADEMY FOR GROWN HORSEMEN: Containing the completest Instructions for Walking, Trotting, Cantering, Galloping, Stumbling, and Tumbling. Illustrated with 27 Coloured Plates, and adorned with a Portrait of the Author. By Geoffrey Gambado, Esq.

REAL LIFE IN IRELAND, or, the Day and Night Scenes of Brian Boru, Esq., and his Elegant Friend, Sir Shawn O'Dogherty. By a Real Paddy. With 19 Coloured Plates by Heath, Marks, etc.

THE ADVENTURES OF JOHNNY NEWCOME IN THE NAVY. By Alfred Burton. With 16 Coloured Plates by T. Rowlandson.

THE OLD ENGLISH SQUIRE: A Poem. By John Careless, Esq. With 20 Coloured Plates after the style of T. Rowlandson.

*THE ENGLISH SPY. By Bernard Blackmantle. With 72 Coloured Plates by R. Cruikshank, and many Illustrations on wood. *Two Volumes.*

PLAIN BOOKS

THE GRAVE: A Poem. By Robert Blair. Illustrated by 12 Etchings executed by Louis Schiavonetti from the original Inventions of William Blake. With an Engraved Title Page and a Portrait of Blake by T. Phillips, R.A.

The illustrations are reproduced in photogravure.

ILLUSTRATIONS OF THE BOOK OF JOB. Invented and engraved by William Blake.

These famous Illustrations—21 in number—are reproduced in photogravure.

ÆSOP'S FABLES. With 380 Woodcuts by Thomas Bewick.

[*Continued.*

ILLUSTRATED POCKET LIBRARY OF PLAIN AND COLOURED BOOKS—*continued*.

WINDSOR CASTLE. By W. Harrison Ainsworth. With 22 Plates and 87 Woodcuts in the Text by George Cruikshank.

THE TOWER OF LONDON. By W. Harrison Ainsworth. With 40 Plates and 58 Woodcuts in the Text by George Cruikshank.

FRANK FAIRLEGH. By F. E. Smedley. With 30 Plates by George Cruikshank.

HANDY ANDY. By Samuel Lover. With 24 Illustrations by the Author.

THE COMPLEAT ANGLER. By Izaak Walton and Charles Cotton. With 14 Plates and 77 Woodcuts in the Text.
This volume is reproduced from the beautiful edition of John Major of 1824.

THE PICKWICK PAPERS. By Charles Dickens. With the 43 Illustrations by Seymour and Phiz, the two Buss Plates, and the 32 Contemporary Onwhyn Plates.

Junior Examination Series

Edited by A. M. M. STEDMAN, M.A. *Fcap. 8vo.* 1s.

This series is intended to lead up to the School Examination Series, and is intended for the use of teachers and students, to supply material for the former and practice for the latter. The papers are carefully graduated, cover the whole of the subject usually taught, and are intended to form part of the ordinary class work. They may be used *vivâ voce* or as a written examination.

JUNIOR FRENCH EXAMINATION PAPERS. By F. Jacob, M.A.

JUNIOR LATIN EXAMINATION PAPERS. By C. G. Botting, M.A. *Third Edition.*

JUNIOR ENGLISH EXAMINATION PAPERS. By W. Williamson, B.A.

JUNIOR ARITHMETIC EXAMINATION PAPERS. By W. S. Beard. *Second Edition.*

JUNIOR ALGEBRA EXAMINATION PAPERS. By S. W. Finn, M.A.

JUNIOR GREEK EXAMINATION PAPERS. By T. C. Weatherhead, M.A.

JUNIOR GENERAL INFORMATION EXAMINATION PAPERS. By W. S. Beard.

*A KEY TO THE ABOVE. *Crown 8vo.* 3s. 6d.

JUNIOR GEOGRAPHY EXAMINATION PAPERS. By W. G. Baker, M.A.

JUNIOR GERMAN EXAMINATION PAPERS. By A. Voegelin, M.A.

Junior School-Books

Edited by O. D. INSKIP, LL.D., and W. WILLIAMSON, B.A.

A series of elementary books for pupils in lower forms, simply written by teachers of experience.

A CLASS-BOOK OF DICTATION PASSAGES. By W. Williamson, B.A. *Eleventh Edition.* Cr. 8vo. 1s. 6d.

THE GOSPEL ACCORDING TO ST. MATTHEW. Edited by E. Wilton South, M.A. With Three Maps. Cr. 8vo. 1s. 6d.

THE GOSPEL ACCORDING TO ST. MARK. Edited by A. E. Rubie, D.D. With Three Maps. Cr. 8vo. 1s. 6d.

A JUNIOR ENGLISH GRAMMAR. By W. Williamson, B.A. With numerous passages for parsing and analysis, and a chapter on Essay Writing. *Third Edition.* Cr. 8vo. 2s.

A JUNIOR CHEMISTRY. By E. A. Tyler, B.A., F.C.S. With 78 Illustrations. *Second Edition.* Cr. 8vo. 2s. 6d.

THE ACTS OF THE APOSTLES. Edited by A. E. Rubie, D.D. Cr. 8vo. 2s.

A JUNIOR FRENCH GRAMMAR. By L. A. Sornet and M. J. Acatos. Cr. 8vo. 2s.

ELEMENTARY EXPERIMENTAL SCIENCE. PHYSICS by W. T. Clough, A.R.C.S. CHEMISTRY by A. E. Dunstan, B.Sc. With 2 Plates and 154 Diagrams. *Third Edition.* Cr. 8vo. 2s. 6d.

A JUNIOR GEOMETRY. By Noel S. Lydon. With 239 Diagrams. *Second Edition.* Cr. 8vo. 2s.

*A JUNIOR MAGNETISM AND ELECTRICITY. By W. T. Clough. Illustrated. Cr. 8vo. 2s. 6d.

ELEMENTARY EXPERIMENTAL CHEMISTRY. By A. E. Dunstan, B.Sc. With 4 Plates and 109 Diagrams. Cr. 8vo. 2s.

A JUNIOR FRENCH PROSE COMPOSITION. By R. R. N. Baron, M.A. Cr. 8vo. 2s.

*THE GOSPEL ACCORDING TO ST. LUKE. With an Introduction and Notes by William Williamson, B.A. With Three Maps. Cr. 8vo. 2s.

Leaders of Religion

Edited by H. C. BEECHING, M.A., Canon of Westminster. *With Portraits.*
Cr. 8vo. 2s. net.

A series of short biographies of the most prominent leaders of religious life and thought of all ages and countries.

CARDINAL NEWMAN. By R. H. Hutton.
JOHN WESLEY. By J. H. Overton, M.A.
BISHOP WILBERFORCE. By G. W. Daniell, M.A.
CARDINAL MANNING. By A. W. Hutton, M.A.
CHARLES SIMEON. By H. C. G. Moule, D.D.
JOHN KEBLE. By Walter Lock, D.D.
THOMAS CHALMERS. By Mrs. Oliphant.
LANCELOT ANDREWES. By R. L. Ottley, D.D. *Second Edition.*
AUGUSTINE OF CANTERBURY. By E. L. Cutts, D.D.

WILLIAM LAUD. By W. H. Hutton, M.A. *Third Edition.*
JOHN KNOX. By F. MacCunn. *Second Edition.*
JOHN HOWE. By R. F. Horton, D.D.
BISHOP KEN. By F. A. Clarke, M.A.
GEORGE FOX, THE QUAKER. By T. Hodgkin, D.C.L.
JOHN DONNE. By Augustus Jessopp, D.D.
THOMAS CRANMER. By A. J. Mason, D.D.
BISHOP LATIMER. By R. M. Carlyle and A. J. Carlyle, M.A.
BISHOP BUTLER. By W. A. Spooner, M.A.

Little Blue Books, The

General Editor, E. V. LUCAS.

Illustrated. Demy 16mo. 2s. 6d.

A series of books for children. The aim of the editor is to get entertaining or exciting stories about normal children, the moral of which is implied rather than expressed.

1. THE CASTAWAYS OF MEADOWBANK. By Thomas Cobb.
2. THE BEECHNUT BOOK. By Jacob Abbott. Edited by E. V. Lucas.
3. THE AIR GUN. By T. Hilbert.
4. A SCHOOL YEAR. By Netta Syrett.
5. THE PEELES AT THE CAPITAL. By Roger Ashton.
6. THE TREASURE OF PRINCEGATE PRIORY. By T. Cobb.
7. MRS. BARBERRY'S GENERAL SHOP. By Roger Ashton.
8. A BOOK OF BAD CHILDREN. By W. T. Webb.
9. THE LOST BALL. By Thomas Cobb.

Little Books on Art

With many Illustrations. Demy 16mo. 2s. 6d. net.

A series of monographs in miniature, containing the complete outline of the subject under treatment and rejecting minute details. These books are produced with the greatest care. Each volume consists of about 200 pages, and contains from 30 to 40 illustrations, including a frontispiece in photogravure.

GREEK ART. H. B. Walters. *Second Edition.*
BOOKPLATES. E. Almack.
REYNOLDS. J. Sime. *Second Edition.*
ROMNEY. George Paston.
WATTS. R. E. D. Sketchley.
LEIGHTON. Alice Corkran.
VELASQUEZ. Wilfrid Wilberforce and A. R. Gilbert.
GREUZE AND BOUCHER. Eliza F. Pollard.
VANDYCK. M. G. Smallwood.
TURNER. Frances Tyrell-Gill.
DÜRER. Jessie Allen.
HOPPNER. H. P. K. Skipton.

HOLBEIN. Mrs. G. Fortescue.
BURNE-JONES. Fortunée de Lisle. *Second Edition.*
REMBRANDT. Mrs. E. A. Sharp
COROT. Alice Pollard and Ethel Birnstingl.
RAPHAEL. A. R. Dryhurst.
MILLET. Netta Peacock.
ILLUMINATED MSS. J. W. Bradley.
*CHRIST IN ART. Mrs. Henry Jenner.
JEWELLERY. Cyril Davenport.
CLAUDE. Edward Dillon.
*THE ARTS OF JAPAN. Edward Dillon.

Little Galleries, The

Demy 16mo.   2s. 6d. net.

A series of little books containing examples of the best work of the great painters. Each volume contains 20 plates in photogravure, together with a short outline of the life and work of the master to whom the book is devoted.

A LITTLE GALLERY OF REYNOLDS.
A LITTLE GALLERY OF ROMNEY.
A LITTLE GALLERY OF HOPPNER.

A LITTLE GALLERY OF MILLAIS.
A LITTLE GALLERY OF ENGLISH POETS.

Little Guides, The

Small Pott 8vo, cloth, 2s. 6d. net.; leather, 3s. 6d. net.

OXFORD AND ITS COLLEGES. By J. Wells, M.A. Illustrated by E. H. New. *Sixth Edition.*
CAMBRIDGE AND ITS COLLEGES. By A. Hamilton Thompson. *Second Edition.* Illustrated by E. H. New.
THE MALVERN COUNTRY. By B. C. A. Windle, D.Sc., F.R.S. Illustrated by E. H. New.
SHAKESPEARE'S COUNTRY. By B. C. A. Windle, D.Sc., F.R.S. Illustrated by E. H. New. *Second Edition.*
SUSSEX. By F. G. Brabant, M.A. Illustrated by E. H. New.
WESTMINSTER ABBEY. By G. E. Troutbeck. Illustrated by F. D. Bedford.
NORFOLK. By W. A. Dutt. Illustrated by B. C. Boulter.
CORNWALL. By A. L. Salmon. Illustrated by B. C. Boulter.
BRITTANY. By S. Baring-Gould. Illustrated by J. Wylie.
HERTFORDSHIRE. By H. W. Tompkins, F.R.H.S. Illustrated by E. H. New.
THE ENGLISH LAKES. By F. G. Brabant, M.A. Illustrated by E. H. New.
KENT. By G. Clinch. Illustrated by F. D. Bedford.

ROME. By C. G. Ellaby. Illustrated by B. C. Boulter.
THE ISLE OF WIGHT. By G. Clinch. Illustrated by F. D. Bedford.
SURREY. By F. A. H. Lambert. Illustrated by E. H. New.
BUCKINGHAMSHIRE. By E. S. Roscoe. Illustrated by F. D. Bedford.
SUFFOLK. By W. A. Dutt. Illustrated by J. Wylie.
DERBYSHIRE. By J. C. Cox, LL.D., F.S.A. Illustrated by J. C. Wall.
THE NORTH RIDING OF YORKSHIRE. By J. E. Morris. ⸸ Illustrated by R. J. S. Bertram.
HAMPSHIRE. By J. C. Cox. Illustrated by M. E. Purser.
SICILY. By F. H. Jackson. With many Illustrations by the Author.
DORSET. By Frank R. Heath. Illustrated.
CHESHIRE. By W. M. Gallichan. Illustrated by Elizabeth Hartley.
*NORTHAMPTONSHIRE. By Wakeling Dry. Illustrated.
*THE EAST RIDING OF YORKSHIRE. By J. E. Morris. Illustrated.
*OXFORDSHIRE. By F. G. Brabant. Illustrated by E. H. New.
*ST. PAUL'S CATHEDRAL. By George Clinch. Illustrated by Beatrice Alcock.

Little Library, The

With Introductions, Notes, and Photogravure Frontispieces.

Small Pott 8vo.   Each Volume, cloth, 1s. 6d. net; leather, 2s. 6d. net.

A series of small books under the above title, containing some of the famous works in English and other literatures, in the domains of fiction, poetry, and belles lettres. The series also contains volumes of selections in prose and verse. The books are edited with the most scholarly care. Each one contains an introduction which gives (1) a short biography of the author; (2) a critical estimate of the book. Where they are necessary, short notes are added at the foot of the page.

Each volume has a photogravure frontispiece, and the books are produced with great care.

Anon. ENGLISH LYRICS, A LITTLE BOOK OF.
Austen (Jane). PRIDE AND PREJUDICE. Edited by E. V. LUCAS. *Two Volumes.*

NORTHANGER ABBEY. Edited by E. V. LUCAS.
Bacon (Francis). THE ESSAYS OF LORD BACON. Edited by EDWARD WRIGHT.

Barham (R. H.). THE INGOLDSBY LEGENDS. Edited by J. B. ATLAY. *Two Volumes.*

Barnett (Mrs. P. A.). A LITTLE BOOK OF ENGLISH PROSE.

Beckford (William). THE HISTORY OF THE CALIPH VATHEK. Edited by E. DENISON ROSS.

Blake (William). SELECTIONS FROM WILLIAM BLAKE. Edited by M. PERUGINI.

Borrow (George). LAVENGRO. Edited by F. HINDES GROOME. *Two Volumes.* THE ROMANY RYE. Edited by JOHN SAMPSON.

Browning (Robert). SELECTIONS FROM THE EARLY POEMS OF ROBERT BROWNING. Edited by W. HALL GRIFFIN, M.A.

Canning (George). SELECTIONS FROM THE ANTI-JACOBIN: with GEORGE CANNING's additional Poems. Edited by LLOYD SANDERS.

Cowley (Abraham). THE ESSAYS OF ABRAHAM COWLEY. Edited by H. C. MINCHIN.

Crabbe (George). SELECTIONS FROM GEORGE CRABBE. Edited by A. C. DEANE.

Craik (Mrs.). JOHN HALIFAX, GENTLEMAN. Edited by ANNE MATHESON. *Two Volumes.*

Crashaw (Richard). THE ENGLISH POEMS OF RICHARD CRASHAW. Edited by EDWARD HUTTON.

Dante (Alighieri). THE INFERNO OF DANTE. Translated by H. F. CARY. Edited by PAGET TOYNBEE, M.A., D.Litt. THE PURGATORIO OF DANTE. Translated by H. F. CARY. Edited by PAGET TOYNBEE, M.A., D.Litt. THE PARADISO OF DANTE. Translated by H. F. CARY. Edited by PAGET TOYNBEE, M.A., D.Litt.

Darley (George). SELECTIONS FROM THE POEMS OF GEORGE DARLEY. Edited by R. A. STREATFEILD.

Deane (A. C.). A LITTLE BOOK OF LIGHT VERSE.

Dickens (Charles). CHRISTMAS BOOKS. *Two Volumes.*

Ferrier (Susan). MARRIAGE. Edited by A. GOODRICH - FREER and LORD IDDESLEIGH. *Two Volumes.* THE INHERITANCE. *Two Volumes.*

Gaskell (Mrs.). CRANFORD. Edited by E. V. LUCAS. *Second Edition.*

Hawthorne (Nathaniel). THE SCARLET LETTER. Edited by PERCY DEARMER.

Henderson (T. F.). A LITTLE BOOK OF SCOTTISH VERSE.

Keats (John). POEMS. With an Introduction by L. BINYON, and Notes by J. MASEFIELD.

Kinglake (A. W.). EOTHEN. With an Introduction and Notes. *Second Edition.*

Lamb (Charles). ELIA, AND THE LAST ESSAYS OF ELIA. Edited by E. V. LUCAS.

Locker (F.). LONDON LYRICS. Edited by A. D. GODLEY, M.A. A reprint of the First Edition.

Longfellow (H. W.). SELECTIONS FROM LONGFELLOW. Edited by L. M. FAITHFULL.

Marvell (Andrew). THE POEMS OF ANDREW MARVELL. Edited by E. WRIGHT.

Milton (John). THE MINOR POEMS OF JOHN MILTON. Edited by H. C. BEECHING, M.A., Canon of Westminster.

Moir (D. M.). MANSIE WAUCH. Edited by T. F. HENDERSON.

Nichols (J. B. B.). A LITTLE BOOK OF ENGLISH SONNETS.

Rochefoucauld (La). THE MAXIMS OF LA ROCHEFOUCAULD. Translated by Dean STANHOPE. Edited by G. H. POWELL.

Smith (Horace and James). REJECTED ADDRESSES. Edited by A. D. GODLEY, M.A.

Sterne (Laurence). A SENTIMENTAL JOURNEY. Edited by H. W. PAUL.

Tennyson (Alfred, Lord). THE EARLY POEMS OF ALFRED, LORD TENNYSON. Edited by J. CHURTON COLLINS, M.A. IN MEMORIAM. Edited by H. C. BEECHING, M.A. THE PRINCESS. Edited by ELIZABETH WORDSWORTH. MAUD. Edited by ELIZABETH WORDSWORTH.

Thackeray (W. M.). VANITY FAIR. Edited by S. GWYNN. *Three Volumes.* PENDENNIS. Edited by S. GWYNN. *Three Volumes.* ESMOND. Edited by S. GWYNN. CHRISTMAS BOOKS. Edited by S. GWYNN.

Vaughan (Henry). THE POEMS OF HENRY VAUGHAN. Edited by EDWARD HUTTON.

Walton (Izaak). THE COMPLEAT ANGLER. Edited by J. BUCHAN.

Waterhouse (Mrs. Alfred). A LITTLE BOOK OF LIFE AND DEATH. Edited by. *Eighth Edition.*

Wordsworth (W.). SELECTIONS FROM WORDSWORTH. Edited by NOWELL C. SMITH.

Wordsworth (W.) and Coleridge (S. T.). LYRICAL BALLADS. Edited by GEORGE SAMPSON.

Miniature Library

Reprints in miniature of a few interesting books which have qualities of humanity, devotion, or literary genius.

EUPHRANOR: A Dialogue on Youth. By Edward FitzGerald. From the edition published by W. Pickering in 1851. *Demy 32mo. Leather, 2s. net.*

POLONIUS: or Wise Saws and Modern Instances. By Edward FitzGerald. From the edition published by W. Pickering in 1852. *Demy 32mo. Leather, 2s. net.*

THE RUBÁIYÁT OF OMAR KHAYYÁM. By Edward FitzGerald. From the 1st edition of 1859, *Third Edition. Leather, 1s. net.*

THE LIFE OF EDWARD, LORD HERBERT OF CHERBURY. Written by himself. From the edition printed at Strawberry Hill in the year 1764. *Medium 32mo. Leather, 2s. net.*

THE VISIONS OF DOM FRANCISCO QUEVEDO VILLEGAS, Knight of the Order of St. James. Made English by R. L. From the edition printed for H. Herringman, 1668. *Leather. 2s. net.*

POEMS. By Dora Greenwell. From the edition of 1848. *Leather, 2s. net.*

Oxford Biographies

Fcap. 8vo. Each volume, cloth, 2s. 6d. net; leather, 3s. 6d. net.

These books are written by scholars of repute, who combine knowledge and literary skill with the power of popular presentation. They are illustrated from authentic material.

DANTE ALIGHIERI. By Paget Toynbee, M.A., D.Litt. With 12 Illustrations. *Second Edition.*

SAVONAROLA. By E. L. S. Horsburgh, M.A. With 12 Illustrations. *Second Edition.*

JOHN HOWARD. By E. C. S. Gibson, D.D., Bishop of Gloucester. With 12 Illustrations.

TENNYSON. By A. C. BENSON, M.A. With 9 Illustrations.

WALTER RALEIGH. By I. A. Taylor. With 12 Illustrations.

ERASMUS. By E. F. H. Capey. With 12 Illustrations.

THE YOUNG PRETENDER. By C. S. Terry. With 12 Illustrations.

ROBERT BURNS. By T. F. Henderson. With 12 Illustrations.

CHATHAM. By A. S. M'Dowall. With 12 Illustrations.

ST. FRANCIS OF ASSISI. By Anna M. Stoddart. With 16 Illustrations.

CANNING. By W. Alison Phillips. With 12 Illustrations.

BEACONSFIELD. By Walter Sichel. With 12 Illustrations.

GOETHE. By H. G. Atkins. With 12 Illustrations.

*FENELON. By Viscount St. Cyres. With 12 Illustrations.

School Examination Series

Edited by A. M. M. STEDMAN, M.A. *Cr. 8vo. 2s. 6d.*

FRENCH EXAMINATION PAPERS. By A. M. M. Stedman, M.A. *Thirteenth Edition.*
A KEY, issued to Tutors and Private Students only to be had on application to the Publishers. *Fifth Edition. Crown 8vo. 6s. net.*

LATIN EXAMINATION PAPERS. By A. M. M. Stedman, M.A. *Thirteenth Edition.*
KEY (*Fourth Edition*) issued as above. 6s. net.

GREEK EXAMINATION PAPERS. By A. M. M. Stedman, M.A. *Eighth Edition.*
KEY (*Third Edition*) issued as above. 6s. net.

GERMAN EXAMINATION PAPERS. By R. J. Morich. *Sixth Edition.*

KEY (*Third Edition*) issued as above. 6s. net.

HISTORY AND GEOGRAPHY EXAMINATION PAPERS. By C. H. Spence, M.A. *Second Edition.*

PHYSICS EXAMINATION PAPERS. By R. E. Steel, M.A., F.C.S.

GENERAL KNOWLEDGE EXAMINATION PAPERS. By A. M. M. Stedman, M.A. *Fifth Edition.*
KEY (*Third Edition*) issued as above. 7s. net.

EXAMINATION PAPERS IN ENGLISH HISTORY. By J. Tait Plowden-Wardlaw, B.A.

Social Questions of To-day

Edited by H. DE B. GIBBINS, Litt.D., M.A. *Crown 8vo. 2s. 6d.*

A series of volumes upon those topics of social, economic, and industrial interest that are foremost in the public mind.

TRADE UNIONISM—NEW AND OLD. By G. Howell. *Third Edition.*

THE COMMERCE OF NATIONS. By C. F. Bastable, M.A. *Third Edition.*

THE ALIEN INVASION. By W. H. Wilkins, B.A.

THE RURAL EXODUS. By P. Anderson Graham.

LAND NATIONALIZATION. By Harold Cox, B.A. *Second Edition.*

A SHORTER WORKING DAY. By H. de B. Gibbins and R. A. Hadfield.

BACK TO THE LAND. An Inquiry into Rural Depopulation. By H. E. Moore.

TRUSTS, POOLS, AND CORNERS. By J. Stephen Jeans.

THE FACTORY SYSTEM. By R. W. Cooke Taylor.

WOMEN'S WORK. By Lady Dilke, Miss Bulley, and Miss Whitley.

SOCIALISM AND MODERN THOUGHT. By M. Kauffmann.

THE PROBLEM OF THE UNEMPLOYED. By J. A. Hobson, M.A.

LIFE IN WEST LONDON By Arthur Sherwell, M.A. *Third Edition.*

RAILWAY NATIONALIZATION. By Clement Edwards.

UNIVERSITY AND SOCIAL SETTLEMENTS. By W. Reason, M.A.

Textbooks of Science.

PRACTICAL MECHANICS. By Sidney H. Wells. *Third Edition. Cr. 8vo. 3s. 6d.*

PRACTICAL PHYSICS. By H. Stroud, D.Sc., M.A. *Cr. 8vo. 3s. 6d.*

PRACTICAL CHEMISTRY. Part I. By W. French, M.A. *Cr. 8vo. Third Edition. 1s.6d.*

PRACTICAL CHEMISTRY. Part II. By W. French, M.A., and T. H. Boardman, M.A.

Cr. 8vo. 1s. 6d.

EXAMPLES IN PHYSICS. By C. E. Jackson, B.A., Science Master at Bradford Grammar School. *Cr. 8vo. 2s. 6d.*

ELEMENTARY ORGANIC CHEMISTRY. By A. E. Dunstan, B.Sc., Head of Chemical Department, East Ham Technical College. Illustrated. *Cr. 8vo. 2s. 6d.*

Technology, Textbooks of

Edited by G. F. GOODCHILD, B.A., B.Sc., and G. R. MILLS, M.A.
Fully Illustrated.

HOW TO MAKE A DRESS. By J. A. E. Wood. *Third Edition. Cr. 8vo. 1s. 6d.*

CARPENTRY AND JOINERY. By F. C. Webber. *Fourth Edition. Cr. 8vo. 3s. 6d.*

MILLINERY, THEORETICAL AND PRACTICAL. By Clare Hill. *Second Edition. Cr. 8vo. 2s.*

TECHNICAL ARITHMETIC AND GEOMETRY. By C. T. Millis, M.I.M.E. *Cr. 8vo.*

3s. 6d.

AN INTRODUCTION TO THE STUDY OF TEXTILE DESIGN. By Aldred F. Barker. *Demy 8vo. 7s. 6d.*

BUILDERS' QUANTITIES. By H. C. Grubb. *Cr. 8vo. 4s. 6d.*

RÉPOUSSÉ METAL WORK. By A. C. Horth. *Cr. 8vo. 2s. 6d.*

Theology, Handbooks of

Edited by R. L. OTTLEY, D.D., Professor of Pastoral Theology at Oxford, and Canon of Christ Church, Oxford.

The series is intended, in part, to furnish the clergy and teachers or students of Theology with trustworthy Textbooks, adequately representing the present position of the questions dealt with ; in part, to make accessible to the reading public an accurate and concise statement of facts and principles in all questions bearing on Theology and Religion.

THE XXXIX. ARTICLES OF THE CHURCH OF ENGLAND. Edited by E. C. S. Gibson, D.D. *Third and Cheaper Edition in one Volume. Demy 8vo. 12s. 6d.*

AN INTRODUCTION TO THE HISTORY OF RELIGION. By F. B. Jevons, M.A., Litt.D. *Third Edition. Demy 8vo. 10s. 6d.*

THE DOCTRINE OF THE INCARNATION. By R. L. Ottley, D.D. *Second and Cheaper Edition. Demy 8vo. 12s. 6d.*

AN INTRODUCTION TO THE HISTORY OF THE CREEDS. By A. E. Burn, B.D. *Demy 8vo. 10s. 6d.*

THE PHILOSOPHY OF RELIGION IN ENGLAND AND AMERICA. By Alfred Caldecott, D.D. *Demy 8vo. 10s. 6d.*

A HISTORY OF EARLY CHRISTIAN DOCTRINE. By J. F. Bethune Baker, M.A. *Demy 8vo. 10s. 6d.*

Westminster Commentaries, The

General Editor, WALTER LOCK, D.D., Warden of Keble College,
Dean Ireland's Professor of Exegesis in the University of Oxford.

The object of each commentary is primarily exegetical, to interpret the author's meaning to the present generation. The editors will not deal, except very subordinately, with questions of textual criticism or philology; but, taking the English text in the Revised Version as their basis, they will try to combine a hearty acceptance of critical principles with loyalty to the Catholic Faith.

THE BOOK OF GENESIS. Edited with Introduction and Notes by S. R. Driver, D.D. *Fourth Edition Demy 8vo.* 10s. 6d.

THE BOOK OF JOB. Edited by E. C. S. Gibson, D.D. *Second Edition. Demy 8vo.* 6s.

THE ACTS OF THE APOSTLES. Edited by R. B. Rackham, M.A. *Demy 8vo. Second and Cheaper Edition.* 10s. 6d.

THE FIRST EPISTLE OF PAUL THE APOSTLE TO THE CORINTHIANS. Edited by H. L. Goudge, M.A. *Demy 8vo.* 6s.

THE EPISTLE OF ST. JAMES. Edited with Introduction and Notes by R. J. Knowling, M.A. *Demy 8vo.* 6s.

PART II.—FICTION

Albanesi (E. Maria). SUSANNAH AND ONE OTHER. *Fourth Edition. Cr. 8vo.* 6s.

THE BLUNDER OF AN INNOCENT. *Second Edition. Cr. 8vo.* 6s.

CAPRICIOUS CAROLINE. *Second Edition. Cr. 8vo.* 6s.

LOVE AND LOUISA. *Second Edition. Cr. 8vo.* 6s.

PETER, A PARASITE. *Cr. 8vo.* 6s.

THE BROWN EYES OF MARY. *Third Edition. Cr. 8vo.* 6s.

Anstey (F.). Author of 'Vice Versâ.' A BAYARD FROM BENGAL. Illustrated by BERNARD PARTRIDGE. *Third Edition. Cr. 8vo.* 3s. 6d.

Bacheller (Irving), Author of 'Eben Holden.' DARREL OF THE BLESSED ISLES. *Third Edition. Cr. 8vo.* 6s.

Bagot (Richard). A ROMAN MYSTERY. *Third Edition. Cr. 8vo.* 6s.

THE PASSPORT. *Fourth Ed. Cr. 8vo.* 6s.

Baring-Gould (S.). ARMINELL. *Fifth Edition. Cr. 8vo.* 6s.

URITH. *Fifth Edition. Cr. 8vo.* 6s.

IN THE ROAR OF THE SEA. *Seventh Edition. Cr. 8vo.* 6s.

CHEAP JACK ZITA. *Fourth Edition. Cr. 8vo.* 6s.

MARGERY OF QUETHER. *Third Edition. Cr. 8vo.* 6s.

THE QUEEN OF LOVE. *Fifth Edition. Cr. 8vo.* 6s.

JACQUETTA. *Third Edition. Cr. 8vo.* 6s.

KITTY ALONE. *Fifth Edition. Cr. 8vo.* 6s.

NOÉMI. Illustrated. *Fourth Edition. Cr. 8vo.* 6s.

THE BROOM-SQUIRE. Illustrated. *Fifth Edition. Cr. 8vo.* 6s.

DARTMOOR IDYLLS. *Cr. 8vo.* 6s.

THE PENNYCOMEQUICKS. *Third Edition. Cr. 8vo.* 6s.

GUAVAS THE TINNER. Illustrated. *Second Edition. Cr. 8vo.* 6s.

BLADYS. Illustrated. *Second Edition. Cr. 8vo.* 6s.

PABO THE PRIEST. *Cr. 8vo.* 6s.

WINEFRED. Illustrated. *Second Edition. Cr. 8vo.* 6s.

ROYAL GEORGIE. Illustrated. *Cr. 8vo.* 6s.

MISS QUILLET. Illustrated. *Cr. 8vo.* 6s.

CHRIS OF ALL SORTS. *Cr. 8vo.* 6s.

IN DEWISLAND. *Second Edition. Cr. 8vo.* 6s.

LITTLE TU'PENNY. *A New Edition.* 6d. See also Strand Novels and Books for Boys and Girls.

Barlow (Jane). THE LAND OF THE SHAMROCK. *Cr. 8vo.* 6s. See also Strand Novels.

Barr (Robert). IN THE MIDST OF ALARMS. *Third Edition. Cr. 8vo.* 6s.

THE MUTABLE MANY. *Third Edition. Cr. 8vo.* 6s.

THE COUNTESS TEKLA. *Third Edition. Cr. 8vo.* 6s.

THE LADY ELECTRA. *Second Edition. Cr. 8vo.* 6s.

THE TEMPESTUOUS PETTICOAT. Illustrated. *Third Edition. Cr. 8vo.* 6s. See also Strand Novels and S. Crane.

Begbie (Harold). THE ADVENTURES OF SIR JOHN SPARROW. *Cr. 8vo.* 6s.

Belloc (Hilaire). EMMANUEL BURDEN, MERCHANT. With 36 Illustrations by G. K. CHESTERTON. *Second Edition. Cr. 8vo.* 6s.

Benson (E. F.) DODO. *Fourth Edition. Cr. 8vo. 6s.* See also Strand Novels.

Benson (Margaret). SUBJECT TO VANITY. *Cr. 8vo. 3s. 6d.*

Bourne (Harold C.). See V. Langbridge.

Burton (J. Bloundelle). THE YEAR ONE: A Page of the French Revolution. Illustrated. *Cr. 8vo. 6s.*

THE FATE OF VALSEC. *Cr. 8vo. 6s.*

A BRANDED NAME. *Cr. 8vo. 6s.* See also Strand Novels.

Capes (Bernard), Author of 'The Lake of Wine.' THE EXTRAORDINARY CONFESSIONS OF DIANA PLEASE. *Third Edition. Cr. 8vo. 6s.*

A JAY OF ITALY. *Fourth Ed. Cr. 8vo. 6s.*

*LOAVES AND FISHES. *Cr. 8vo. 6s.*

Chesney (Weatherby). THE TRAGEDY OF THE GREAT EMERALD. *Cr. 8vo. 6s.*

THE MYSTERY OF A BUNGALOW. *Second Edition. Cr. 8vo. 6s.* See also Strand Novels.

Clifford (Hugh). A FREE LANCE OF TO-DAY. *Cr. 8vo. 6s.*

Clifford (Mrs. W. K.). See Strand Novels and Books for Boys and Girls.

Cobb (Thomas). A CHANGE OF FACE. *Cr. 8vo. 6s.*

Corelli (Marie). A ROMANCE OF TWO WORLDS. *Twenty-Sixth Edition. Cr. 8vo. 6s.*

VENDETTA. *Twenty-Second Edition. Cr. 8vo. 6s.*

THELMA. *Thirty-Third Edition. Cr. 8vo. 6s.*

ARDATH: THE STORY OF A DEAD SELF. *Sixteenth Edition. Cr. 8vo. 6s.*

THE SOUL OF LILITH. *Thirteenth Edition. Cr. 8vo. 6s.*

WORMWOOD. *Fourteenth Edition. Cr. 8vo. 6s.*

BARABBAS: A DREAM OF THE WORLD'S TRAGEDY. *Fortieth Edition. Cr. 8vo. 6s.*

THE SORROWS OF SATAN. *Fiftieth Edition. Cr. 8vo. 6s.*

THE MASTER CHRISTIAN. 167*th Thousand. Cr. 8vo. 6s.*

TEMPORAL POWER: A STUDY IN SUPREMACY. 130*th Thousand. Cr. 8vo. 6s.*

GOD'S GOOD MAN: A SIMPLE LOVE STORY. 134*th Thousand. Cr. 8vo. 6s.*

THE MIGHTY ATOM. *A New Edition. Cr. 8vo. 6s.*

BOY. *A New Edition. Cr. 8vo. 6s.*

JANE. *A New Edition. Cr. 8vo. 6s.*

Crockett (S. R.), Author of 'The Raiders,' etc. LOCHINVAR. Illustrated. *Third Edition. Cr. 8vo. 6s.*

THE STANDARD BEARER. *Cr. 8vo. 6s.*

Croker (B. M.). THE OLD CANTONMENT. *Cr. 8vo. 6s.*

JOHANNA. *Second Edition. Cr. 8vo. 6s.*

THE HAPPY VALLEY. *Third Edition. Cr. 8vo. 6s.*

A NINE DAYS' WONDER. *Third Edition. Cr. 8vo. 6s.*

PEGGY OF THE BARTONS. *Sixth Edition. Cr. 8vo. 6s.*

ANGEL. *Fourth Edition. Cr. 8vo. 6s.*

A STATE SECRET. *Third Edition. Cr. 8vo. 3s. 6d.*

Dawson (Francis W.). THE SCAR. *Cr. 8vo. 6s.*

Dawson (A. J.). DANIEL WHYTE. *Cr. 8vo. 3s. 6d.*

Doyle (A. Conan), Author of 'Sherlock Holmes,' 'The White Company,' etc. ROUND THE RED LAMP. *Ninth Edition. Cr. 8vo. 6s.*

Duncan (Sara Jeannette) (Mrs. Everard Cotes). THOSE DELIGHTFUL AMERICANS. Illustrated. *Third Edition. Cr. 8vo. 6s.* See also Strand Novels.

Findlater (J. H.). THE GREEN GRAVES OF BALGOWRIE. *Fifth Edition. Cr. 8vo. 6s.* See also Strand Novels.

Findlater (Mary). A NARROW WAY. *Third Edition. Cr. 8vo.. 6s.*

THE ROSE OF JOY. *Third Edition. Cr. 8vo. 6s.* See also Strand Novels.

Fitzpatrick (K.) THE WEANS AT ROWALLAN. Illustrated. *Second Edition. Cr. 8vo. 6s.*

Fitzstephen (Gerald). MORE KIN THAN KIND. *Cr. 8vo. 6s.*

Fletcher (J. S.). LUCIAN THE DREAMER. *Cr. 8vo. 6s.*

Fraser (Mrs. Hugh), Author of 'The Stolen Emperor.' THE SLAKING OF THE SWORD. *Cr. 8vo. 6s.*

*THE SHADOW OF THE LORD. *Cr. 8vo. 6s.*

*Fuller-Maitland (Mrs.),** Author of 'The Day Book of Bethia Hardacre.' BLANCHE ESMEAD. *Cr. 8vo. 6s.*

Gerard (Dorothea), Author of 'Lady Baby.' THE CONQUEST OF LONDON. *Second Edition. Cr. 8vo. 6s.*

HOLY MATRIMONY. *Second Edition. Cr. 8vo. 6s.*

MADE OF MONEY. *Cr. 8vo. 6s.*

THE BRIDGE OF LIFE. *Cr. 8vo. 6s.*

THE IMPROBABLE IDYL. *Third Edition. Cr. 8vo. 6s.* See also Strand Novels.

Gerard (Emily). THE HERONS' TOWER. *Cr. 8vo. 6s.*

Gissing (George), Author of 'Demos,' 'In the Year of Jubilee,' etc. THE TOWN TRAVELLER. *Second Ed. Cr. 8vo. 6s.*

THE CROWN OF LIFE. *Cr. 8vo. 6s.*

Gleig (Charles). BUNTER'S CRUISE. Illustrated. *Cr. 8vo. 3s. 6d.*

Harraden (Beatrice). IN VARYING MOODS. *A New Edition. Cr. 8vo. 6s.*

*THE SCHOLAR'S DAUGHTER. *Cr. 8vo. 6s.*

Harrod (F.) (Frances Forbes Robertson). THE TAMING OF THE BRUTE. *Cr. 8vo. 6s.*

Herbertson (Agnes G.). PATIENCE DEAN. *Cr. 8vo. 6s.*

Hichens (Robert). THE PROPHET OF BERKELEY SQUARE. *Second Edition. Cr. 8vo. 6s.*
TONGUES OF CONSCIENCE. *Second Edition. Cr. 8vo. 6s.*
FELIX. *Fifth Edition. Cr. 8vo. 6s.*
THE WOMAN WITH THE FAN. *Sixth Edition. Cr. 8vo. 6s.*
BYEWAYS. *Cr. 8vo. 3s. 6d.*
THE GARDEN OF ALLAH. *Twelfth Edition. Cr. 8vo. 6s.*
THE BLACK SPANIEL. *Cr. 8vo. 6s.*

Hobbes (John Oliver), Author of 'Robert Orange.' THE SERIOUS WOOING. *Cr. 8vo. 6s.*

Hope (Anthony). THE GOD IN THE CAR. *Tenth Edition. Cr. 8vo. 6s.*
A CHANGE OF AIR, *Sixth Edition. Cr. 8vo. 6s.*
A MAN OF MARK. *Fifth Edition. Cr. 8vo. 6s.*
THE CHRONICLES OF COUNT ANTONIO. *Sixth Edition. Cr. 8vo. 6s.*
PHROSO. Illustrated by H. R. MILLAR. *Sixth Edition. Cr. 8vo. 6s.*
SIMON DALE. Illustrated. *Sixth Edition. Cr. 8vo. 6s.*
THE KING'S MIRROR. *Fourth Edition. Cr. 8vo. 6s.*
QUISANTE. *Fourth Edition. Cr. 8vo. 6s.*
THE DOLLY DIALOGUES. *Cr. 8vo. 6s.*
A SERVANT OF THE PUBLIC. Illustrated. *Fourth Edition. Cr. 8vo. 6s.*

Hope (Graham), Author of 'A Cardinal and his Conscience,' etc., etc. THE LADY OF LYTE. *Second Ed. Cr. 8vo. 6s.*

Hough (Emerson). THE MISSISSIPPI BUBBLE. Illustrated. *Cr. 8vo. 6s.*

Housman (Clemence). THE LIFE OF SIR AGLOVALE DE GALIS. *Cr. 8vo. 6s.*

Hyne (C. J. Cutcliffe), Author of 'Captain Kettle.' MR. HORROCKS, PURSER. *Third Edition. Cr. 8vo. 6s.*

Jacobs (W. W.). MANY CARGOES. *Twenty-Eighth Edition. Cr. 8vo. 3s. 6d.*
SEA URCHINS. *Twelfth Edition. Cr. 8vo. 3s. 6d.*
A MASTER OF CRAFT. Illustrated. *Sixth Edition. Cr. 8vo. 3s. 6d.*
LIGHT FREIGHTS. Illustrated. *Fifth Edition. Cr. 8vo. 3s. 6d.*

James (Henry). THE SOFT SIDE. *Second Edition. Cr. 8vo. 6s.*
THE BETTER SORT. *Cr. 8vo. 6s.*
THE AMBASSADORS. *Second Edition. Cr. 8vo. 6s.*
THE GOLDEN BOWL. *Third Edition. Cr. 8vo. 6s.*

Janson (Gustaf). ABRAHAM'S SACRIFICE. *Cr. 8vo. 6s.*

Keays (H. A. Mitchell). HE THAT EATETH BREAD WITH ME. *Cr. 8vo. 6s.*

Langbridge (V.) and **Bourne (C. Harold.).** THE VALLEY OF INHERITANCE. *Cr. 8vo. 6s.*

Lawless (Hon. Emily). WITH ESSEX IN IRELAND. *Cr. 8vo. 6s.*
See also Strand Novels.

Lawson (Harry), Author of 'When the Billy Boils.' CHILDREN OF THE BUSH. *Cr. 8vo. 6s.*

Le Queux (W.). THE HUNCHBACK OF WESTMINSTER. *Third Edition. Cr. 8vo. 6s.*
THE CLOSED BOOK. *Third Edition. Cr. 8vo. 6s.*
THE VALLEY OF THE SHADOW. Illustrated. *Third Edition. Cr. 8vo. 6s.*
BEHIND THE THRONE. *Third Edition. Cr. 8vo. 6s.*

Levett-Yeats (S.). ORRAIN. *Second Edition. Cr. 8vo. 6s.*

Long (J. Luther), Co-Author of 'The Darling of the Gods.' MADAME BUTTERFLY. *Cr. 8vo. 3s. 6d.*
SIXTY JANE. *Cr. 8vo. 6s.*

Lowis (Cecil). THE MACHINATIONS OF THE MYO-OK. *Cr. 8vo. 6s.*

Lyall (Edna). DERRICK VAUGHAN, NOVELIST. *42nd Thousand. Cr. 8vo. 3s. 6d.*

M'Carthy (Justin H.), Author of 'If I were King.' THE LADY OF LOYALTY HOUSE. Illustrated. *Third Edition. Cr. 8vo. 6s.*
THE DRYAD. *Second Edition. Cr. 8vo. 6s.*

Macdonald (Ronald). THE SEA MAID. *Cr. 8vo. 6s.*

Macnaughtan (S.). THE FORTUNE OF CHRISTINA MACNAB. *Third Edition. Cr. 8vo. 6s.*

Malet (Lucas). COLONEL ENDERBY'S WIFE. *Fourth Edition. Cr. 8vo. 6s.*
A COUNSEL OF PERFECTION. *New Edition. Cr. 8vo. 6s.*
THE WAGES OF SIN. *Fourteenth Edition. Cr. 8vo. 6s.*
THE CARISSIMA. *Fourth Edition. Cr. 8vo. 6s.*
THE GATELESS BARRIER. *Fourth Edition. Cr. 8vo. 6s.*
THE HISTORY OF SIR RICHARD CALMADY. *Seventh Edition. Cr. 8vo. 6s.*
See also Books for Boys and Girls.

Mann (Mrs. M. E.). OLIVIA'S SUMMER. *Second Edition. Cr. 8vo. 6s.*
A LOST ESTATE. *A New Edition. Cr. 8vo. 6s.*
THE PARISH OF HILBY. *A New Edition. Cr. 8vo. 6s.*
THE PARISH NURSE. *Fourth Edition. Cr. 8vo. 6s.*

GRAN'MA'S JANE. *Cr. 8vo. 6s.*

MRS. PETER HOWARD. *Cr. 8vo. 6s.*

A WINTER'S TALE. *A New Edition. Cr. 8vo. 6s.*

ONE ANOTHER'S BURDENS. *A New Edition. Cr. 8vo. 6s.*

ROSE AT HONEYPOT. *Second Ed. Cr. 8vo. 6s.* See also Books for Boys and Girls.

Marriott (Charles), Author of 'The Column.' GENEVRA. *Second Edition. Cr. 8vo. 6s.*

Marsh (Richard). THE TWICKENHAM PEERAGE. *Second Edition. Cr. 8vo. 6s.*

A DUEL. *Cr. 8vo. 6s.*

THE MARQUIS OF PUTNEY. *Second Edition. Cr. 8vo. 6s.*
See also Strand Novels.

Mason (A. E. W.), Author of 'The Four Feathers,' etc. CLEMENTINA. *Illustrated. Second Edition. Cr. 8vo. 6s.*

Mathers (Helen), Author of 'Comin' thro' the Rye.' HONEY. *Fourth Edition. Cr. 8vo. 6s.*

GRIFF OF GRIFFITHSCOURT. *Cr. 8vo. 6s.*

THE FERRYMAN. *Second Edition. Cr. 8vo. 6s.*

Maxwell (W. B.), Author of 'The Ragged Messenger.' VIVIEN. *Seventh Edition. Cr. 8vo. 6s.*

THE RAGGED MESSENGER. *Third Edition. Cr. 8vo. 6s.*

FABULOUS FANCIES. *Cr. 8vo. 6s.*

Meade (L. T.). DRIFT. *Second Edition. Cr. 8vo. 6s.*

RESURGAM. *Cr. 8vo. 6s.*

VICTORY. *Cr. 8vo. 6s.*
See also Books for Girls and Boys.

Meredith (Ellis). HEART OF MY HEART. *Cr. 8vo. 6s.*

'Miss Molly' (The Author of). THE GREAT RECONCILER. *Cr. 8vo. 6s.*

Mitford (Bertram). THE SIGN OF THE SPIDER. *Illustrated. Sixth Edition. Cr. 8vo. 3s. 6d.*

IN THE WHIRL OF THE RISING. *Third Edition. Cr. 8vo. 6s.*

THE RED DERELICT. *Second Edition. Cr. 8vo. 6s.*

Montresor (F. F.), Author of 'Into the Highways and Hedges.' THE ALIEN. *Third Edition. Cr. 8vo. 6s.*

Morrison (Arthur). TALES OF MEAN STREETS. *Sixth Edition. Cr. 8vo. 6s.*

A CHILD OF THE JAGO. *Fourth Edition. Cr. 8vo. 6s.*

TO LONDON TOWN. *Second Edition. Cr. 8vo. 6s.*

CUNNING MURRELL. *Cr. 8vo. 6s.*

THE HOLE IN THE WALL. *Fourth Edition. Cr. 8vo. 6s.*

DIVERS VANITIES. *Cr. 8vo. 6s.*

Nesbit (E.). (Mrs. E. Bland). THE RED HOUSE. *Illustrated. Fourth Edition. Cr. 8vo. 6s.*
See also Strand Novels.

Norris (W. E.). THE CREDIT OF THE COUNTY. *Illustrated. Second Edition. Cr. 8vo. 6s.*

THE EMBARRASSING ORPHAN. *Cr. 8vo. 6s.*

NIGEL'S VOCATION. *Cr. 8vo. 6s.*

BARHAM OF BELTANA. *Second Edition. Cr. 8vo. 6s.*
See also Strand Novels.

Ollivant (Alfred). OWD BOB, THE GREY DOG OF KENMUIR. *Eighth Edition. Cr. 8vo. 6s.*

Oppenheim (E. Phillips). MASTER OF MEN. *Third Edition. Cr. 8vo. 6s.*

Oxenham (John), Author of 'Barbe of Grand Bayou.' A WEAVER OF WEBS. *Second Edition. Cr. 8vo. 6s.*

THE GATE OF THE DESERT. *Fourth Edition. Cr. 8vo. 6s.*

Pain (Barry). THREE FANTASIES. *Cr. 8vo. 1s.*

LINDLEY KAYS. *Third Edition. Cr. 8vo. 6s.*

Parker (Gilbert). PIERRE AND HIS PEOPLE. *Sixth Edition.*

MRS. FALCHION. *Fifth Edition. Cr. 8vo. 6s.*

THE TRANSLATION OF A SAVAGE. *Second Edition. Cr. 8vo. 6s.*

THE TRAIL OF THE SWORD. *Illustrated. Ninth Edition. Cr. 8vo. 6s.*

WHEN VALMOND CAME TO PONTIAC: The Story of a Lost Napoleon. *Fifth Edition. Cr. 8vo. 6s.*

AN ADVENTURER OF THE NORTH: The Last Adventures of 'Pretty Pierre.' *Third Edition. Cr. 8vo. 6s.*

THE SEATS OF THE MIGHTY. *Illustrated. Fourteenth Edition. Cr. 8vo. 6s.*

THE BATTLE OF THE STRONG: a Romance of Two Kingdoms. *Illustrated. Fifth Edition. Cr. 8vo. 6s.*

THE POMP OF THE LAVILETTES. *Second Edition. Cr. 8vo. 3s. 6d.*

Pemberton (Max). THE FOOTSTEPS OF A THRONE. *Illustrated. Third Edition. Cr. 8vo. 6s.*

I CROWN THEE KING. *With Illustrations by Frank Dadd and A. Forrestier. Cr. 8vo. 6s.*

Phillpotts (Eden). LYING PROPHETS. *Cr. 8vo. 6s.*

CHILDREN OF THE MIST. *Fifth Edition. Cr. 8vo. 6s.*

THE HUMAN BOY. *With a Frontispiece. Fourth Edition. Cr. 8vo. 6s.*

SONS OF THE MORNING. *Second Edition. Cr. 8vo. 6s.*

THE RIVER. *Third Edition. Cr. 8vo. 6s.*

THE AMERICAN PRISONER. *Third Edition. Cr. 8vo. 6s.*

THE SECRET WOMAN. *Fourth Edition. Cr. 8vo. 6s.*

KNOCK AT A VENTURE. With a Frontispiece. *Third Edition. Cr. 8vo. 6s.*

*THE PORTREEVE. *Cr. 8vo. 6s.*
See also Strand Novels.

Pickthall (Marmaduke). SAÏD THE FISHERMAN. *Fifth Edition. Cr. 8vo. 6s.*

BRENDLE. *Second Edition. Cr. 8vo. 6s.*

'Q,' Author of 'Dead Man's Rock.' THE WHITE WOLF. *Second Edition. Cr. 8vo. 6s.*

THE MAYOR OF TROY. *Cr. 8vo. 6s.*

Rhys (Grace). THE WOOING OF SHEILA. *Second Edition. Cr. 8vo. 6s.*

THE PRINCE OF LISNOVER. *Cr. 8vo. 6s.*

Rhys (Grace) and Another. THE DIVERTED VILLAGE. Illustrated by DOROTHY GWYN JEFFREYS. *Cr. 8vo. 6s.*

Ridge (W. Pett). LOST PROPERTY. *Second Edition. Cr. 8vo. 6s.*

'ERB. *Second Edition. Cr. 8vo. 6s.*

A SON OF THE STATE. *A New Edition. Cr. 8vo. 3s. 6d.*

A BREAKER OF LAWS. *A New Edition. Cr. 8vo. 3s. 6d.*

MRS. GALER'S BUSINESS. Illustrated. *Second Edition. Cr. 8vo. 6s.*

SECRETARY TO BAYNE, M.P. *Cr. 8vo. 3s. 6d.*

Ritchie (Mrs. David G.). THE TRUTHFUL LIAR. *Cr. 8vo. 6s.*

Roberts (C. G. D.). THE HEART OF THE ANCIENT WOOD. *Cr. 8vo. 3s. 6d.*

Russell (W. Clark). MY DANISH SWEETHEART. Illustrated. *Fifth Edition. Cr. 8vo. 6s.*

HIS ISLAND PRINCESS. Illustrated. *Second Edition. Cr. 6vo. 6s.*

ABANDONED. *Cr. 8vo. 6s.*
See also Books for Boys and Girls.

Sergeant (Adeline). ANTHEA'S WAY. *Cr. 8vo. 6s.*

THE PROGRESS OF RACHAEL. *Cr. 8vo. 6s.*

THE MYSTERY OF THE MOAT. *Second Edition. Cr. 8vo. 6s.*

MRS. LYGON'S HUSBAND. *Cr. 8vo. 6s.*

THE COMING OF THE RANDOLPHS. *Cr. 8vo. 6s.*
See also Strand Novels.

Shannon (W. F.). THE MESS DECK. *Cr. 8vo. 3s. 6d.*
See also Strand Novels.

Sonnischsen (Albert). DEEP-SEA VAGABONDS. *Cr. 8vo. 6s.*

Thompson (Vance). SPINNERS OF LIFE. *Cr. 8vo. 6s.*

Urquhart (M.), A TRAGEDY IN COMMONPLACE. *Second Ed. Cr. 8vo. 6s.*

Waineman (Paul). BY A FINNISH LAKE. *Cr. 8vo. 6s.*

THE SONG OF THE FOREST. *Cr. 8vo. 6s.* See also Strand Novels.

Waltz (E. C.). THE ANCIENT LANDMARK : A Kentucky Romance. *Cr. 8vo. 6s.*

Watson (H. B. Marriott). ALARUMS AND EXCURSIONS. *Cr. 8vo. 6s.*

CAPTAIN FORTUNE. *Third Edition. Cr. 8vo. 6s.*

TWISTED EGLANTINE. With 8 Illustrations by FRANK CRAIG. *Second Edition. Cr. 8vo. 6s.*

*THE HIGH TOBY. With a Frontispiece. *Cr. 8vo. 6s.* See also Strand Novels.

Wells (H. G.). THE SEA LADY. *Cr. 8vo. 6s.*

Weyman (Stanley), Author of 'A Gentleman of France.' UNDER THE RED ROBE. With Illustrations by R. C. WOODVILLE. *Nineteenth Edition. Cr. 8vo. 6s.*

White (Stewart E.), Author of 'The Blazed Trail.' CONJUROR'S HOUSE. A Romance of the Free Trail. *Second Edition. Cr. 8vo. 6s.*

White (Percy). THE SYSTEM. *Third Edition. Cr. 8vo. 6s.*

THE PATIENT MAN. *Second Edition. Cr. 8vo. 6s.*

Williamson (Mrs. C. N.), Author of 'The Barnstormers.' THE ADVENTURE OF PRINCESS SYLVIA. *Cr. 8vo. 3s. 6d.*

THE WOMAN WHO DARED. *Cr. 8vo. 6s.*

THE SEA COULD TELL. *Second Edition. Cr. 8vo. 6s.*

THE CASTLE OF THE SHADOWS. *Third Edition. Cr. 8vo. 6s.*

PAPA. *Cr. 8vo. 6s.*

*LADY BETTY ACROSS THE WATER. *Cr. 8vo. 6s.*

Williamson (C. N. and A. M.). THE LIGHTNING CONDUCTOR : Being the Romance of a Motor Car. Illustrated. *Thirteenth Edition. Cr. 8vo. 6s.*

THE PRINCESS PASSES. Illustrated. *Sixth Edition. Cr. 8vo. 6s.*

MY FRIEND THE CHAUFFEUR. With 16 Illustrations. *Sixth Edition. Cr. 8vo. 6s.*

*Wyllarde (Dolf), Author of 'Uriah the Hittite.' THE PATHWAY OF THE PIONEER. *Cr. 8vo. 6s.*

The Strand Novels

Cr. 8vo.   Cloth, 1s. net.

ENCOURAGED by the great and steady sale of their Sixpenny Novels, Messrs. Methuen have determined to issue a new series of fiction at a low price under the title of 'THE STRAND NOVELS.' These books are well printed and well bound in *cloth*, and the excellence of their quality may be gauged from the names of those authors who contribute the early volumes of the series.

Messrs. Methuen would point out that the books are as good and as long as a six shilling novel, that they are bound in cloth and not in paper, and that their price is One Shilling *net*. They feel sure that the public will appreciate such good and cheap literature, and the books can be seen at all good booksellers.

The first volumes are—

Balfour (Andrew). VENGEANCE IS MINE.
TO ARMS.
Baring=Gould (S.). MRS. CURGENVEN OF CURGENVEN.
*DOMITIA.
*THE FROBISHERS.
Barlow (Jane), Author of 'Irish Idylls.' FROM THE EAST UNTO THE WEST
A CREEL OF IRISH STORIES.
*THE FOUNDING OF FORTUNES.
Barr (Robert). THE VICTORS.
Bartram (George). THIRTEEN EVENINGS.
Benson (E. F.), Author of 'Dodo.' THE CAPSINA.
Bowles (G. Stewart). A STRETCH OFF THE LAND.
Brooke (Emma). THE POET'S CHILD.
Bullock (Shan F.). THE BARRYS.
THE CHARMER.
THE SQUIREEN.
THE RED LEAGUERS.
Burton (J. Bloundelle). ACROSS THE SALT SEAS.
THE CLASH OF ARMS.
DENOUNCED.
*FORTUNE'S MY FOE.
Capes (Bernard). AT A WINTER'S FIRE.
Chesney (Weatherby). THE BAPTIST RING.
THE BRANDED PRINCE.
THE FOUNDERED GALLEON.
JOHN TOPP.
Clifford (Mrs. W. K.). A FLASH OF SUMMER.
Collingwood (Harry). THE DOCTOR OF THE 'JULIET.'
Cornford (L. Cope). SONS OF ADVERSITY.
Crane (Stephen). WOUNDS IN THE RAIN.
Denny (C. E.). THE ROMANCE OF UPFOLD MANOR.
Dickson (Harris). THE BLACK WOLF'S BREED.
Dickinson (Evelyn). THE SIN OF ANGELS.

*Duncan (Sara J.). THE POOL IN THE DESERT.
*A VOYAGE OF CONSOLATION.
Embree (C. F.). A HEART OF FLAME.
Fenn (G. Manville). AN ELECTRIC SPARK.
Findlater (Jane H.). THE DAUGHTER OF STRIFE.
*Findlater (Mary). OVER THE HILLS.
Forrest (R. E.). THE SWORD OF AZRAEL.
Francis (M. E.). MISS ERIN.
Gallon (Tom). RICKERBY'S FOLLY.
Gerard (Dorothea). THINGS THAT HAVE HAPPENED.
Glanville (Ernest). THE DESPATCH RIDER.
THE LOST REGIMENT.
THE KLOOF BRIDE.
THE INCA'S TREASURE.
Gordon (Julien). MRS. CLYDE.
WORLD'S PEOPLE.
Goss (C. F.). THE REDEMPTION OF DAVID CORSON.
*Gray (E. M'Queen). MY STEWARD-SHIP.
Hales (A. G.). JAIR THE APOSTATE.
Hamilton (Lord Ernest). MARY HAMILTON.
Harrison (Mrs. Burton). A PRINCESS OF THE HILLS. Illustrated.
Hooper (I.). THE SINGER OF MARLY.
Hough (Emerson). THE MISSISSIPPI BUBBLE.
'Iota' (Mrs. Caffyn). ANNE MAULEVERER.
*Jepson (Edgar). KEEPERS OF THE PEOPLE.
Kelly (Florence Finch). WITH HOOPS OF STEEL.
Lawless (Hon. Emily). MAELCHO.
Linden (Annie). A WOMAN OF SENTIMENT.
*Lorimer (Norma). JOSIAH'S WIFE.
Lush (Charles K.). THE AUTOCRATS.
Macdonnell (A.). THE STORY OF TERESA.
Macgrath (Harold). THE PUPPET CROWN.

Mackie (Pauline Bradford). THE VOICE IN THE DESERT.

Marsh (Richard). THE SEEN AND THE UNSEEN.

*GARNERED.

*A METAMORPHOSIS.

MARVELS AND MYSTERIES.

BOTH SIDES OF THE VEIL.

Mayall (J. W.). THE CYNIC AND THE SYREN.

Monkhouse (Allan). LOVE IN A LIFE.

Moore (Arthur). THE KNIGHT PUNCTILIOUS.

Nesbit (Mrs. Bland). THE LITERARY SENSE.

Norris (W. E.). AN OCTAVE.

Oliphant (Mrs.). THE LADY'S WALK.

SIR ROBERT'S FORTUNE.

THE TWO MARY'S.

Penny (Mrs. F. A.). A MIXED MARRIAGE.

Phillpotts (Eden). THE STRIKING HOURS.

FANCY FREE.

Randall (J.). AUNT BETHIA'S BUTTON.

*Raymond (Walter).** FORTUNE'S DARLING.

*Rayner (Olive Pratt).** ROSALBA.

Rhys (Grace). THE DIVERTED VILLAGE.

Rickert (Edith). OUT OF THE CYPRESS SWAMP.

Roberton (M. H.). A GALLANT QUAKER.

Saunders (Marshall). ROSE A CHARLITTE.

Sergeant (Adeline). ACCUSED AND ACCUSER.

BARBARA'S MONEY.

THE ENTHUSIAST.

A GREAT LADY.

*THE LOVE THAT OVERCAME.

THE MASTER OF BEECHWOOD.

UNDER SUSPICION.

*THE YELLOW DIAMOND.

Shannon (W. F.). JIM TWELVES.

*Strain (E. H.).** ELMSLIE'S DRAG NET.

Stringer (Arthur). THE SILVER POPPY.

Stuart (Esmè). CHRISTALLA.

Sutherland (Duchess of). ONE HOUR AND THE NEXT.

Swan (Annie). LOVE GROWN COLD.

Swift (Benjamin). SORDON.

Tanqueray (Mrs. B. M.). THE ROYAL QUAKER.

Trafford-Taunton (Mrs. E. W.). SILENT DOMINION.

*Upward (Allen).** ATHELSTANE FORD.

Waineman (Paul). A HEROINE FROM FINLAND.

Watson (H. B. Marriott). THE SKIRTS OF HAPPY CHANCE.

Books for Boys and Girls

Illustrated. Crown 8vo. 3s. 6d.

THE GETTING WELL OF DOROTHY. By Mrs. W. K. Clifford. *Second Edition.*

THE ICELANDER'S SWORD. By S. Baring-Gould.

ONLY A GUARD-ROOM DOG. By Edith E. Cutheil.

THE DOCTOR OF THE JULIET. By Harry Collingwood.

LITTLE PETER. By Lucas Malet. *Second Edition.*

MASTER ROCKAFELLAR'S VOYAGE. By W. Clark Russell.

THE SECRET OF MADAME DE MONLUC. By the Author of "Mdlle. Mori."

SYD BELTON : Or, the Boy who would not go to Sea. By G. Manville Fenn.

THE RED GRANGE. By Mrs. Molesworth.

A GIRL OF THE PEOPLE. By L. T. Meade. *Second Edition.*

HEPSY GIPSY. By L. T. Meade. 2s. 6d.

THE HONOURABLE MISS. By L. T. Meade.

THERE WAS ONCE A PRINCE. By Mrs. M. E. Mann.

WHEN ARNOLD COMES HOME. By Mrs. M. E. Mann.

The Novels of Alexandre Dumas

Price 6d. Double Volumes, 1s.

THE THREE MUSKETEERS. With a long Introduction by Andrew Lang. Double volume.

THE PRINCE OF THIEVES. *Second Edition.*

ROBIN HOOD. A Sequel to the above.

THE CORSICAN BROTHERS.

GEORGES.

CROP-EARED JACQUOT; JANE; Etc.

TWENTY YEARS AFTER. Double volume.

AMAURY.

THE CASTLE OF EPPSTEIN.

THE SNOWBALL, and SULTANETTA.

CECILE ; OR, THE WEDDING GOWN.

ACTÉ.